HARCOURT ART EVERYWHERE

Teacher Edition

AUTHORS

Jacqueline Chanda
Kristen Pederson Marstaller

CONSULTANTS

Katherina Danko-McGhee
María Teresa García-Pedroche

Harcourt
SCHOOL PUBLISHERS

Orlando   Austin   New York   San Diego   Toronto   London

Visit *The Learning Site!*
www.harcourtschool.com

S0-ARV-875

Printed in the United States of America

ISBN 0-15-336453-X
    0-15-342013-8

2 3 4 5 6 7 8 9 10   030   13 12 11 10 09 08 07 06 05

Authors

Jacqueline Chanda

Chair, Division of Art Education and Art History, School of Visual Arts, University of North Texas; Co-Director, North Texas Institute for Educators on the Visual Arts

Research contributions: thematic instruction, literacy through art, art history

Kristen Pederson Marstaller

Instructional Coordinator of Fine Arts, Austin Independent School District; President, Texas Art Education Association, 2003–2005

Research contributions: teacher preparation, classroom management, creative expression

CONSULTANTS

Katherina Danko-McGhee

Early Childhood Art Education Coordinator, University of Toledo, Art Department—Center for the Visual Arts; Early Childhood Consultant, Toledo Museum of Art

Research contributions: aesthetic preferences of young children, museum studies

María Teresa García-Pedroche

Head of Family Programs and Community Outreach, Dallas Museum of Art; Visual Artist

Research contributions: school–home and community connections, museum studies, art and culture

How to Use
Art Everywhere

Art Everywhere is a comprehensive program that teaches the elements of art, the principles of design, and other art concepts. Thirty lessons and twelve cross-curricular features are organized into six thematic units designed to help children think critically about art and the world around them.

Plan

Use the **Planning Guide** and **Artist's Workshops Preview** to identify lesson objectives and plan production activities. Gather resources from a variety of options:

- Art Prints
- Teacher Resource Book
- Artist's Workshop Activities: English and Spanish
- Art Transparencies

 Electronic Art Gallery CD-ROM, Primary

 Visit *The Learning Site* www.harcourtschool.com

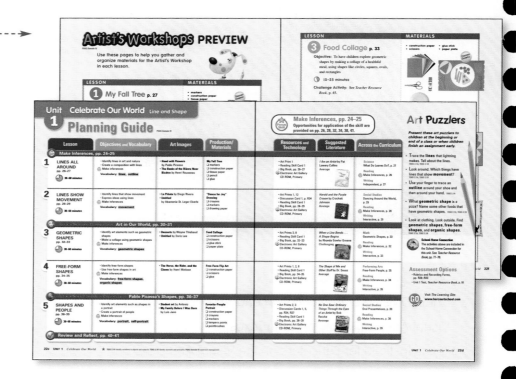

Provide Instruction

Teach the **elements of art**, the **principles of design**, and other **art concepts** through a variety of well-known and culturally diverse art images as well as student artworks. Encourage children's creativity and problem-solving skills through **Artist's Workshop** activities.

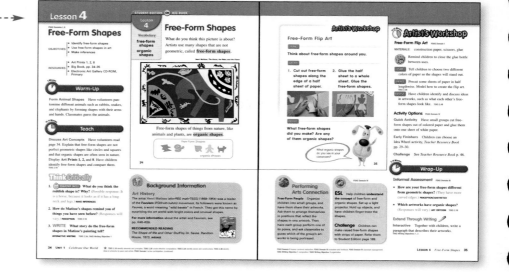

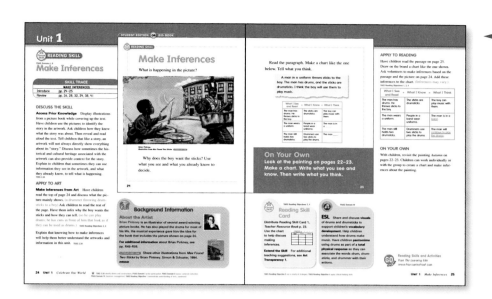

Support Reading

At the beginning of each unit, introduce a key **Reading Skill** that children will apply to artworks and to text throughout the unit.

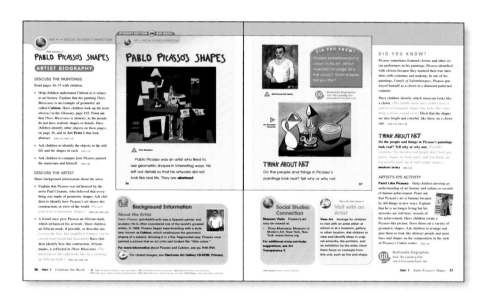

Make Connections

Make **meaningful cross-curricular connections** between art and other disciplines, including reading/literature, social studies, math, and science.

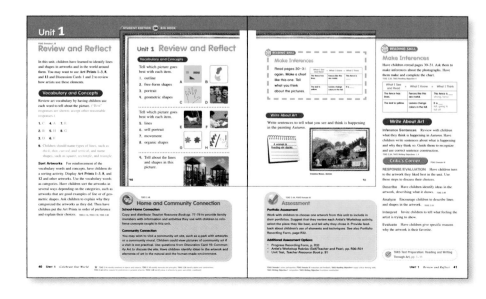

Review and Extend

Assess children's understanding of unit concepts with **Review and Reflect**. Extend the learning with additional **reading and writing** activities and opportunities for **response/evaluation**.

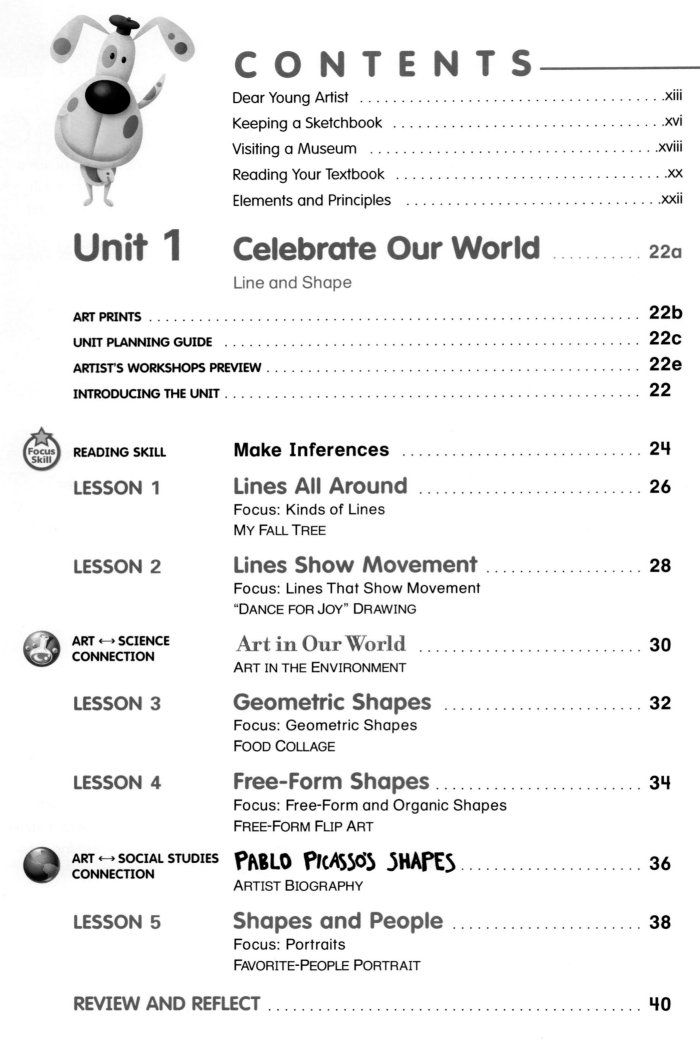

CONTENTS

Unit 1   Celebrate Our World 22a
Line and Shape

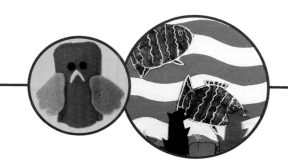

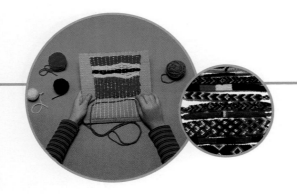

Unit 4

Surprises Everywhere 82a

Form and Space

Focus Skill

LESSON 16   **Shapes and Forms** **86**
Focus: Forms
DECORATED CLAY BOWL

LESSON 17   **Sculpted Forms** **88**
Focus: Sculpted Forms, Space
FOIL SCULPTURE

ART ↔ SOCIAL STUDIES CONNECTION   Cowboys and Cowgirls in Art **90**
ART AND CULTURE

LESSON 18   **Relief Sculpture** **92**
Focus: Forms in Relief
CLAY TILE RELIEF SCULPTURE

LESSON 19   **Architecture** **94**
Focus: Form in Architecture
AMAZING SCHOOL MODEL

ART ↔ SOCIAL STUDIES CONNECTION   Frank Lloyd Wright's Buildings **96**
ARTIST BIOGRAPHY

LESSON 20   **Landscapes** **98**
Focus: Foreground, Background, and Horizon Line
3-D LANDSCAPE PAINTING

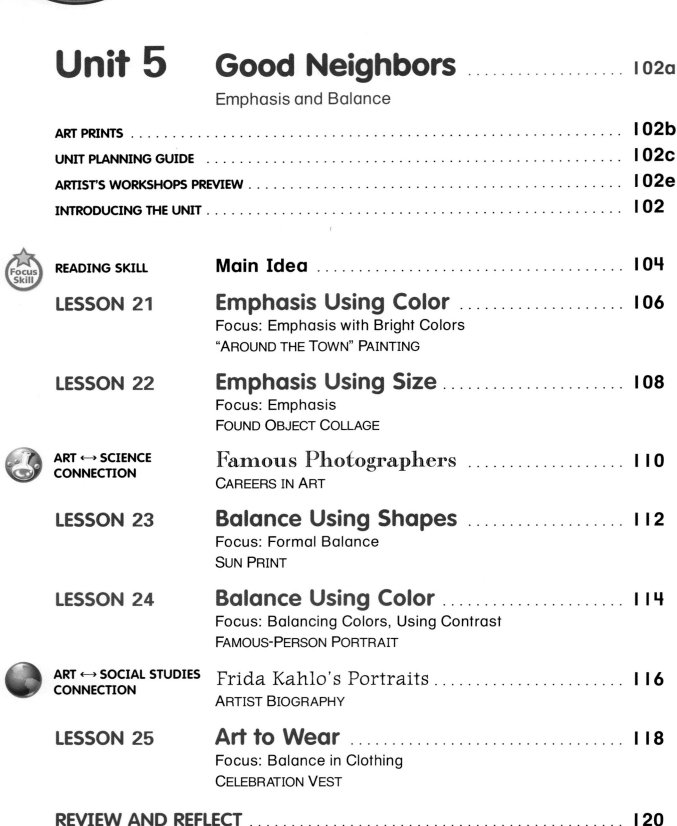

RESOURCES

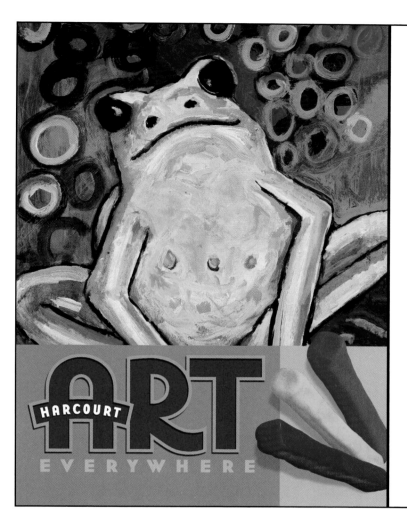

EVERYWHERE

AUTHORS
Jacqueline Chanda
Kristen Pederson Marstaller

CONSULTANTS
Katherina Danko-McGhee
María Teresa García-Pedroche

Harcourt
SCHOOL PUBLISHERS

Orlando   Austin   New York   San Diego   Toronto   London

Visit *The Learning Site!*
www.harcourtschool.com

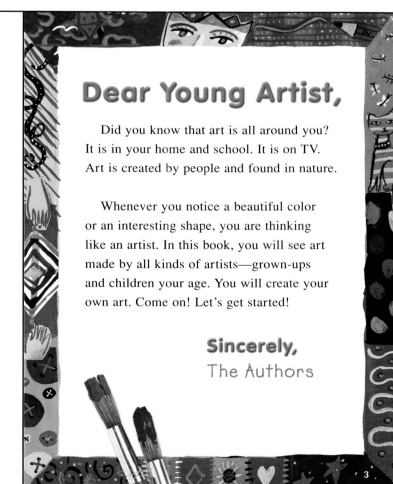

Dear Young Artist,

Did you know that art is all around you? It is in your home and school. It is on TV. Art is created by people and found in nature.

Whenever you notice a beautiful color or an interesting shape, you are thinking like an artist. In this book, you will see art made by all kinds of artists—grown-ups and children your age. You will create your own art. Come on! Let's get started!

Sincerely,
The Authors

CONTENTS

AT A GLANCE

Art Production

Elements and Principles

10

Media

Cross-Curricular Connections

11

Keeping a Sketchbook

Introduce Sketchbooks If possible, share with children an example of a sketchbook or journal that has sketches or written ideas. Ask children whether they already use a sketchbook and what they put in it. Explain that many artists use sketchbooks to plan artworks, practice making certain parts of an artwork, try new styles, or put other ideas on paper.

Read the Pages Read aloud pages 12–13 as children follow along in their books. Ask how the top and bottom pictures on page 12 are the same and how they are different. (They both show a large dinosaur, but the picture on the bottom shows a final version of the dinosaur in a different pose.) Explain that the top picture is a sketch made by artist William Joyce when he was planning his book *Dinosaur Bob*. The bottom picture shows the final artwork he made from one of his sketches. It shows the actual cover of the book.

Share Ideas Draw children's attention to the drawings, pictures, and other images on the sketchbook pages on page 13. Ask children what kinds of things they would like to draw and keep in sketchbooks of their own.

Artists have many creative ideas. Often, they sketch their ideas.

▲ *Dinosaur Bob* by William Joyce   LITERATURE LINK

The artist William Joyce used the ideas in his sketchbook to make a book.

12

 Background Information

About the Artist

William Joyce (1957–) sketched many dinosaurs as a child but now he really enjoys drawing robots, spaceships, and bugs. Joyce credits two of his art teachers with encouraging his talent. In college, he studied art and animation because he enjoyed telling stories in pictures. After college, he started writing and illustrating children's books. Joyce plans all his books with pencil drawings and then does paintings of them.

LITERATURE LINK   Share other illustrations from *Dinosaur Bob* by William Joyce. HarperCollins 1995.

CHALLENGING

Keep an art sketchbook. Draw what you see. Sketch your ideas, and write about them.

This leaf is my favorite fall color.

Keep other things like pictures, notes, and colors in your sketchbook.

spiral shell

pyramid

spiral

13

See pages R28–R33 for Assessment Options.

Student Self-Assessment

Have children make and keep several sketchbooks over the course of the school year. At the end of the year, they can look back at early sketchbooks and express ideas about their artwork and how they have grown as artists. Have children choose artworks they like that they have made in their sketchbooks and give reasons for their preferences. See pages R28–R33 for Assessment Options. TEKS 2.4A

MAKING A SKETCHBOOK

Model for children one way to make a sketchbook.

1. Cut out and staple a pocket to thin cardboard.

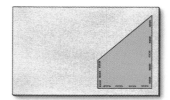

2. Staple drawing paper to the cardboard.

3. Make and decorate a cover.

My Sketchbook

USING A SKETCHBOOK

Encourage children to use their sketchbooks often. Share with children some of the following points about keeping and using a sketchbook.

- Their sketchbooks are their very own.

- They can practice drawing skills, try out new ideas, and sketch any kind of pictures they like in their sketchbooks. TEKS 2.2C

- They can use their sketchbooks to help them remember what they observe.

- Children can use their sketchbooks when they are studying other subjects, such as to record plant growth in science or to get ideas for their writing.

- Children can write notes and tape or glue pictures—or examples of other things they like—onto the pages or keep them in the pocket.

Visiting a Museum

Access Prior Knowledge Have children share their experiences viewing art. Encourage them to talk about sculptures, murals, and other artworks in their community. Ask children to share the kinds of artworks they like most and why. Then read and discuss pages 14–15 with children.

Discuss Museum Features Help children brainstorm a list of ways that visiting a museum is different from viewing art in a book. Use these ideas to get them started:

- You can see actual artworks rather than photographs, or reproductions, of them.
- You can see a sculpture from different sides.
- You can find and read the labels that tell about each artwork.
- You can ask a museum guide, or docent, questions about the artworks.

Have children tell you whether the pictures of artworks in their books are reproductions or actual artworks. (reproductions) Discuss, and then encourage volunteers to share their experiences visiting museums. Ask them where the museum was located and what they saw. Then tell children that the artworks in their *Student Editions* are located in museums around the world. Read the museum names on pages 14–15.

LOCATE IT Have children turn to *Student Edition* page 22, and point out the Locate It logo at the bottom of the page. Explain to children that when they see this logo, they can turn to the Maps of Museums and Art Sites on pages 144–147 to see where the artwork shown on that page is located.

Visiting a Museum

▲ Guggenheim Museum, New York City, New York

Walk slowly. Look at the art.

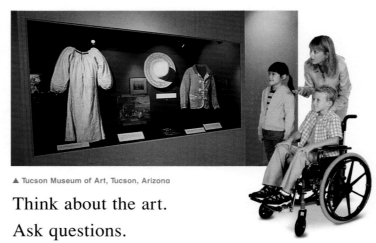

▲ Tucson Museum of Art, Tucson, Arizona

Think about the art.
Ask questions.

14

Home and Community Connection

Visiting a Museum

A class field trip to a museum in your region is a valuable way to enrich the art curriculum. Children can expand their ability to think critically about what they see by observing firsthand. Before your visit, talk with the museum education staff or with a docent. Prepare children for the visit by introducing the museum's major artists or exhibit themes.

▲ Whitney Museum of American Art, New York City, New York

Talk quietly. Tell what you think about the art. Find out what others think.

▲ Dallas Museum of Art, Dallas, Texas

Sketch what you see. Draw or write ideas the art makes you think of.

15

Art Prints

Virtual Tour

If you are unable to arrange a museum visit, display the **Art Prints** to provide children with a similar experience. Refer to the backs of the **Art Prints** for discussion ideas.

 For additional artworks, see **Electronic Art Gallery CD-ROM, Primary.**

ESL You can support children's **language acquisition** by using the additional teaching suggestions and resources in each lesson. See also Meeting Individual Needs, pages R24–R27, for ESL teaching strategies related to art education.

LOOKING AT ART

Discuss Art Criticism Help children understand that art criticism is the process of describing an artwork and what it means and then forming an opinion about it based on reasons. Explain that they should use art vocabulary to tell about artworks in their own words. See also page R34 for Teacher Discussion Card 2.

MODEL

Display **Art Print 3**. Tell children that it is a painting by Leonardo da Vinci. Model the steps below using the Art Print. Encourage children to share their own ideas for each step.

DESCRIBE Say: **This painting shows a portrait of a woman. She is smiling a little. Behind her are landforms. The artist used mostly dark colors.**

ANALYZE Discuss how the artist used principles of design. Say: **The woman's oval face stands out. Her hair and clothes show mostly smooth textures.** Children will become increasingly successful with this step as their art vocabulary grows. For more information about the elements of art and the principles of design, see *Student Edition* pages 18–21 and 170–181.

INTERPRET Say: **The lady lived a long time ago. Her clothes tell me this. She is smiling a little, but I'm not sure what she is thinking. I think the artist wanted to show her feelings.**

EVALUATE Say: **I like this painting because it shows how a person lived a long time ago. I like that the lady's smile makes me think about how she might be feeling.** Encourage children to explain why they like or dislike the painting.

Reading Your Textbook

Access Prior Knowledge Display an illustrated children's storybook and a nonfiction picture book or textbook that is familiar to children. Ask children questions such as these:

- Which book tells a story about made-up characters?
- Which book is nonfiction and gives information about real people, things, or places?

Explain to children that they will be learning more about how to read a nonfiction book but will be using one that gives information about art and artists.

Discuss Lesson Parts Have children turn to page 16 in their art book. Have volunteers read each of the sidebars on the page, pointing to and reading aloud each corresponding part in the student facsimile. Discuss children's ideas about how these parts can help them learn more about the art and the artists. Explain that the highlighted words are vocabulary words and that children should pay special attention to their meaning.

STUDENT EDITION OR BIG BOOK

Reading Your Textbook

A **title** tells what a lesson is about.

Lesson
10

Vocabulary
seascape
horizon line

Colors in Seascapes

What is going on in this painting? A **seascape** is an artwork that shows a water setting, like the sea. What colors did the artist use to show water? Why?

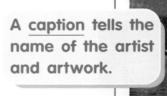

Winslow Homer, *Gloucester Harbor*

A **caption** tells the name of the artist and artwork.

Highlighted words help you learn art vocabulary.

Can you find the line where the sky and the water meet? This is called the **horizon line**.

16

58

Look for other important parts of your book.
- Title Page
- Contents
- Glossary

Artist's Workshop

Crayon-Resist Seascape

PLAN

Think about all the things you can find on the ocean and in the ocean.

CREATE

1. Draw a horizon line. Use crayons to draw boats. Add plants and animals under the water.

2. Paint watercolor over the picture. Make it darker at the bottom.

The steps are in order. They tell how to make an artwork.

REFLECT

What colors did you use? What does the water look like?

Where can you find a seascape in your town?

59

17

Technology

Tell children that they can find more information about art and artists by using a computer. Discuss with children some of the information and activities available to them with your supervision.

GO ONLINE Visit *The Learning Site* www.harcourtschool.com

ESL Help children identify the parts of their book by **naming and pointing to** the different parts and then pointing to different parts and asking volunteers to identify them. Ask **yes/no questions** about each of the parts.

Discuss Artist's Workshops Have children read the sidebar on page 17. Explain to children that every lesson in their book will include an artist's workshop activity. Have children discuss their experiences with following directions, and point out that the directions in their books are numbered and show pictures of the steps. Ask children why it is important to follow the steps in order. Then point out and discuss these additional parts of the workshops:

- **photographs** (show steps in order)
- **questions or tips** (have children apply what they have learned to what they observe in their environment—with the help of an art mascot)

Discuss Book Parts Point out that the little dog mascot at the top of the page will appear from time to time to help children learn more about art. Have children read the text in the speech balloon, and then have them locate each of these important book parts. Do a walk-through of the Student Handbook in the children's book (pages 142–206), which contains each of these sections:

- **Maps of Museums and Art Sites** (tells the location of artworks, museums, and art sites)
- **Art Safety** (guidelines for using tools and materials)
- **Art Techniques** (instructions for making different kinds of art)
- **Elements and Principles** (images for the art elements and design principles)
- **Gallery of Artists** (pictures and information about artists in the book)
- **Glossary** (definitions, pictures, and pronunciations for vocabulary terms)
- **Index of Artists and Artworks** (list of artists and artworks in the book with page references)
- **Index** (tells where to find information about a topic)

Elements of Art

Access Prior Knowledge Play a game with children in which you give clues about classroom objects and they guess the objects. Use elements such as line, shape, and color in your clues. For example, "I see a big white circle. It has two straight black lines coming from its center and many short lines around it. What is it?" (possible response: wall clock)

Tell children that they will learn more about ways of observing art and objects in the world around them.

Discuss the Pages Read aloud pages 18–19 as children follow along in their books. Talk about the pictures for each element and what children may already know. Tell children that they will learn more about these elements of art throughout the year. Invite volunteers to identify art elements such as lines, shapes, and colors in the classroom.
TEKS 2.1B

Elements and Principles

Elements of Art

Art is made up of parts called **elements**. Here are elements you will learn about.

line ▼

shape ▼

SCHOOL

color ▲

18

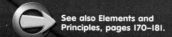

See also Elements and
Principles, pages 170–181.

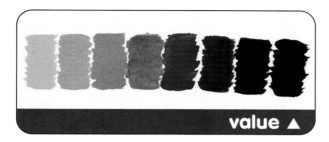

value ▲

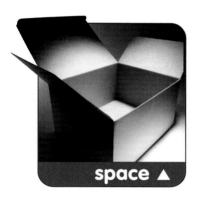

space ▲

texture ▼

form ▼

OLD FASHIONED OATS 100% Natural

19

See also Elements and Principles
pages R7–R9 and *Student Edition*
pages 170–181.

Art Center

Bulletin Board Display the *Posters of Elements, Principles, and Safety*
for children's reference. Introduce children to the Art Center, and show
them where materials are stored. Discuss the importance of safety in
handling art materials.

Principles of Design

Discuss the Pages Read the top of page 20 aloud as children follow along. Discuss the principles shown, and the picture for each principle. Encourage children to describe patterns in their clothing and elsewhere in the room. Tell children that they will learn more about the principles of design as they look at and create artworks.
TEKS 2.1B

Principles of Design

Artists use art elements in different ways according to **principles**. Here are principles you will learn about.

balance ▲

emphasis ▼

pattern ▲

20

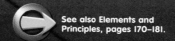 See also Elements and Principles, pages 170–181.

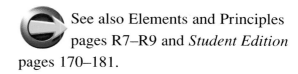 See also Elements and Principles pages R7–R9 and *Student Edition* pages 170–181.

rhythm ▼

movement ▼

unity ▲

variety ▲

21

Unit 1
Line and Shape

Celebrate Our World

Throughout time, artists have created art to celebrate the world around them. In this unit, children learn how artists use line and shape to look at the world in new ways.

Resources

- Unit 1 Art Prints (1–3)
- Additional Art Prints (8, 12)
- Art Transparencies 1–3
- Test Preparation: Reading and Writing Through Art, pp. 1–11
- Artist's Workshop Activities: English and Spanish, pp. 1–10
- Encyclopedia of Artists and Art History, pp. R48–R59
- Picture Cards Collection, Cards 35, 47, 70, 100, 122

Using the Art Prints

- Discussion Cards, pp. R34–R42
- Teaching Suggestions, backs of Art Prints
- Art Print Teaching Suggestions: Spanish

Teacher Resource Book

- Vocabulary Cards in English and Spanish, pp. 7–8
- Reading Skill Card 1, p. 23
- Copying Masters, pp. 29, 30, 31, 42
- Challenge Activities, pp. 43–47
- School-Home Connection: English/Spanish, pp. 77–78
- Unit Test, p. 91

Technology Resources

 Electronic Art Gallery CD-ROM, Primary
Picture Card Bank CD-ROM

 Visit *The Learning Site* www.harcourtschool.com

- Multimedia Art Glossary
- Multimedia Biographies
- Reading Skills and Activities

Art Prints for This Unit

ART PRINT 1

Colombe avec Fleurs (Dove with Flowers)
by Pablo Picasso

ART PRINT 2

People and Dog in Front of the Sun
by Joan Miró

ART PRINT 8

Fall Plowing
by Grant Wood

ART PRINT 3

Mona Lisa
by Leonardo da Vinci

ART PRINT 12

Interior of the Guggenheim Museum
designed by Frank Lloyd Wright

Planning Guide

PDAS Domain IV

Lesson	Objectives and Vocabulary	Art Images	Production/Materials
Focus Skill — Make Inferences, pp. 24–25			
1 **LINES ALL AROUND** pp. 26–27 — 30–60 minutes	• Identify lines in art and nature • Create a composition with lines • Make inferences **Vocabulary: lines , outline**	• **Hand with Flowers** by Pablo Picasso • **The Banks of the Bièvre Near Bicêtre** by Henri Rousseau	**My Fall Tree** ❏ markers ❏ construction paper ❏ tissue paper ❏ pencil ❏ glue
2 **LINES SHOW MOVEMENT** pp. 28–29 — 30–60 minutes	• Identify lines that show movement • Express ideas using lines • Make inferences **Vocabulary: movement**	• **La Piñata** by Diego Rivera • **Untitled** by Abastenia St. Leger Eberle	**"Dance for Joy" Drawing** ❏ crayons ❏ markers ❏ drawing paper
Art ←→ Science Connection: Art in Our World, pp. 30–31			
3 **GEOMETRIC SHAPES** pp. 32–33 — 30–60 minutes	• Identify art elements such as geometric shapes • Make a collage using geometric shapes • Make inferences **Vocabulary: geometric shapes**	• **Desserts** by Wayne Thiebaud • **Untitled** by Doris Lee	**Food Collage** ❏ construction paper ❏ scissors ❏ glue stick ❏ paper plate
4 **FREE-FORM SHAPES** pp. 34–35 — 30–60 minutes	• Identify free-form shapes • Use free-form shapes in art • Make inferences **Vocabulary: free-form shapes, organic shapes**	• **The Horse, the Rider, and the Clown** by Henri Matisse	**Free-Form Flip Art** ❏ construction paper ❏ scissors ❏ glue
Art ←→ Social Studies Connection: Pablo Picasso's Shapes, pp. 36–37			
5 **SHAPES AND PEOPLE** pp. 38–39 — 30–60 minutes	• Identify art elements such as shapes in a portrait • Create a portrait of people • Make inferences **Vocabulary: portrait , self-portrait**	• **Student art** by Antavio • **My Family Before I Was Born** by Luis Jaso	**Favorite-People Portrait** ❏ construction paper ❏ crayons ❏ markers ❏ tempera paints ❏ paintbrushes
Review and Reflect, pp. 40–41			

Make Inferences, pp. 24–25

Focus Skill

Opportunities for application of the skill are provided on pp. 26, 28, 32, 34, 38, 41.

Art Puzzlers

Resources and Technology	Suggested Literature	Across the Curriculum
• Art Print 1 • Reading Skill Card 1 • Big Book, pp. 26–27 • Electronic Art Gallery CD-ROM, Primary	*I Am an Artist* by Pat Lowery Collins **Average** 	**Science** What Do Leaves Do?, p. 27 **Reading** Make Inferences, p. 26 **Writing** Independent, p. 27
• Art Prints 1, 12 • Discussion Card 1, p. R34 • Reading Skill Card 1 • Big Book, pp. 28–29 • Electronic Art Gallery CD-ROM, Primary	*Harold and the Purple Crayon* by Crockett Johnson **Average** 	**Social Studies** Dancing Around the World, p. 29 **Reading** Make Inferences, p. 28 **Writing** Interactive, p. 29
• Art Prints 3, 8 • Reading Skill Card 1 • Big Book, pp. 32–33 • Electronic Art Gallery CD-ROM, Primary	*When a Line Bends . . . A Shape Begins* by Rhonda Gowler Greene **Challenging** 	**Math** Geometric Shapes, p. 33 **Reading** Make Inferences, p. 32 **Writing** Interactive, p. 33
• Art Prints 1, 2, 8 • Reading Skill Card 1 • Big Book, pp. 34–35 • Electronic Art Gallery CD-ROM, Primary	*The Shape of Me and Other Stuff* by Dr. Seuss **Average** 	**Performing Arts** Free-Form People, p. 35 **Reading** Make Inferences, p. 34 **Writing** Interactive, p. 35
• Art Prints 2, 3 • Discussion Cards 1, 5, pp. R34, R37 • Reading Skill Card 1 • Big Book, pp. 38–39 • Electronic Art Gallery CD-ROM, Primary	*No One Saw: Ordinary Things Through the Eyes of an Artist* by Bob Raczka **Average** 	**Social Studies** Oral Presentations, p. 39 **Reading** Make Inferences, p. 38 **Writing** Interactive, p. 39

Present these art puzzlers to children at the beginning or end of a class or when children finish an assignment early.

- Trace the **lines** that lightning makes. Tell about the lines.
  TEKS 2.1A, TEKS 2.1B

- Look around. Which things have lines that show **movement**?
  TEKS 2.1A, TEKS 2.1B

- Use your finger to trace an **outline** around your shoe and then around your hand. TEKS 2.1A

- What **geometric shape** is a pizza? Name some other foods that have geometric shapes. TEKS 2.1A, TEKS 2.1B

- Look at clothing. Look outside. Find **geometric shapes**, **free-form shapes**, and **organic shapes**.
  TEKS 2.1A, TEKS 2.1B

School-Home Connection
The activities above are included in the School-Home Connection for this unit. See *Teacher Resource Book,* pp. 77–78.

Assessment Options

- Rubrics and Recording Forms, pp. R28–R33
- Unit 1 Test, *Teacher Resource Book*, p. 91

Visit *The Learning Site*:
www.harcourtschool.com

Artist's Workshops PREVIEW

PDAS Domain IV

Use these pages to help you gather and organize materials for the Artist's Workshop in each lesson.

LESSON	MATERIALS

1 My Fall Tree p. 27

Objective: To have children draw the outline of a tree using different kinds of lines, and then add tissue-paper autumn leaves

🕐 15–25 minutes

Challenge Activity: See *Teacher Resource Book,* p. 43.

- markers
- construction paper
- tissue paper
- pencil
- glue

FINISHED EXAMPLE

LESSON

2 "Dance for Joy" Drawing p. 29

Objective: To have children explore lines that show movement by drawing themselves dancing and other things moving across the scene

🕐 15–25 minutes

Challenge Activity: See *Teacher Resource Book,* p. 44.

- crayons
- markers
- drawing paper

FINISHED EXAMPLE

Safety Tips
For safety information, see Art Safety, page R4; the Art Safety Poster; or Big Book page 148.

For information on media and techniques, see pages R15–R23.

LESSON	MATERIALS

3 Food Collage p. 33

Objective: To have children explore geometric shapes by making a collage of a healthful meal, using shapes like circles, squares, ovals, and rectangles

🕐 15–25 minutes

Challenge Activity: See *Teacher Resource Book,* p. 45.

- construction paper
- scissors
- glue stick
- paper plate

FINISHED EXAMPLE

LESSON

4 Free-Form Flip Art p. 35

Objective: To have children explore shapes by cutting and gluing organic and free-form shapes to create images in the style of Matisse

🕐 15–25 minutes

Challenge Activity: See *Teacher Resource Book,* p. 46.

- construction paper
- scissors
- glue

FINISHED EXAMPLE

LESSON

5 Favorite-People Portrait p. 39

Objective: To have children create portraits of families or other groups, using lines and shapes

🕐 15–25 minutes

Challenge Activity: See *Teacher Resource Book,* p. 47.

- construction paper
- crayons
- markers
- tempera paints
- paintbrushes

FINISHED EXAMPLE

Unit 1

PDAS Domains I, II

Celebrate Our World

PREVIEW THE UNIT

Do a Walk-Through   Have children use the Contents on page 4 to find the page on which Unit 1 begins and then turn to the correct page. Tell children that they will learn how artists express their feelings about themselves and the world around them. Point out the lesson titles, art captions, and art production activities. Discuss the importance of following safety rules. (See Art Safety, *Student Edition*, pp. 148–149.)

SHARE THE POEM

Read the poem to children as they view the art. Then reread the poem aloud with them.

How does the poem add to your feelings about this painting? (Possible response: I feel even happier after looking at the farm and then reading about a blue sky and green grass.)
TAKS Reading Objectives 1, 4

STEP INTO THE ART

Have children look carefully at the painting and describe what they see and feel. Then ask:

Would you like to visit the place shown in the painting? Why or why not? (Yes. It looks happy, and I like animals.) **PERSONAL RESPONSE**

SHARE BACKGROUND INFORMATION

Tell children that "Grandma" Moses is known by that name because she did not begin painting until she was nearly 80 years old. Have children identify a story they see in Grandma Moses's painting.
TEKS 2.3A

 LOCATE IT   See *Using the Maps of Museums and Art Sites*, pp. R2–R3.

▲ Grandma Moses, *Autumn*

LOCATE IT

This painting is in the Bennington Museum in Bennington, Vermont.

See Maps of Museums and Art Sites, pages 144–147.

22

Background Information

About the Artist

Anna Mary Robertson ("Grandma") Moses (1860–1961) lived and worked on farms most of her life. Moses began painting when she was 77 years old. She was discovered when a collector saw her paintings in a drugstore window. At a time when American art was moving toward the abstract, Grandma Moses became famous for her more traditional style.

For additional information about Grandma Moses, see pp. R48–R59.

For related images, see **Electronic Art Gallery CD-ROM, Primary.**

★ **TEKS 2.1B** identify elements and principles; **TEKS 2.2C** identify and practice skills; **TEKS 2.3A** identify stories and constructions; **PDAS Domain I** active participation; **PDAS Domain II** learner-centered instruction; **PDAS Domain IV** classroom management; *(continued)*

Unit 1

Line and Shape

Celebrate Our World

I'm Glad

I'm glad the sky is
painted blue,
And the earth is
painted green,
With such a lot of
nice fresh air
All sandwiched
in between.

Anonymous

ABOUT THE ARTIST

See Gallery of Artists, pages 182–191.

Unit Vocabulary

lines
outline
movement
geometric shapes

free-form shapes
organic shapes
portrait
self-portrait

 GO ONLINE Multimedia Art Glossary
Visit *The Learning Site*
www.harcourtschool.com

23

Have volunteers read aloud the vocabulary words. Ask children to tell the meanings of familiar words and point to examples in the art or in the classroom that illustrate their meaning. Tell children they will learn about these words in this unit.

lines marks that extend some distance. Lines can be any size, color, or thickness.

outline the line along the edge of a shape

movement a feeling of motion through an artwork—often achieved by patterns or lines that curve and bend

geometric shapes flat spaces that are enclosed by a line, such as circles, squares, and triangles

free-form shapes shapes that are irregular or are not geometric

organic shapes free-form shapes that show things in nature, such as the shapes of most leaves and animals

portrait a picture of a person or group of people

self-portrait an artist's picture of himself or herself

Vocabulary Resources

- Vocabulary Cards in English and Spanish: *Teacher Resource Book*, pp. 7–8
- Student Edition Glossary, pp. 192–201

 GO ONLINE Multimedia Art Glossary
English/Spanish
Visit *The Learning Site*
www.harcourtschool.com

Sketchbook

Before beginning this unit, direct children's attention to *Student Edition* pages 12–13. Help them create a sketchbook. Have children use their sketchbooks to practice the skills necessary for producing a variety of artworks. TEKS 2.2C

TEKS 2.1B; PDAS Domain IV

 ## Art Center

Materials markers, crayons, pencils, pens, geometric shapes, traceable objects

Ongoing Activity
Have children draw and identify lines and shapes they observe.

Big Book Put the *Big Book* in the Art Center for children to use.

TEKS 2.1B; PDAS Domain IV

 ## Classroom Management

Create several stations with materials for exploring different art media. Whenever time permits, have children work in small groups to explore and identify the elements of line and shape, using materials such as tempera paints, watercolors, clay, and oil pastels.

TAKS Reading Objective 1 demonstrate understanding of texts; **TAKS Reading Objective 4** apply critical-thinking skills

UNIT 1 *Celebrate Our World* **23**

Focus Skill READING SKILL

PDAS Domains I, II

Make Inferences

SKILL TRACE	
MAKE INFERENCES	
Introduce	pp. 24–25
Review	pp. 26, 28, 32, 34, 38, 41

DISCUSS THE SKILL

Access Prior Knowledge   Display illustrations from a picture book while covering up the text. Have children use the pictures to identify the story in the artwork. Ask children how they knew what the story was about. Then reveal and read aloud the text. Tell children that like a story, an artwork will not always directly show everything about its "story." Discuss how sometimes the historical and cultural heritage associated with the artwork can also provide context for the story. Explain to children that sometimes they can use information they see in the artwork, and what they already know, to tell what is happening.
TEKS 2.3A

APPLY TO ART

Make Inferences from Art   Have children read the top of page 24 and discuss what the picture mainly shows. (a drummer throwing drumsticks to a boy) Ask children to read the rest of the page. Have them infer why the boy wants the sticks and how they can tell. (so he can play drums; he has cans in front of him that look as if they can be used as drums.)   TAKS Reading Objectives 3, 4

Explain that knowing how to make inferences will help them better understand the artworks and information in this unit.   TEKS 2.3A

Focus Skill READING SKILL

Make Inferences

What is happening in the picture?

Brian Pinkney,
illustration from *Max Found Two Sticks*   LITERATURE LINK

Why does the boy want the sticks? Use what you see and what you already know to decide.

24

FYI Background Information

About the Artist

Brian Pinkney is an illustrator of several award-winning picture books. He has also played the drums for most of his life. His musical experience gave him the idea for the book that includes the picture shown on page 24.

For additional information about Brian Pinkney, see pp. R48–R59.

LITERATURE LINK   Share other illustrations from *Max Found Two Sticks* by Brian Pinkney. Simon & Schuster, 1994.

AVERAGE

★ TEKS 2.3A identify stories and constructions; **PDAS Domain I** active participation; **PDAS Domain II** learner-centered instruction; **PDAS Domain IV** classroom management; **TAKS Reading Objective 1** demonstrate understanding of texts; *(continued)*

Read the paragraph. Make a chart like the one below. Tell what you think.

> A man in a uniform throws sticks to the boy. The man has drums, and the sticks are drumsticks. I think the boy will use them to play music.

What I See and Read	+ What I Know	= What I Think
The man has drums. He throws sticks to the boy.	The sticks are drumsticks.	The boy can play music with them.
The man wears a uniform.	People in a band wear uniforms.	The man is in a ____.
The man still holds two drumsticks.	Drummers use two sticks to play the drums.	The man ____.

On Your Own

Look at the painting on pages 22–23. Make a chart. Write what you see and know. Then write what you think.

25

APPLY TO READING

Have children read the passage on page 25. Draw on the board a chart like the one shown. Ask volunteers to make inferences based on the passage and the picture on page 24. Add these inferences to the chart. (Inferences may vary.)
TAKS Reading Objectives 1, 3, 4

What I See and Read	+ What I Know	= What I Think
The man has drums. He throws sticks to the boy.	The sticks are drumsticks.	The boy can play music with them.
The man wears a uniform.	People in a band wear uniforms.	The man is in a band.
The man still holds two drumsticks.	Drummers use two sticks to play the drums.	The man will continue to play the drums.

ON YOUR OWN

With children, revisit the painting *Autumn* on pages 22–23. Children can work individually or with the group to create a chart and make inferences about the painting.

TAKS Reading Objectives 3, 4

Reading Skill Card

Distribute Reading Skill Card 1, *Teacher Resource Book* p. 23. Use the chart to help discuss making inferences.

Extend the Skill For additional teaching suggestions, see **Art Transparency 1**.

PDAS Domain IV

ESL Share and discuss **visuals** of drums and drumsticks to support children's **vocabulary development**. Help children understand how drums make music. Have children **pantomime** using drums as part of a **total physical response** so they can associate the words *drum*, *drumsticks*, and *drummer* with their actions.

Reading Skills and Activities
Visit *The Learning Site*
www.harcourtschool.com

Lesson 1

Lines All Around

PDAS Domains I, II

OBJECTIVES
- Identify lines in art and nature
- Create a composition with lines
- Make inferences

RESOURCES
- Art Print 1
- Big Book, pp. 26–27
- Electronic Art Gallery CD-ROM, Primary

5 Minutes

Warm-Up

Trace Lines in Objects Have each child choose an object and use his or her finger to trace around it in one continuous line. Ask children to discuss how their fingers moved as they traced. TEKS 2.2C

10–15 Minutes

Teach

Discuss Art Concepts Ask volunteers to read pages 26–27. Have children answer the questions. Then help them identify kinds of lines in each of the artworks. Display **Art Print 1**. Ask children which two artworks are by the same artist. Have them explain how they could tell. TEKS 2.1B

Think Critically

1. **(Focus Skill) READING SKILL** Why do you think the hands are holding flowers in Picasso's artwork? (Possible response: to show friendship and people sharing) MAKE INFERENCES
TEKS 2.3A; TAKS Reading Objective 4

2. **How are the lines in these artworks alike?** (Possible response: They both use many straight and curved lines.)
PERCEPTION/COMPARE AND CONTRAST   TEKS 2.1B

3. **WRITE** Which artwork's lines do you think look more real? Tell why.
INTERACTIVE WRITING   TEKS 2.1B; TAKS Writing Objective 1

Lesson 1

Vocabulary
lines
outline

Lines All Around

What do you see in these artworks?

Pablo Picasso,
Hand with Flowers   A

Artists use many kinds of **lines**. Find lines like these in the art.

| thin | thick | curved | vertical | horizontal | diagonal |

26

Background Information

About the Artists

Pablo Picasso (pih•KAHS•soh) (1881–1973) was mainly a painter, but he also created sculptures, prints, and ceramics. Picasso began drawing as a child.

Henri Rousseau (ahn•REE roo•SOH) (1844–1910) was a French artist with no artistic training. His paintings are known for their strong, cheerful colors and imaginative subject matter. Trees are often featured in his landscapes.

For additional information about the artists, see pp. R48–R59.

★ TEKS 2.1B identify elements and principles; TEKS 2.2A express ideas and feelings; TEKS 2.2B create effective compositions; TEKS 2.2C identify and practice skills; TEKS 2.3A identify stories and constructions; TEKS 2.4B identify ideas in artworks by peers and artists; *(continued)*

An **outline** is the line along the edge of a shape.
Use your finger. Trace an outline in each picture.

Henri Rousseau,
*The Banks of the
Bièvre Near Bicêtre*

My Fall Tree

1. **Draw the outline of a tree. Use many kinds of lines.**

2. **Glue on paper leaves.**

27

My Fall Tree

MATERIALS: construction paper, tissue paper, glue, pencil, markers

TECHNIQUE TIP: Children can draw in pencil, make changes, and then use markers.

PLAN Have children identify skills needed for drawing realistic trees and practice drawing them, using a variety of lines. TEKS 2.2C

CREATE Model how to make leaves from tissue paper. Ask children to express their ideas and feelings using a variety of lines. TEKS 2.2A, TEKS 2.2B

REFLECT Volunteers share their art, and classmates identify ideas in the art. TEKS 2.4B

Activity Options PDAS Domain IV

Quick Activity Have children draw a large tree on chart paper and have each child add leaves.

Early Finishers Children may draw the outline of a flower and then cut out and glue petals on it.

Challenge See *Teacher Resource Book* p. 43.

Wrap-Up

Informal Assessment PDAS Domain III

- **Which artwork has lines most like your fall tree?** (Responses will vary.) PERCEPTION/AESTHETICS

- **What kinds of lines did others use in their trees?** (Responses will vary.) ART CRITICISM
TEKS 2.1B

Extend Through Writing

Independent Have volunteers write their names, using different types of lines. TEKS 2.1B

Science Connection

What Do Leaves Do? Provide two plants for children to observe. Have children fold a piece of paper in half and draw one plant on each side. Then cover the leaves of one plant in tin foil. Keep the plants in the sun and water them. After a week, have children draw the two plants again. Discuss them.

PDAS Domain IV

ESL Use **visuals** to support **comprehensible input**. Display a picture of a tree. Help children point to and name its parts.

Use *Picture Cards Collection* card 122. See also *Picture Card Bank* **CD-ROM**, Categories: Plants, Parts of Plants.

tree

PDAS Domain I active participation; PDAS Domain II learner-centered instruction; PDAS Domain III evaluation and feedback; PDAS Domain IV classroom management;
TAKS Reading Objective 4 apply critical-thinking skills; TAKS Writing Objective 1 composition
LESSON 1 *Lines All Around* **27**

Lesson 2

PDAS Domains I, II

Lines Show Movement

OBJECTIVES
- Identify lines that show movement
- Express ideas using lines
- Make inferences

RESOURCES
- Art Prints 1 and 12
- Discussion Card 1
- Big Book, pp. 28–29
- Electronic Art Gallery CD-ROM, Primary

5 Minutes

Warm-Up

Action Poses Have children demonstrate an action, such as jumping rope or running in place. Have them tell how their legs and arms moved.

10-15 Minutes

Teach

Discuss Art Concepts Have children read the text and answer the questions on page 28. Use Discussion Card 1 to ask additional questions. Point out how the curving lines lead their eyes through each artwork, giving a sense of movement. Then have children compare lines in **Art Prints 1** and **12**. TEKS 2.1B

Think Critically

1. **(Focus Skill) READING SKILL How can you tell this dancer is moving?** (Possible response: Her arms and legs are bent in zigzag lines.)
   MAKE INFERENCES TEKS 2.4B; TAKS Reading Objective 4

2. **How are the lines in the artworks alike?** (Possible response: Both show long, curved lines.) **PERCEPTION/COMPARE AND CONTRAST** TEKS 2.1B

3. **WRITE In which direction is the piñata moving? How do the lines help you tell?**
   INTERACTIVE WRITING TAKS Writing Objective 1

STUDENT EDITION **OR** BIG BOOK

Lesson 2

Vocabulary
movement

Lines Show Movement

What is going on in each artwork?
What actions do you see in each one?

A Diego Rivera, *La Piñata*

Lines that curve and bend through an artwork can show **movement**. Which lines show movement in these artworks?

Abastenia St. Leger Eberle, *Untitled* **B**

28

FYI

Background Information

About the Artists

Abastenia St. Leger Eberle (ab•uh•STEE•nee•uh saynt LEJ•er EB•er•lee) (1878–1942) was a New York City artist who made realistic sculptures of people. Much of her work reflects the lives of poor people who came to America.

Diego Rivera (DYAY•goh ree•VAY•rah) (1886–1957) was a Mexican artist who became famous for his huge, boldly colorful murals.

For more information about the artists, see pp. R48–R59.

★ **TEKS 2.1B** identify elements and principles; **TEKS 2.2A** express ideas and feelings; **TEKS 2.2B** create effective compositions; **TEKS 2.2C** identify and practice skills; **TEKS 2.4A** define reasons for preferences in personal artworks; **TEKS 2.4B** identify ideas in artworks by peers and artists; *(continued)*

Artist's Workshop

"Dance for Joy" Drawing

PLAN

Think about how your arms and legs bend when you are dancing.

CREATE

1. **Draw yourself dancing. Show your arms and legs moving.**

2. **Use lines to show things around you moving.**

REFLECT

Did you bend, jump, or twirl? What kinds of lines did you use to show movement?

What actions do you see in your classroom?

29

Artist's Workshop

15-25 Minutes

"Dance for Joy" Drawing

MATERIALS: crayons, markers, drawing paper

TECHNIQUE TIP: Model how to use the sides of crayons to draw soft motion lines.

PLAN Have children identify skills for producing drawings and practice drawing figures with lines to show movement. TEKS 2.2C

CREATE Ask children to express their ideas and feelings about dancing by using straight, curved, and zigzag lines. TEKS 2.2A, TEKS 2.2B

REFLECT Ask volunteers to share how they used lines to show movement. TEKS 2.2A

Activity Options PDAS Domain IV

Quick Activity Draw starter outlines of people in motion on butcher paper. Have each child add lines to show movement. TEKS 2.2C

Early Finishers Have children complete an activity from the Idea Wheel, *Teacher Resource Book,* pages 29–30.

Challenge See *Teacher Resource Book* p. 44.

5-10 Minutes

Wrap-Up

Informal Assessment PDAS Domain III

- **What kind of lines best show movement?**
  (Possible response: curved) PERCEPTION/AESTHETICS TEKS 2.4A
- **How did classmates use lines like yours?**
  (Responses will vary.) ART CRITICISM TEKS 2.4B

Extend Through Writing

Interactive Have children "share the pen" to write sentences about their dance drawings. Have volunteers capitalize the beginning of each sentence. TAKS Writing Objectives 1, 2, 4

Social Studies Connection

Dancing Around the World
Explain to children that different cultures have traditional dances. Then teach them the "Mexican Hat Dance" or another dance you choose. Place a hat in the center of the room. Play music, and have children dance around the hat while clapping to the beat.

 PDAS Domain IV

ESL Use **total physical response** and **visuals** to develop an understanding of movement. Demonstrate and talk about actions such as dancing.

Use *Picture Cards Collection* cards 35, 70, and 100. See also *Picture Card Bank* **CD-ROM,** Category: Fun and Games.

run

PDAS Domain I active participation; PDAS Domain II learner-centered instruction; PDAS Domain III evaluation and feedback; PDAS Domain IV classroom management; TAKS Reading Objective 4 apply critical-thinking skills; TAKS Writing Objective 1 composition; TAKS Writing Objective 2 conventions; TAKS Writing Objective 4 sentence construction

LESSON 2 *Lines Show Movement* **29**

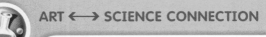

ART ←→ SCIENCE CONNECTION

PDAS Domains I, II

Art in Our World

ART IN THE ENVIRONMENT

DISCUSS THE PHOTOGRAPHS

Have children read pages 30–31.

- Help children develop and organize ideas from the environment. Have them identify variations in objects and subjects from the environment using the senses. Tell children that the environment is made up of all the living and nonliving things around them. Explain that lines, shapes, and colors can be found in nature and in human-made objects. Have children tell which images show something in nature and which show something human-made. **TEKS 2.1A**

- Point out that the iron fence and the zebras are similar in that they both have straight and curved black lines. Ask children to use their sense of sight to identify other variations in line, shape, and color between the photographs. Have them tell how the subjects of the photographs are alike and different. **TEKS 2.1A, TEKS 2.1B**

- Ask children to tell what senses other than sight they could use to learn about these objects and subjects in the environment. (smell for bluebonnets, sound for roller coaster, touch for gate, and smell for plants and animals) **TEKS 2.1A, TEKS 2.1B**

- Display **Art Print 8**, and have children identify lines, shapes, and colors. Have them compare the subject and the other objects shown in the painting to those in the photographs. Have children do the same for the use of line. **TEKS 2.1A, TEKS 2.1B**

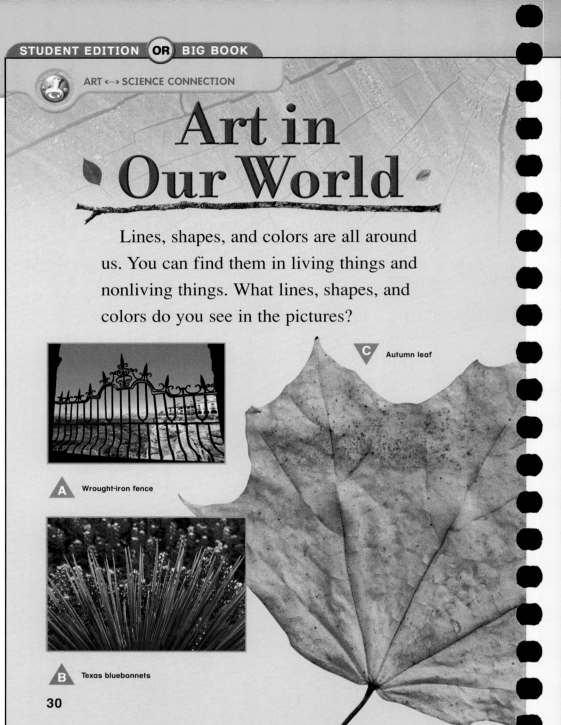

Art in Our World

Lines, shapes, and colors are all around us. You can find them in living things and nonliving things. What lines, shapes, and colors do you see in the pictures?

C Autumn leaf

A Wrought-iron fence

B Texas bluebonnets

30

FYI

Background Information

Art History

The roots of **roller coasters** lie in Russia in the 1600s. During the cold winters in the area that is now St. Petersburg, Russian ice slides were built. The structures were made of lumber with a sheet of ice several inches thick covering the surface. People would climb up stairs and slide down the icy slope. The tradition caught on in other countries that had milder climates. The ice slides eventually evolved into structures with cars that had wheels so they could be enjoyed in all temperatures.

 You may wish to have children look for other artworks inspired by nature on the **Electronic Art Gallery CD-ROM, Primary.**

★ **TEKS 2.1A** identify variations in objects and subjects; **TEKS 2.1B** identify elements and principles; **TEKS 2.2A** express ideas and feelings; **TEKS 2.2C** identify and practice skills; **TEKS 2.4B** identify ideas in artworks by peers and artists; **PDAS Domain I** active participation; **PDAS Domain II** learner-centered instruction

D Zebras

DID YOU KNOW?

The lines on a zebra help keep it safe. These stripes blend in with the lines of tall grass to hide the zebra.

Think About Art

What lines, shapes, and colors do you see in your classroom?

E Railroad crossing sign

F Roller coaster

Science Connection

Warning Colors Tell children that yellow and black on signs mean "warning." Discuss how these colors mimic colors of animals. Have children use yellow and black to create signs.

For additional cross-curricular teaching suggestions, see Art Transparency 2.

TEKS 2.4B; PDAS Domain II

Student Art Show

Display Artworks During this unit, have children create an exhibit of their portfolios and finished artworks. Ask children to view and identify ideas in one another's original artworks, portfolios, and the exhibit as a whole. Have them focus on line and shape. See also Student Art Exhibitions, page 142.

DID YOU KNOW?

The contrasting shapes and lines that make up the stripes on a zebra's coat serve to "break up" the shape of the animal into irregular shapes. When looking from a distance or watching the animal in motion, the eye has a difficult time seeing a solid shape. The stripes break up the zebra's outline so it does not stand out against the background. This helps keep zebras from being seen easily by predators.

Help children name other animals that have lines for camouflage, such as tigers. TEKS 2.1B

Think About Art

What lines, shapes, and colors do you see in your classroom? (Responses will vary but should include examples of elements from human-made products as well as from living things in the classroom, such as plants and class pets.)

IMPORTANT DETAILS TEKS 2.1A, TEKS 2.1B

ARTIST'S EYE ACTIVITY

Bifold Art Have children choose two objects that have similar lines, one from the natural environment and one from the human-made environment. Ask them to draw the natural example on the top half of a folded sheet of paper and the human-made example on the bottom half. As children work, have them identify and practice skills necessary for producing drawings. Ask them to use a variety of lines to express their ideas and feelings. Then have children identify art elements, such as line, in one another's artworks.
TEKS 2.1A, TEKS 2.1B, TEKS 2.2A, TEKS 2.2C

Lesson 3

PDAS Domains I, II

Geometric Shapes

OBJECTIVES
- Identify art elements such as geometric shapes
- Make a collage using geometric shapes
- Make inferences

RESOURCES
- Art Prints 3 and 8
- Big Book, pp. 32–33
- Electronic Art Gallery CD-ROM, Primary

5 Minutes

Warm-Up

Find Shapes   Draw an outline of a circle, triangle, and square on the board, reviewing that a line along the edge of something is called an outline. Have children find and share examples of each drawing in classroom objects.   TEKS 2.1B

10-15 Minutes

Teach

Discuss Art Concepts   Read pages 32–33 with children. Draw an oval on the board, and help children distinguish it from a circle. Display **Art Prints 3** and **8**, and have children identify shapes in all the artworks.   TEKS 2.1B

Think Critically

1. **READING SKILL   Why did these artists use geometric shapes?** (Possible response: because the foods they painted have geometric shapes) MAKE INFERENCES

2. **Which artist uses more geometric shapes? Which do you see?** (Possible response: Thiebaud—triangles, rectangles, squares, circles) PERCEPTION/COMPARE AND CONTRAST

3. **WRITE   Tell how these foods might taste.**
   INTERACTIVE WRITING   TAKS Writing Objective 1

Lesson 3

Vocabulary
geometric shapes

Geometric Shapes

What does this art show? What shapes can you find? Shapes like circles, squares, and triangles are **geometric shapes**.

A   Wayne Thiebaud, *Desserts*

circle   oval   triangle   square   rectangle

32

Background Information

About the Artists
Wayne Thiebaud (TEE·boh) (1920–) is an American artist who became famous in the 1960s for his paintings of cakes, pies, and other foods.

Doris Lee (1905–1983) was an American artist who grew up among people who sewed quilts and made crafts. Her paintings are known for their simple folk-art style.

For more information about the artists, see pp. R48–R59.

RECOMMENDED READING
When a Line Bends . . . A Shape Begins by Rhonda Gowler Greene. Houghton, 1997. CHALLENGING

 TEKS 2.1B identify elements and principles; TEKS 2.2B create effective compositions; TEKS 2.2C identify and practice skills; TEKS 2.4A define reasons for preferences in personal artworks; TEKS 2.4B identify ideas in artworks by peers and artists; PDAS Domain I active participation; *(continued)*

Trace some geometric shapes in the art. What kinds of lines did the artists use to make the shapes?

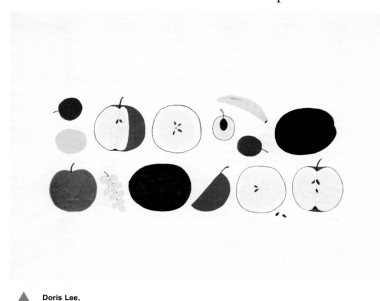

B Doris Lee,
Untitled

Food Collage

1. **Cut out geometric shapes to show a meal you like.**

2. **Glue everything to a paper place mat.**

33

Food Collage

MATERIALS: construction paper, glue stick, scissors, paper plate

 Safety Tips Review with children how to handle scissors carefully.

PLAN Encourage children to arrange their shapes in the way they like best before gluing. TEKS 2.2C

CREATE Model how to cut shapes. TEKS 2.2B

REFLECT Ask volunteers to tell why they chose particular shapes to represent different kinds of food. TEKS 2.4A

Activity Options PDAS Domain IV

Quick Activity Provide children with precut shapes, and have small groups work together.

Early Finishers Have children make another shape collage—one that forms their name.

Challenge See *Teacher Resource Book* p. 45.

Wrap-Up

Informal Assessment PDAS Domain III

- **How did looking at the paintings help you put shapes together to look like food?** (Responses will vary.) PERCEPTION/AESTHETICS TEKS 2.1B

- **Which collages look the most like real foods? Why?** (Responses will vary.) ART CRITICISM TEKS 2.4A, TEKS 2.4B

Extend Through Writing

Interactive Have children "share the pen" to write about foods in the collages. Then have volunteers check and add the correct end mark to each sentence. TAKS Writing Objectives 1, 2, 4

 ## Math Connection

Geometric Shapes Have children cut out large geometric shapes and then cut them apart to form new shapes. Ask children to identify each new shape and to compare and contrast their attributes. Then have children combine the small shapes in new ways to create larger shapes.

 PDAS Domain IV

ESL Cut shapes out of construction paper. Point to each shape, say the word, and have children repeat it to help them make associations with **visuals**.

Special Needs If children have motor disabilities, give them spring-action scissors to make cutting easier.

PDAS Domain II learner-centered instruction; PDAS Domain III evaluation and feedback; PDAS Domain IV classroom management; TAKS Writing Objective 1 composition; TAKS Writing Objective 2 conventions; TAKS Writing Objective 4 sentence construction

LESSON 3 *Geometric Shapes* **33**

Lesson 4

PDAS Domains I, II

Free-Form Shapes

OBJECTIVES
- Identify free-form shapes
- Use free-form shapes in art
- Make inferences

RESOURCES
- Art Prints 1, 2, 8
- Big Book, pp. 34–35
- Electronic Art Gallery CD-ROM, Primary

Warm-Up
5 Minutes

Form Animal Shapes Have volunteers pantomime different animals such as rabbits, snakes, and elephants by forming shapes with their arms and hands. Classmates guess the animals.

Teach
10–15 Minutes

Discuss Art Concepts Have volunteers read page 34. Explain that free-form shapes are not perfect geometric shapes like circles and squares and that organic shapes are often seen in nature. Display **Art Prints 1, 2,** and **8.** Have children identify free-form shapes and compare them.
TEKS 2.1B

Think Critically

1. (Focus Skill) **READING SKILL** **What do you think the reddish shape is? Why?** (Possible response: It is a horse, because it looks as if it has a long neck and legs.) **MAKE INFERENCES**

2. **How do Matisse's shapes remind you of things you have seen before?** (Responses will vary.) **PERCEPTION** TEKS 2.1B

3. **WRITE** **What story do the free-form shapes in Matisse's artwork tell?**
INTERACTIVE WRITING TEKS 2.3A; TAKS Writing Objective 1

Lesson 4

Free-Form Shapes

Vocabulary
free-form shapes
organic shapes

What do you think this picture is about? Artists use many shapes that are not geometric, called **free-form shapes**.

Henri Matisse, *The Horse, the Rider, and the Clown*

Free-form shapes of things from nature, like animals and plants, are **organic shapes**.

Free-Form Shapes

organic shapes

34

Background Information

Art History

The artist **Henri Matisse** (ahn•REE mah•TEES) (1869–1954) was a leader of the **Fauvism** (FOH•vih•zuhm) movement. Its followers were known as *Fauves*, a word meaning "wild beasts" in French. They got this name by surprising the art world with bright colors and unusual shapes.

For more information about the artist and Fauvism, see pp. R48–R59.

RECOMMENDED READING
The Shape of Me and Other Stuff by Dr. Seuss. Random House, 1973. **AVERAGE**

★ TEKS 2.1B identify elements and principles; TEKS 2.2B create effective compositions; TEKS 2.3A identify stories and constructions; TEKS 2.4B identify ideas in artworks by peers and artists; **PDAS Domain I** active participation; *(continued)*

Artist's Workshop

Free-Form Flip Art

PLAN

Think about free-form shapes around you.

CREATE

1. Cut out free-form shapes along the edge of a half sheet of paper.

2. Glue the half sheet to a whole sheet. Glue the free-form shapes.

REFLECT

What free-form shapes did you make? Are any of them organic shapes?

What organic shapes do you see in your classroom?

35

Artist's Workshop

Free-Form Flip Art PDAS Domain I

MATERIALS: construction paper, scissors, glue

Safety Tips Remind children to close the glue bottle between uses.

PLAN Tell children to choose two different colors of paper so the shapes will stand out.

CREATE Precut some sheets of paper in half lengthwise. Model how to create the flip art. TEKS 2.2B

REFLECT Have children identify and discuss ideas in artworks, such as what each other's free-form shapes look like. TEKS 2.4B

Activity Options PDAS Domain IV

Quick Activity Have small groups cut free-form shapes out of colored paper and glue them onto one sheet of white paper.

Early Finishers Children can choose an Idea Wheel activity, *Teacher Resource Book* pp. 29–30.

Challenge See *Teacher Resource Book* p. 46.

Wrap-Up

5-10 Minutes

Informal Assessment PDAS Domain III

- **How are your free-form shapes different from geometric shapes?** (They have more curved edges.) PERCEPTION/AESTHETICS

- **Which artworks have organic shapes?** (Responses will vary.) ART CRITCISM TEKS 2.1B

Extend Through Writing

Interactive Together with children, write a paragraph that describes their artworks.
TAKS Writing Objectives 1, 3

Performing Arts Connection

Free-Form People Organize children into small groups, and have them share their artworks. Ask them to arrange themselves in positions that reflect the shapes in one artwork. Then have each group perform one of its poses, and ask classmates to guess which of the group's artworks is being portrayed.

PDAS Domain IV

ESL Help children **understand the concept** of free-form and organic shapes. Set up a light projector. Hold up objects, and have children finger-trace the shapes.

Challenge Children can make raised free-form shapes with strips of paper. Refer them to Student Edition page 169.

PDAS Domain II learner-centered instruction; **PDAS Domain III** evaluation and feedback; **PDAS Domain IV** classroom management; **TAKS Writing Objective 1** composition; **TAKS Writing Objective 3** organization

LESSON 4 *Free-Form Shapes* 35

ART ←→ SOCIAL STUDIES CONNECTION

PDAS Domains I, II

PABLO PICASSO'S SHAPES

ARTIST BIOGRAPHY

DISCUSS THE PAINTINGS

Read pages 36–37 with children.

- Help children understand Cubism as it relates to art history. Explain that the painting *Three Musicians* is an example of geometric art called **Cubism**. Have children look up the term *abstract* in the Glossary, page 192. Point out that *Three Musicians* is abstract, as the people do not have realistic shapes or details. Have children identify other objects on these pages, on page 26, and in **Art Print 1** that look abstract.   TEKS 2.1A, TEKS 2.1B

- Ask children to identify the objects in the still life and the shapes in each.   TEKS 2.1B

- Ask children to compare how Picasso painted the musicians and himself.   TEKS 2.3B

DISCUSS THE ARTIST

Share background information about the artist.

- Explain that Picasso was influenced by the artist Paul Cézanne, who believed that everything was made of geometric shapes. Ask children to identify how Picasso's art shows this construction, or view of the world. (Picasso used a lot of geometric shapes.)   TEKS 2.3A, TEKS 2.4B

- A friend once gave Picasso an African mask, which influenced his artwork. Show children an African mask, if possible, or describe one. (covers the face, has simplified features, can be carved from wood and decorated) Have children identify how this construction, African masks, is reflected in *Three Musicians*. (The musician on the right looks like he is wearing an African mask.)   TEKS 2.3A, TEKS 2.4B

STUDENT EDITION **OR** BIG BOOK

ART ←→ SOCIAL STUDIES CONNECTION

PABLO PICASSO'S SHAPES

 Three Musicians

Pablo Picasso was an artist who liked to use geometric shapes in interesting ways. He left out details so that his artworks did not look like real life. They are **abstract**.

36

Background Information

About the Artist
Pablo Picasso (pih•KAHS•soh) was a Spanish painter and sculptor. He is often considered one of the world's greatest artists. In 1907, Picasso began experimenting with a style later known as **Cubism**, which emphasizes the geometric shapes of a subject, showing it in a flat, fragmented way. Picasso once painted a picture that an art critic said looked like "little cubes."

For more information about Picasso and Cubism, see pp. R48–R59.

 For related images, see **Electronic Art Gallery CD-ROM, Primary.**

36   UNIT 1 *Celebrate Our World*   ★ **TEKS 2.1A** identify variations in objects and subjects; **TEKS 2.1B** identify elements and principles; **TEKS 2.3A** identify stories and constructions; **TEKS 2.3B** compare artworks showing individuals/families; **TEKS 2.4B** identify ideas in artworks by peers and artists; **PDAS Domain I** active participation; *(continued)*

B *Self-Portrait with Palette*

Multimedia Biographies
Visit *The Learning Site*
www.harcourtschool.com

C
The Enameled Casserole

THINK ABOUT ART

Do the people and things in Picasso's paintings look real? Tell why or why not.

37

Social Studies Connection

Museum Visits   Picasso's art may be viewed at:

- *Three Musicians*, Museum of Modern Art, New York, New York. www.moma.org

For additional cross-curricular suggestions, see Art Transparency 3.

TEKS 2.4B; PDAS Domain II
Visit with an Artist

View Art   Arrange for children to visit with an artist either at school or at a museum, gallery, or other location. Ask children to view and identify ideas in original artworks, the portfolio, and an exhibition by the artist. Have them focus on concepts from this unit, such as line and shape.

DID YOU KNOW?

Picasso sometimes featured clowns and other circus performers in his paintings. Picasso identified with clowns because they masked their true identities with costumes and makeup. In one of his paintings, *Family of Saltimbanques*, Picasso portrayed himself as a clown in a diamond-patterned costume.

Have children identify which musician looks like a clown. (The middle musician's clothes have a pattern of triangular shapes that looks like something a clown would wear.) Elicit that the shapes are also bright and colorful, like those on a clown suit.   TEKS 2.1B, TEKS 2.3A

THINK ABOUT ART

Do the people and things in Picasso's paintings look real? Tell why or why not. (Possible response: No, because real people don't have geometric shapes for body parts, and real things are not usually made up of such simple shapes.)
IMPORTANT DETAILS   TEKS 2.3A

ARTIST'S EYE ACTIVITY

Paint Like Picasso   Help children develop an understanding of art history and culture as records of human achievement. Point out that Picasso's art is famous because he did things in new ways. Explain that he is no longer living but his artworks are still here, records of his achievement. Have children create a Picasso-like picture. Have them cut a variety of geometric shapes. Ask children to arrange and glue them to look like abstract people and paint lines and shapes on the composition in the style of Picasso's Cubist works.   TEKS 2.3A

Multimedia Biographies
Visit *The Learning Site*
www.harcourtschool.com

Lesson 5
Shapes and People

PDAS Domains I, II

OBJECTIVES
- Identify art elements such as shapes in a portrait
- Create a portrait of people
- Make inferences

RESOURCES
- Art Prints 2 and 3
- Discussion Cards 1, 5
- Big Book, pp. 38–39
- Electronic Art Gallery CD-ROM, Primary

5 Minutes
Warm-Up

Find Shapes in Faces Ask children to look at each other's faces, or faces in magazines, and to identify shapes they would use to draw them.

10-15 Minutes
Teach

Discuss Art Concepts Have children read the text on page 38. Share Art History. Use Discussion Card 1 for additional questions. Then display **Art Prints 2** and **3**. Have children identify and compare shapes in all four portraits.
TEKS 2.1B; TAKS Reading Objective 1

Think Critically

1. **(Focus Skill) READING SKILL** Why do you think the family is wearing old-fashioned clothes? (Possible response: They lived a long time ago.) **MAKE INFERENCES** TEKS 2.3B

2. **How are the shapes in the artworks alike and different?** (Possible response: They both have round shapes, but the painting has more details.) **PERCEPTION/COMPARE AND CONTRAST** TEKS 2.1B

3. **WRITE** Luis Jaso's family is dressed up. Tell what they might do next.
INTERACTIVE WRITING TEKS 2.3A; TAKS Writing Objective 1

Lesson 5
Shapes and People

Shapes and People

Vocabulary

portrait
self-portrait

What shapes do you see in these artworks? A **portrait** shows what a person or a group looks like. In a **self-portrait**, an artist paints himself or herself.

A Luis Jaso, *My Family Before I Was Born*

B Antavio, Student art

38

FYI
Background Information

Art History
A **portrait** can have at least one of three main purposes. It shows (1) what a person or group looks like, (2) the mood or character of that person or group, (3) the wealth or importance of a person or group.

For information about the artist Luis Jaso (loo•EES HAH•soh), see pp. R48–R59.

RECOMMENDED READING
No One Saw: Ordinary Things Through the Eyes of an Artist by Bob Raczka. Millbrook, 2002. **AVERAGE**

38 UNIT 1 *Celebrate Our World* ⭐ **TEKS 2.1B** identify elements and principles; **TEKS 2.2A** express ideas and feelings; **TEKS 2.2B** create effective compositions; **TEKS 2.2C** identify and practice skills; **TEKS 2.3A** identify stories and constructions; **TEKS 2.3B** compare artworks showing individuals/families; *(continued)*

Artist's Workshop

Favorite-People Portrait

PLAN ....

Think about your family or another group of people you would like to paint.

CREATE ....

1. **Fold the edges of your paper to make a frame.**

2. **Draw a group portrait. Paint it. Decorate the frame.**

REFLECT ....

What lines and shapes did you use in your portrait?

Where have you seen portraits? What did they look like?

39

Social Studies Connection

Oral Presentations Have each child present his or her portrait to the group. Ask children to introduce family members or friends in their portrait and tell why they chose certain lines and shapes for each person. Then invite them to tell one nice thing about the group as a whole.

PDAS Domain IV

ESL Point to individual family members on pictures of families, say their names, and have children repeat. Then have volunteers point to and name each one.

Use **Picture Cards Collection**, card 47. See also **Picture Card Bank CD-ROM**, Category: My Family.

family

Artist's Workshop

15-25 Minutes

Favorite-People Portrait

MATERIALS: construction paper, brushes, tempera paints, crayons, markers

TECHNIQUE TIP: Have children sketch their ideas for a portrait. Discuss how to use shapes like ovals, circles, triangles, and free-form shapes.

PLAN Have children identify and practice the skills necessary for painting a portrait. TEKS 2.2C

CREATE Model how to make a frame. Ask children to use shapes and colors to express their ideas and feelings. TEKS 2.2A, TEKS 2.2B

REFLECT Ask children to compare and contrast how they made their portraits. TEKS 2.3B

Activity Options PDAS Domain IV

Quick Activity Have each child draw one family member or a friend with crayons.

Early Finishers Children can use Discussion Card 5 with their portraits.

Challenge See *Teacher Resource Book* p. 47.

Wrap-Up

5-10 Minutes

Informal Assessment PDAS Domain III

- **How did you paint your family members differently than Luis Jaso did?** (Responses will vary.) PERCEPTION/AESTHETICS TEKS 2.3B

- **What kinds of shapes did your classmates use?** (Responses will vary.) ART CRITICISM TEKS 2.1B

Extend Through Writing

Interactive Help children write on a card a title for their portraits. Have them proofread the titles for correct capitalization of important words.
TAKS Writing Objective 6

PDAS Domain I active participation; **PDAS Domain II** learner-centered instruction; **PDAS Domain III** evaluation and feedback; **PDAS Domain IV** classroom management; **TAKS Reading Objective 1** demonstrate understanding of texts; **TAKS Writing Objective 1** composition; **TAKS Writing Objective 6** proofreading

LESSON 5 *Shapes and People* **39**

Unit **1**

PDAS Domains I, III

Review and Reflect

In this unit, children have learned to identify lines and shapes in artworks and in the world around them. You may want to use **Art Prints 1–3**, **8**, and **12** and Discussion Cards 1 and 2 to review how artists use these elements.

Vocabulary and Concepts

Review art vocabulary by having children use each word to tell about the picture. ("Best" responses are shown; accept other reasonable responses.)

1. C   **4.** A   **7.** E

2. B   **5.** H   **8.** G

3. D   **6.** F

9. Children should name types of lines, such as *thick*, *thin*, *curved*, and *vertical*, and name shapes, such as *square*, *rectangle*, and *triangle*.

Sort Artworks   For reinforcement of the vocabulary words and concepts, have children do a sorting activity. Display **Art Prints 1–3**, **8**, and **12** and other artworks. Use the vocabulary words as categories. Have children sort the artworks in several ways depending on the categories, such as artworks that are good examples of line or of geometric shapes. Ask children to explain why they categorized the artworks as they did. Then have children put the Art Prints in order of preference and explain their choices.   TEKS 2.1A, TEKS 2.1B, TEKS 2.4B

Unit **1** Review and Reflect

Vocabulary and Concepts

Tell which picture goes best with each item.

1. outline
2. free-form shapes
3. portrait
4. geometric shapes

 **A**
 B
 C
 D

Tell which picture goes best with each item.

5. lines
6. self-portrait
7. movement
8. organic shapes

 E
 F
 **G**
 **H**

9. Tell about the lines and shapes in this picture.

40

TEKS 2.4B

Home and Community Connection

School-Home Connection

Copy and distribute *Teacher Resource Book* pp. 77–78 to provide family members with information and activities they use with children to reinforce concepts taught in this unit.

Community Connection

You may wish to visit a community art site, such as a park with artworks or a community mural. Children could view pictures of community art if a visit is not practical. Use questions from Discussion Card 10: Community Art to discuss the site. Have children identify ideas in the artwork and elements of art in the natural and the human-made environment.

★ **TEKS 2.1A** identify variations in objects and subjects; **TEKS 2.1B** identify elements and principles; **TEKS 2.3A** identify stories and constructions; **TEKS 2.4A** define reasons for preferences in personal artworks; **TEKS 2.4B** identify ideas in artworks by peers and artists; *(continued)*

Make Inferences

Read pages 30–31 again. Make a chart like this one. Tell what you think about the pictures.

What I See and Read	+ What I Know	= What I Think
The fence has lines.	Fences like this are metal.	This fence is ____.
The leaf is yellow.	Leaves change colors in the fall.	It is ____.

Write About Art

Write sentences to tell what you see and think is happening in the painting *Autumn*.

A woman is feeding six ducks.

Grandma Moses, *Autumn*

41

TEKS 2.4A; PDAS Domain III

Assessment

Portfolio Assessment

Work with children to choose one artwork from this unit to include in their portfolios. Suggest that they review each Artist's Workshop activity, select the piece they like best, and tell why they chose it. Provide feedback about children's use of elements and techniques. See also Portfolio Recording Form, page R32.

Additional Assessment Options

- Progress Recording Form, p. R33
- Artist's Workshop Rubrics (Self/Teacher and Peer), pp. R30–R31
- Unit Test, *Teacher Resource Book* p. 91

 **READING SKILL**

Make Inferences

Have children reread pages 30–31. Ask them to make inferences about the photographs. Have them make and complete the chart.
TEKS 2.3A; TAKS Reading Objective 4

What I See and Read	+ What I Know	= What I Think
The fence has lines.	Fences like this are metal.	This fence is ____. strong; fancy
The leaf is yellow.	Leaves change colors in the fall.	It is ____. fall; going to fall off

Write About Art

Inference Sentences Review with children what they think is happening in *Autumn*. Have children write sentences about what is happening and why they think so. Guide them to recognize and use correct sentence construction.
TEKS 2.3A; TAKS Writing Objectives 1, 4

Critic's Corner   PDAS Domain III

RESPONSE/EVALUATION Have children turn to the artwork they liked best in the unit. Use these steps to discuss their choices.

Describe Have children identify ideas in the artwork, describing what it shows. TEKS 2.4B

Analyze Encourage children to describe lines and shapes in the artwork. TEKS 2.1B

Interpret Invite children to tell what feeling the artist is trying to show.

Evaluate Have children give specific reasons why the artwork is their favorite.

 TAKS Test Preparation: Reading and Writing Through Art, pp. 1–11

PDAS Domain I active participation; **PDAS Domain III** evaluation and feedback; **TAKS Reading Objective 4** apply critical-thinking skills; **TAKS Writing Objective 1** composition; **TAKS Writing Objective 4** sentence construction

UNIT 1 *Review and Reflect* **41**

Unit 2 Color and Value

Mix and Match

Color is a beautiful element artists use to express feelings. In this unit, children explore how artists use colors to express themselves, recording stories of the times in which they live.

Resources

- Unit 2 Art Prints (4–6)
- Additional Art Prints (17, 18)
- Art Transparencies 4–6
- Test Preparation: Reading and Writing Through Art, p. 12
- Artist's Workshop Activities: English and Spanish, pp. 11–20
- Encyclopedia of Artists and Art History, pp. R48–R59
- Picture Cards Collection, Cards 5, 29, 55, 58, 65, 68, 95, 101

Using the Art Prints

- Discussion Cards, pp. R34–R42
- Teaching Suggestions, backs of Art Prints
- Art Print Teaching Suggestions: Spanish

Teacher Resource Book

- Vocabulary Cards in English and Spanish, pp. 9–12
- Reading Skill Card 2, p. 24
- Copying Masters, pp. 29, 30, 31, 32, 39
- Challenge Activities, pp. 48–52
- School-Home Connection: English/Spanish, pp. 79–80
- Unit Test, p. 92

Technology Resources

 Electronic Art Gallery CD-ROM, Primary Picture Card Bank CD-ROM

 Visit *The Learning Site* www.harcourtschool.com

- Multimedia Art Glossary
- Multimedia Biographies
- Reading Skills and Activities

Art Prints for This Unit

ART PRINT 4

Girl with Sunflowers
by Diego Rivera

ART PRINT 5

Poppy
by Georgia O'Keeffe

ART PRINT 6

Breezing Up (A Fair Wind)
by Winslow Homer

ART PRINT 17

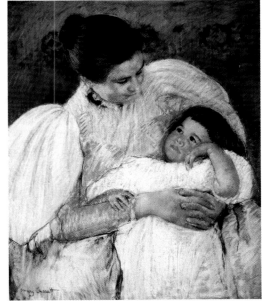

Nurse and Child
by Mary Cassatt

ART PRINT 18

Flowers in a Vase
by Henri Rousseau

Unit 2
Mix and Match Color and Value

Planning Guide
PDAS Domain IV

Lesson	Objectives and Vocabulary	Art Images	Production/Materials
Focus Skill Story Elements, pp. 44–45			
6 **COLORS WORK TOGETHER** pp. 46–47 🕐 30–60 minutes	• Identify and make primary and secondary colors • Practice skills necessary for producing constructions (Focus Skill) Identify story elements **Vocabulary: primary colors, secondary colors**	• **Balloons for a Dime** by Jonathan Green	**Rainbow Pinwheel** ❏ white paper ❏ scissors ❏ tempera paints ❏ glue stick ❏ brad ❏ drinking straw ❏ paintbrushes
7 **WARM AND COOL COLORS** pp. 48–49 🕐 30–60 minutes	• Identify warm and cool colors • Express feelings by using a variety of colors in artworks (Focus Skill) Identify story elements **Vocabulary: warm colors, cool colors**	• **La Era** by Diego Rivera • **The Waterlily Pond** by Claude Monet	**Mood Painting** ❏ white paper ❏ tempera paints— red, blue, yellow ❏ paintbrushes
Art ↔ Science Connection: Georgia O'Keeffe's Seasons, pp. 50–51			
8 **LIGHT AND DARK COLORS** pp. 52–53 🕐 30–60 minutes	• Understand values, tints, and shades • Create effective compositions using color and value (Focus Skill) Identify story elements **Vocabulary: value, tint, shade**	• **Violet Light** by Gustavo, age 7 • **Bouquet and Cat** by Suzanne Valadon	**Fall Bouquet Painting** ❏ construction paper ❏ wallpaper sample ❏ scissors ❏ glue stick ❏ tempera paints ❏ paintbrushes
9 **COLORS TELL STORIES** pp. 54–55 🕐 30–60 minutes	• Identify mood and stories in art • Express ideas in artworks (Focus Skill) Identify story elements **Vocabulary: mood**	• **First Steps, after Millet** by Vincent van Gogh	**Story Puppet Scene** ❏ construction paper ❏ scissors ❏ craft sticks ❏ glue ❏ oil pastels ❏ crayons, markers
Art ↔ Technology Connection: Edna Crawford, Animator, pp. 56–57			
10 **COLORS IN SEASCAPES** pp. 58–59 🕐 30–60 minutes	• Identify seascapes and horizon lines • Create an effective seascape (Focus Skill) Identify story elements **Vocabulary: seascape, horizon line**	• **Gloucester Harbor** by Winslow Homer	**Crayon-Resist Seascape** ❏ white paper ❏ watercolor paints ❏ paintbrushes ❏ oil pastels ❏ crayons
✓ Review and Reflect, pp. 60–61			

★ TEKS 2.1A identify variations in objects and subjects; TEKS 2.1B identify elements and principles; PDAS Domain IV classroom management

Story Elements, pp. 44–45

Focus Skill

Opportunities for application of the skill are provided on pp. 46, 48, 52, 54, 58, 61.

Art Puzzlers

Resources and Technology	Suggested Literature	Across the Curriculum
• Art Prints 4, 5, 18 • Discussion Card 3, p. R35 • Reading Skill Card 2 • Big Book, pp. 46–47 • Electronic Art Gallery CD-ROM, Primary	*Mouse Paint* by Ellen Stoll Walsh **Easy** 	**Math** Create a Bar Graph, p. 47 **Reading** Focus Skill Story Elements, p. 46 **Writing** Independent, p. 47
• Art Prints 4, 5, 6, 17 • Reading Skill Card 2 • Big Book, pp. 48–49 • Electronic Art Gallery CD-ROM, Primary	*A Blue Butterfly: A Story About Claude Monet* by Bijou Le Tord **Easy** 	**Science** Colors for Hot Days, p. 49 **Reading** Focus Skill Story Elements, p. 48 **Writing** Independent, p. 49
• Art Prints 4, 5, 6, 17, 18 • Discussion Card 9, p. R41 • Reading Skill Card 2 • Big Book, pp. 52–53 • Electronic Art Gallery CD-ROM, Primary	*Rainbow Joe and Me* by Maria Diaz Strom **Challenging** 	**Science** Basic Needs, p. 53 **Reading** Focus Skill Story Elements, p. 52 **Writing** Interactive, p. 53
• Art Prints 6, 17 • Discussion Card 2, p. R34 • Reading Skill Card 2 • Big Book, pp. 54–55 • Electronic Art Gallery CD-ROM, Primary	*In the Garden with Van Gogh* by Julie Merberg and Suzanne Bober **Average** 	**Drama** Puppets of the World, p. 55 **Reading** Focus Skill Story Elements, p. 54 **Writing** Interactive, p. 55
• Art Print 6 • Discussion Card 1, p. R34 • Reading Skill Card 2 • Big Book, pp. 58–59 • Electronic Art Gallery CD-ROM, Primary	*Little Blue and Little Yellow* by Leo Lionni **Average** 	**Science** Water on Planet Earth, p. 59 **Reading** Focus Skill Story Elements, p. 58 **Writing** Shared, p. 59

Present these art puzzlers to children at the beginning or end of a class or when children finish an assignment early.

• Name the **colors** of some fruits and vegetables. TEKS 2.1A, TEKS 2.1B

• How do you feel? What **colors** describe your **mood**? TEKS 2.1B

• Look around. Point to **light colors** and **dark colors**. TEKS 2.1B

• What **colors** would be in a **story** that is loud and full of action? In a story that is quiet and still? TEKS 2.1B

• Name things you might see in a **seascape**, such as the color blue. TEKS 2.1A

 School-Home Connection
The activities above are included in the School-Home Connection for this unit. See *Teacher Resource Book,* pp. 79–80.

Assessment Options

• Rubrics and Recording Forms, pp. R28–R33
• Unit 2 Test, *Teacher Resource Book*, p. 92

 Visit *The Learning Site*:
www.harcourtschool.com

Artist's Workshops PREVIEW

Use these pages to help you gather and organize materials for the Artist's Workshop in each lesson.

LESSON	MATERIALS

6 Rainbow Pinwheel
p. 47

Objective: To have children mix primary colors to create secondary colors, paint them in rainbow order, and then make a pinwheel

🕐 15–25 minutes

Challenge Activity: See *Teacher Resource Book,* p. 48.

- square white paper
- scissors
- tempera paints—red, blue, yellow
- paintbrushes
- glue stick
- brad
- drinking straw

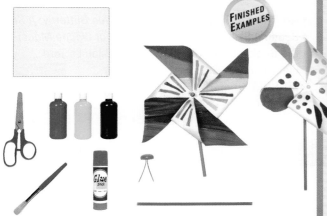

FINISHED EXAMPLES

LESSON

7 Mood Painting p. 49

Objective: To have children choose cool or warm colors to show emotion in a painting of themselves doing their favorite activity

🕐 15–25 minutes

Challenge Activity: See *Teacher Resource Book,* p. 49.

- white paper
- tempera paints—red, blue, yellow
- paintbrushes

FINISHED EXAMPLES

Safety Tips

For safety information, see Art Safety, page R4; the Art Safety Poster; or Big Book page 148.

For information on media and techniques, see pages R15–R23.

LESSON	MATERIALS

8 Fall Bouquet Painting p. 53

- construction paper
- wallpaper sample
- scissors
- glue stick
- tempera paints— red, blue, yellow, black, white
- brushes

FINISHED EXAMPLE

Objective: To have children explore color and practice the process of painting by making tints and shades in a painting of a bouquet of flowers

🕐 15–25 minutes

Challenge Activity: See *Teacher Resource Book,* p. 50.

LESSON

9 Story Puppet Scene p. 55

- construction paper
- scissors
- craft sticks
- glue
- oil pastels
- crayons
- markers

FINISHED EXAMPLE

Objective: To have children make puppets and scenery to create a story scene that uses color to show mood

🕐 15–25 minutes

Challenge Activity: See *Teacher Resource Book,* p. 51.

LESSON

10 Crayon-Resist Seascape p. 59

- white paper
- watercolor paints
- paintbrushes
- oil pastels
- crayons

FINISHED EXAMPLE

Objective: To have children use their knowledge of horizon line and colors to create a seascape, first by coloring with crayons or oil pastels and then painting with watercolors, using the crayon-resist technique

🕐 15–25 minutes

Challenge Activity: See *Teacher Resource Book,* p. 52.

Unit 2

PDAS Domains I, II

Mix and Match

PREVIEW THE UNIT

Do a Walk-Through   Have children use the
Contents on page 5 to find the page on which
Unit 2 begins and turn to that page. Tell children
that in this unit they will learn how artists express
feelings and ideas. Point out the lesson titles, art
captions, and Artist's Workshop activities.
Remind children to follow safety rules.

SHARE THE POEM

Read the poem to children as they view the art.
Then reread the poem aloud with them.

How are the poem and the painting alike?
(Possible response: The poem is about friends,
and the painting shows girls happily playing chess
together, like friends do.)   **TAKS Reading Objective 4**

STEP INTO THE ART

Have children read the title of the painting and
describe the colors. Then ask:

Who do you think is winning the game?
Why do you think that? (Possible response:
The girl on the left is winning because she is fac-
ing us and smiling.) **DRAW CONCLUSIONS**   **TEKS 2.3A**

SHARE BACKGROUND INFORMATION

Help children understand the historical and cultural significance of a woman of this time period
being a painter. Explain that most painters were
men. Ask children how they can tell *The Chess
Game* was painted long ago. Then have children
compare and contrast this portrait to the portraits
on page 38 and ones they have drawn of their
own families.   **TEKS 2.3B**

LOCATE IT   See *Using the Maps of Museums
and Art Sites,* pp. R2–R3.

▲ Sofonisba Anguissola, *The Chess Game*

LOCATE IT

This painting is in the National Museum
in Poznan, Poland.

See Maps of Museums and Art Sites, pages 144–147.

42

 Poland

 Background Information

About the Artist

Sofonisba Anguissola (soh•foh•NIS•bah ahn•GWEES•soh•lah) (about
1532–1625) was an Italian painter who specialized in portraits.
Anguissola had contact with well-known artists, including Michelangelo.
She was appointed to the court of King Philip II of Spain because of her
renowned talent for portraiture.

For more information about the artist and the Renaissance movement,
see pp. R48–R59.

For related images, see **Electronic Art Gallery CD-ROM, Primary**.

2

Mix and Match

Friends

Two friends are better than one,
And three are better than two.
And four are much better still.

Just

think

what

four friends can do!

Anonymous

ABOUT THE ARTIST

See Gallery of Artists,
pages 182–191.

Unit Vocabulary

primary colors	value
	tint
secondary colors	shade
warm colors	mood
cool colors	seascape
	horizon line

GO ONLINE Multimedia Art Glossary
Visit *The Learning Site*
www.harcourtschool.com

43

Unit Vocabulary

Have volunteers read aloud the vocabulary words. Work with children to make a word web about the topic *Color*, using the vocabulary words and definitions. Encourage children to tell what they already know about color.

primary colors one of three basic colors from which all other colors are made: red, blue, and yellow

secondary colors colors made by mixing two primary colors: orange, green, and violet

warm colors colors, such as red, orange, and yellow, that remind us of things that are warm and energetic

cool colors colors, such as green, blue, and violet, that remind us of things that are cool and calm

value the lightness or darkness of a color

tint a lighter color made by adding a color to white

shade a darker color made by adding black to a color

mood a feeling produced by a color or an artwork

seascape an artwork that shows the sea or another water setting

horizon line the line where water or land meets the sky

Vocabulary Resources

- Vocabulary Cards in English and Spanish: *Teacher Resource Book*, pp. 9–12
- Student Edition Glossary, pp. 192–201

GO ONLINE Multimedia Art Glossary
English/Spanish
Visit *The Learning Site*
www.harcourtschool.com

Sketchbook

Encourage children to use their sketchbooks to record ideas and to practice skills for producing artworks. TEKS 2.2C

TEKS 2.2A, TEKS 2.2C;
PDAS Domain IV

Art Center

Materials crayons, drawing paper, natural and human-made objects

Ongoing Activity
Have children make crayon rubbings of natural and human-made objects. Invite them to experiment by choosing different colors to express different ideas and feelings.

PDAS Domain IV

Classroom Management

Prepare a dishpan or similar container with materials for each small group of children to share. This makes the distribution and cleanup of materials easier.

Display Discussion Cards, pages R34–R42, and the Idea Wheel, *Teacher Resource Book*, pp. 29–30 for early finishers.

Unit 2

Focus Skill **READING SKILL**

PDAS Domains I, II

Story Elements

SKILL TRACE
STORY ELEMENTS

Introduce	pp. 44–45
Review	pp. 46, 48, 52, 54, 58, 61

DISCUSS THE SKILL

Access Prior Knowledge   Tell children that stories have these elements—**characters** (the people or animals in a story), a **setting** (the time and place in which the story happens), and a **plot** (what happens, including the problem and how it is solved). Explain that many artworks also have these elements. Then have children think of a story they have read recently. Ask:

Who is in the story?
Where and when does it take place?
What is the problem? How was it solved?

Tell children that thinking about story elements as they read a story or look at an artwork will help them better understand and enjoy it.

IMPORTANT DETAILS   TAKS Reading Objectives 1, 2

APPLY TO ART

Story Elements in Art   Ask children to read page 44 and answer the questions. (People are working in a garden. Children, dogs, and a cat are relaxing. A man on a ladder is painting a rainbow in the sky.) Have children compare the group in this picture with the family in the portrait on page 38. Then have them tell about the setting. (Most of the characters are outside of a house in the yard. It is daytime.) **TEKS 2.3B**

Ask children to identify the story in this artwork. Have them tell their versions of the story, including all the story elements. **TEKS 2.3A**

Focus Skill **READING SKILL**

Story Elements

A picture can tell a story. Who is in this picture?
What are these **characters** doing?

Eric Carle, illustration from *Draw Me a Star* **LITERATURE LINK**

A story also has a setting. The **setting** is the time and place. Tell about the setting in this artwork.

44

Background Information

About the Artist

Eric Carle (1929–) says that his ideas come from his experiences, his feelings, and the things he loves. Because he is a nature lover, it is no surprise that many of Carle's books tell stories about animals. He has written and illustrated dozens of children's books, many of which are award-winning.

For more information about Eric Carle, see pp. R48–R59.

LITERATURE LINK   Discuss story elements in other illustrations from *Draw Me a Star* by Eric Carle. Philomel Books, 1992.

AVERAGE

★ TEKS 2.3A identify stories and constructions; TEKS 2.3B compare artworks showing individuals/families; PDAS Domain I active participation;
PDAS Domain II learner-centered instruction; PDAS Domain IV classroom management; TAKS Reading Objective 1 demonstrate understanding of texts; *(continued)*

Read the paragraph. Then make a story map.
Tell a story about the art on page 44.

> Men, women, children, and pets are working together. Someone is in the house. Others are outside in the garden. It is starting to rain. A man is painting a rainbow. Maybe this will help stop the rain.

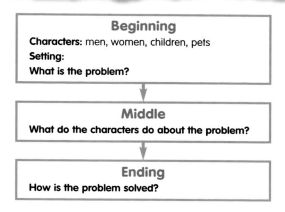

Beginning
Characters: men, women, children, pets
Setting:
What is the problem?

↓

Middle
What do the characters do about the problem?

↓

Ending
How is the problem solved?

On Your Own
Make a story map about the painting on pages 42–43. Use your map to tell a story.

45

Story Elements in Text Have children read the passage on page 45. Display a story map, and ask volunteers to identify story elements from the passage and the picture. Work with them to record their responses. TAKS Reading Objectives 1, 2

Beginning
Characters: men, women, children, pets
Setting: daytime; in a yard outside a house with a garden
What is the problem? The people want to be outside but it is starting to rain.

↓

Middle
What do the characters do about the problem? A man paints a rainbow in the sky. The people keep working and playing outside.

↓

Ending
How is the problem solved? When the rainbow is all painted, the rain stops.

ON YOUR OWN

Revisit the painting *The Chess Game* on pages 42–43. Children can work individually or with the whole group to identify story elements in the painting, complete a story map, and tell a story.
TEKS 2.3A; TAKS Reading Objectives 1, 2, 3; TAKS Writing Objectives 1, 3

TAKS Reading Objectives 1, 2

(Focus Skill)
Reading Skill Card

Distribute Reading Skill Card 2, *Teacher Resource Book* p. 24. Have children use the story map to discuss story elements in artworks.

Extend the Skill
For additional teaching suggestions, see **Art Transparency 4**.

(MEETING INDIVIDUAL NEEDS)
PDAS Domain IV

ESL Display **visuals** to support **comprehensible input**, using *Picture Cards Collection* cards that show items from the artwork: *artist* (5), *cloud* (29), *garden* (58), *house* (68), *rain* (95), *rainbow* (95).

See also *Picture Cards Bank* CD-ROM, Category: Weather.

house

Reading Skills and Activities
Visit *The Learning Site*
www.harcourtschool.com

TAKS Reading Objective 2 apply knowledge of literary elements; **TAKS Reading Objective 3** use a variety of strategies;
TAKS Writing Objective 1 composition; **TAKS Writing Objective 3** organization

UNIT 2 *Story Elements* **45**

Lesson 6

PDAS Domains I, II

Colors Work Together

OBJECTIVES
- Identify and make primary and secondary colors
- Practice skills necessary for producing constructions
- Identify story elements

RESOURCES
- Art Prints 4, 5, 18
- Discussion Card 3
- Big Book pp. 46–47
- Electronic Art Gallery CD-ROM, Primary

Warm-Up
5 Minutes

Play "I Spy a Color" Have children make up and solve riddles about classroom objects that are red, yellow, or blue, for example, *I spy something the color of a banana.* TEKS 2.1A

Teach
10-15 Minutes

Discuss Art Concepts Read pages 46–47 with children. Talk about the color wheel, and tell children that colors are also called **hues**. Explain how mixing a primary and secondary color makes an **intermediate color**. Display **Art Prints 4**, **5**, and **18**. Have children identify colors and compare with the colors in *Balloons for a Dime.*
TEKS 2.1A, TEKS 2.1B

Think Critically

1. **READING SKILL** **Tell about the characters, setting, and plot in the painting.**
   (Responses will vary.) STORY ELEMENTS TEKS 2.3A

2. **Which primary colors make green, orange, and violet?** PERCEPTION (blue + yellow; red + yellow; blue + red) TEKS 2.1B

3. **WRITE** **Tell which color is your favorite and why.** INDEPENDENT WRITING TAKS Writing Objective 1

Lesson 6

Colors Work Together

Vocabulary

primary colors

secondary colors

Can you find a red hat, a yellow shirt, and a blue balloon in this painting? Red, yellow, and blue are **primary colors**. What other colors do you see?

Jonathan Green, *Balloons for a Dime*

Primary colors can be mixed to make the **secondary colors**—orange, green, and violet.

46

FYI Background Information

About the Artist

Jonathan Green (1955–) is a painter and printmaker from South Carolina, raised in the Gullah culture of the coastal Southeast. Many of the African Americans in this area are descended from slaves. Green's brightly colored paintings of people and places he knows bring to life and preserve Gullah culture.

For more information about Green, see pp. R48–R59.

RECOMMENDED READING

Mouse Paint by Ellen Stoll Walsh. Harcourt, 1989. EASY

★ TEKS 2.1A identify variations in objects and subjects; TEKS 2.1B identify elements and principles; TEKS 2.2A express ideas and feelings; TEKS 2.2B create effective compositions; TEKS 2.2C identify and practice skills; TEKS 2.3A identify stories and construction; *(continued)*

A **color wheel** shows colors in rainbow order.
What two colors make orange? Green? Violet?

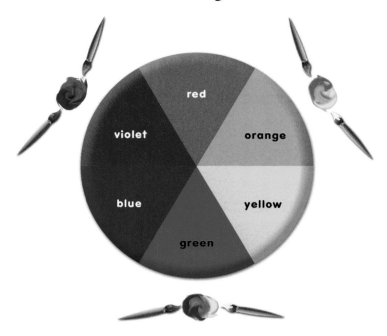

Artist's Workshop

Rainbow Pinwheel

1. **Mix colors and paint them in rainbow order.**

2. **Cut in from each corner. Fold to the middle. Glue.**

47

Artist's Workshop

15-25 Minutes

Rainbow Pinwheel

MATERIALS: white paper, tempera paints, brushes, scissors, glue stick, brad, straw

TECHNIQUE TIP: For help, children refer to p. 168 to make a paper square and to the Pinwheel, *Teacher's Resource Book* p. 39.

PLAN Have children identify and practice the skills necessary for constructing a pinwheel.
TEKS 2.2C

CREATE Model mixing colors, and have children practice. Encourage them to be creative.
TEKS 2.2B, TEKS 2.2C

REFLECT Children share pinwheels and tell how they used colors to express ideas and feelings.
TEKS 2.2A

Activity Options   PDAS Domain IV

Quick Activity Have children paint a series of balloons in rainbow colors.

Early Finishers Children may use Discussion Card 3: Elements, p. R35.

Challenge See *Teacher Resource Book* p. 48.

5-10 Minutes

Wrap-Up

Informal Assessment   PDAS Domain III

- **What happens when your pinwheel spins?** (The colors mix together.) **PERCEPTION/AESTHETICS**

- **Would your pinwheel look as nice if you used only primary colors? Why or why not?** (Responses will vary.) **ART CRITICISM**

Extend Through Writing

Independent Have children list the colors in rainbow order and proofread for correct spelling. They can write them on the Color Wheel, *Teacher Resource Book*, p. 32.   TEKS 2.1B; TAKS Writing Objective 6

Math Connection

Create a Bar Graph Ask children to choose a favorite color from the color wheel. Help them construct a bar graph and interpret it.

Favorite Colors

5					
4	Kyle			Remy	
3	Dillon		Sean	Rosa	
2	Monica	Alex	Laura	George	Matt	
	Paula	Kaitlin	Nikki	Josh	Kelly	Chandra
1	Alonzo	James	Carlos	Katie	Chen	David
	Red	Orange	Yellow	Green	Blue	Violet

PDAS Domain IV

ESL To foster **language acquisition**, write *red* on a sheet of red paper, *blue* on blue, and so on. Place the sheets face down on the floor. Children name the colors and flip them over to check.

Special Needs Provide paints in containers labeled with color names for children who are colorblind.

PDAS Domain I active participation; **PDAS Domain II** learner-centered instruction; **PDAS Domain III** evaluation and feedback; **PDAS Domain IV** classroom management; **TAKS Writing Objective 1** composition; **TAKS Writing Objective 6** proofreading

LESSON 6 *Colors Work Together* **47**

Lesson 7

Warm and Cool Colors

OBJECTIVES
- Identify warm and cool colors
- Express feelings by using a variety of colors in artworks
- Identify story elements

RESOURCES
- Art Prints 4, 5, 6, 17
- Big Book, pp. 48–49
- Electronic Art Gallery CD-ROM, Primary

5 Minutes

Warm-Up

Color Role-Play Hold up colored paper one sheet at a time. Have children act out how they feel, name the feeling, and tell why.

10-15 Minutes

Teach

Discuss Art Concepts Read and discuss pages 48–49 with children. Have them compare the colors in each painting. Then display **Art Prints 4, 5, 6,** and **17**. Have children tell which painting makes them feel warm or cool and why.
TEKS 2.1B, TEKS 2.4B

Think Critically

1. (Focus Skill) **READING SKILL** How are the settings of the paintings different? (a sunny day in a warm place; a cool, shady pond) **STORY ELEMENTS** TAKS Reading Objective 2

2. **What colors are used in these paintings? How do they make you feel?** (Rivera: warm colors; a hot feeling; Monet: cool colors; a peaceful feeling) **PERCEPTION** TEKS 2.1B

3. **WRITE** What colors would show your feelings about being in the woods? Why?
INDEPENDENT WRITING TAKS Writing Objective 1

Lesson 7

Warm and Cool Colors

Vocabulary
warm colors
cool colors

How does each painting make you feel? Colors can make us feel certain ways. Red, orange, and yellow are **warm colors**. Blue, green, and violet are **cool colors**.

Diego Rivera,
La Era

warm colors

cool colors

48

Background Information

About the Artists
Diego Rivera (DYAY•goh ree•VAY•rah) (1886–1957) is best known for his large murals. He painted on the sides of buildings in Mexico and in large public spaces in the United States.

Claude Monet (KLOHD moh•NAY) (1840–1926), a French Impressionist, painted outdoors. He often painted the same scene at different times. This painting is one of a series of his garden at Giverny.

For more information about the artists, see pp. R48–R59.

RECOMMENDED READING
A Blue Butterfly by Bijou Le Tord. Doubleday, 1995. **EASY**

★ **TEKS 2.1B** identify elements and principles; **TEKS 2.2A** express ideas and feelings; **TEKS 2.2B** create effective compositions; **TEKS 2.2C** identify and practice skills; **TEKS 2.4A** define reasons for preferences in personal artworks; **TEKS 2.4B** identify ideas in artworks by peers and artists; **PDAS Domain I** active participation; **PDAS Domain II** learner-centered instruction; **PDAS Domain III** evaluation and feedback; **PDAS Domain IV** classroom management; *(continued)*

B Claude Monet,
The Waterlily Pond

Cool colors can help make pictures feel cool and calm. Warm colors give art more energy and can make pictures seem hot.

Artist's Workshop

Mood Painting

Paint a picture of yourself doing your favorite thing. Use mostly warm or cool colors to show how you feel.

49

Science Connection

Colors for Hot Days Tell children that certain colors can help them stay cooler on a hot day. Give partners a sheet of black paper and a sheet of white paper. Have them leave the papers in the sun and then feel which is warmer. Explain that light colors *reflect* sunlight and dark colors *absorb* sunlight.

PDAS Domain IV

ESL Use **visuals** to support **comprehensible input** for names of feelings. Display *Picture Cards Collection* cards *happy* (65) and *sad* (101) and have children pantomime each. Have volunteers **pantomime** other feelings for classmates to guess.

happy

TAKS Reading Objective 2 apply knowledge of literary elements; TAKS Writing Objective 1 composition; TAKS Writing Objective 4 sentence construction; TAKS Writing Objective 6 proofreading

Artist's Workshop
15-25 Minutes

Mood Painting

MATERIALS: white paper, tempera paints (red, yellow, blue), paintbrushes

TECHNIQUE TIP: Remind children to rinse their paintbrushes after using each color.

PLAN Have children talk about feelings they associate with favorite activities. Have them identify the skills needed to produce an effective mood painting. TEKS 2.2C

CREATE Have children practice mixing colors. Then have them choose colors to express their feelings and ideas. TEKS 2.2A, TEKS 2.2B, TEKS 2.2C

REFLECT Ask volunteers to share their artwork and explain their color choices.

Activity Options   PDAS Domain IV

Quick Activity Have children use oil pastels instead of paints.

Early Finishers Children can choose from the Idea Wheel, *Teacher Resource Book*, pp. 29–30.

Challenge See *Teacher Resource Book* p. 49.

Wrap-Up
5-10 Minutes

Informal Assessment   PDAS Domain III

- **Do you like warm or cool colors? Why?** (Responses will vary.) **PERCEPTION/AESTHETICS** TEKS 2.4A
- **How did classmates use colors to show feelings?** (Responses will vary.) **ART CRITICISM** TEKS 2.4B

Extend Through Writing

Independent Have children write a statement, a question, and an exclamation about their artwork, using names of warm or cool colors. Have them proofread for the correct end marks.
TAKS Writing Objectives 1, 4, 6

ART ←→ SCIENCE CONNECTION

PDAS Domains I, II
Georgia O'Keeffe's Seasons

ARTIST BIOGRAPHY

DISCUSS THE PAINTINGS

Read pages 50–51 with children.

- Explain that Georgia O'Keeffe is well known for large close-up paintings of flowers. She also painted scenes from the Southwest, where she lived for many years. She used color to express shapes from nature.

- Have children note the brown hues in *Autumn Leaves*. Explain that **neutral colors** like brown and gray can be made by mixing two colors that are opposites on the color wheel. Ask children to identify other colors in the painting and tell what colors they think Georgia O'Keeffe mixed to create them. TEKS 2.1B

- Display **Art Print 5**: *Poppy* by Georgia O'Keeffe. Have children compare and contrast art elements such as colors, lines, and shapes in *Poppy*, *Apple Blossoms*, and *Autumn Leaves, Lake George, N.Y.*. Ask them to describe how they feel as they look at each painting. TEKS 2.1B, TEKS 2.4B

DISCUSS THE ARTIST

Share background information about the artist.

- Georgia O'Keeffe first received art lessons at home, where her family recognized her talent.

- O'Keeffe became frustrated by trying to paint in a realistic style and stopped painting for four years, even after winning an important art prize. When she started painting again, it was in a style that was completely her own.

Georgia O'Keeffe's Seasons

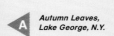
Autumn Leaves, Lake George, N.Y.

Georgia O'Keeffe is famous for her paintings of flowers and other objects in nature. She looked closely at them and painted them large. She wanted to show how she felt about the colors.

50

Background Information

About the Artist

Georgia O'Keeffe (1887–1986) is a well-known American painter. She started her career as an art teacher in Texas. O'Keeffe married photographer Alfred Stieglitz. She may have borrowed photography techniques, because she often painted large close-ups of plants and flowers as if she were looking at them through the zoom lens of a camera.

For more information about Georgia O'Keeffe, see pp. R48–R59.

50 UNIT 2 *Mix and Match* ★ **TEKS 2.1A** identify variations in objects and subjects; **TEKS 2.1B** identify elements and prinniples; **TEKS 2.2B** create effective compositions; **TEKS 2.2C** identify and practice skills; **TEKS 2.4B** identify ideas in artworks by peers and artists; **PDAS Domain I** active participation; **PDAS Domain II** learner-centered instruction

B *Apple Blossoms*

Think About Art

How do you feel when you look at these paintings? What colors do you see?

Multimedia Biographies
Visit *The Learning Site*
www.harcourtschool.com

51

Think About Art

How do you feel when you look at these paintings? What colors do you see? (Possible responses: *Autumn Leaves*, with its red and orange colors, makes me feel warm and reminds me of the sounds and feeling of dry fall leaves. *Apple Blossoms*, with its soft pinks and greens, makes me think of a spring day, calm and happy.)
TEKS 2.1B, TEKS 2.4B

ARTIST'S EYE ACTIVITY

Close-Up Paintings Invite children to imagine they are insects. Have them examine a flower, leaf, or other natural object. Ask children to use their senses to identify the variations in the objects and to discuss them. Then have them practice important painting skills and paint the object from an insect's point of view, filling the entire sheet of paper as Georgia O'Keeffe did.
TEKS 2.1A, TEKS 2.2B, TEKS 2.2C

Multimedia Biographies
Visit *The Learning Site*
www.harcourtschool.com

Science Connection

Autumn or Spring? Explain that in the fall, leaves stop making chlorophyll. Then other colors in the leaves are seen. Have children look at autumn and spring pictures and identify the seasons.

For additional cross-curricular suggestions, see Art Transparency 5.

TEKS 2.4B; PDAS Domain II

Visit with an Artist

View Art Arrange for children to visit with an artist either at school or at a museum, gallery, or other location. Ask children to view and identify ideas in original artworks, the portfolio, and an exhibition by the artist. Have them focus on concepts from this unit, such as color and value.

Lesson 8

PDAS Domains I, II
Light and Dark Colors

OBJECTIVES
- Understand values, tints, and shades
- Create effective compositions using color and value
- Identify story elements

RESOURCES
- Art Prints 4, 5, 6, 17, 18
- Big Book, pp. 52–53
- Discussion Card 9
- Electronic Art Gallery CD-ROM, Primary

5 Minutes
Warm-Up

Lighter and Darker Point out classroom items that have different values of the same color. Ask which is lighter and which is darker.

10-15 Minutes
Teach

Discuss Art Concepts Read and discuss page 52 with children. Explain that black, white, gray, and brown are *neutral* colors that can be used to make tints and shades. Ask children to identify tints and shades in **Art Prints 4, 5, 6, 17, and 18.**
TEKS 2.1B

Think Critically

1. **(Focus Skill) READING SKILL** **Tell a story about one of the paintings.** (Responses will vary.)
   STORY ELEMENTS   TEKS 2.3A; TAKS Reading Objective 2

2. **How are the colors in the paintings alike?** (Both have purple; both have light and dark parts.) PERCEPTION/COMPARE AND CONTRAST   TEKS 2.1B

3. **WRITE** **Which color in the paintings do you like best? Write about it and tell how it was made.** INDEPENDENT WRITING
   TEKS 2.4B; TAKS Writing Objective 1

Lesson 8

Vocabulary
value
tint
shade

Light and Dark Colors

What do these paintings show? Which parts are light colors? The **value** of a color is how light or dark it is.

A Gustavo, age 7, *Violet Light*

B Suzanne Valadon, *Bouquet and Cat*

Make a **tint**, or lighter color, by mixing a color with white. Make a **shade**, or darker color, by mixing a color with black.

52

Background Information

Art History
Suzanne Valadon (1865–1938) is a Post-Impressionist painter. Artists of this period also include Vincent van Gogh, Paul Gauguin, Paul Cézanne, and others. Artists of this movement are often classified by their focus on emotion and composition.

For more information about Valadon and Post-Impressionism, see pp. R48–R59.

RECOMMENDED READING
Rainbow Joe and Me by Maria Diaz Strom. Lee & Low, 1999. **CHALLENGING**

★ **TEKS 2.1B** identify elements and principles; **TEKS 2.2A** express ideas and feelings; **TEKS 2.2B** create effective compositions; **TEKS 2.2C** identify and practice skills; **TEKS 2.3A** identify stories and constructions; **TEKS 2.4A** define reasons for preferences in personal artworks; **TEKS 2.4B** identify ideas in artworks by peers and artists; *(continued)*

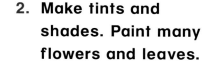

Fall Bouquet Painting

PLAN ....

Think about your favorite flowers.

CREATE ....

1. Cut out a vase. Glue it onto a sheet of paper.

2. Make tints and shades. Paint many flowers and leaves.

REFLECT ....

Which parts of your flowers are light? Which parts are dark?

Are the colors of your clothes light or dark?

53

Science Connection

Basic Needs Ask children to identify the two kinds of living things in *Bouquet and Cat.* (plants, animals) Elicit from children the basic needs of plants (water, light, air) and animals. (water, food, air, shelter) Work together to make a chart.

Plants	Animals

PDAS Domain IV

ESL Use **visuals** to review flower parts, such as *flower*, *petal*, *leaf*, *stem*, and *roots*. When children finish their paintings, have them identify their flowers' parts. Use **Picture Cards Collection** card 55. See also **Picture Card Bank CD-ROM**, Category: Parts of Plants.

flower

Artist's Workshop

Fall Bouquet Painting

MATERIALS: construction paper, glue stick, wallpaper, scissors, tempera paints (red, yellow, blue, black, white), paintbrushes

TECHNIQUE TIP: To save paint, remind children to add only a few drops of color to white to create tints.

PLAN Have children brainstorm favorite flowers and think about fall colors.

CREATE Have children identify and practice skills necessary to make the art. Ask them to use a variety of colors to express ideas and feelings. TEKS 2.2A, TEKS 2.2B, TEKS 2.2C

REFLECT Ask children to point out shades or tints that they like in their art and tell why. TEKS 2.4A

Activity Options PDAS Domain IV

Quick Activity Provide pre-cut vase shapes.

Early Finishers Have children use Discussion Card 9, p. R41.

Challenge See *Teacher Resource Book* p. 50.

Wrap-Up

Informal Assessment PDAS Domain III

- **How did you make the flower that you like the best?** (Responses will vary.) PERCEPTION/AESTHETICS TEKS 2.4A

- **Does your bouquet look the way you planned? Tell why or why not.** (Responses will vary.) ART CRITICISM TEKS 2.4A

Extend Through Writing ✏

Interactive "Share the pen" with children to write the steps for making tints and shades. Have children check the order of the steps.
TAKS Writing Objectives 1, 3

PDAS Domain I active participation; PDAS Domain II learner-centered instruction; PDAS Domain III evaluation and feedback; PDAS Domain IV classroom management; TAKS Reading Objective 2 apply knowledge of literary elements; TAKS Writing Objective 1 composition; TAKS Writing Objective 3 organization

LESSON 8 *Light and Dark Colors* **53**

Lesson 9

Colors Tell Stories

PDAS Domains I, II

OBJECTIVES
- Identify mood and stories in art
- Express ideas in artworks
- Identify story elements

RESOURCES
- Art Prints 6, 17
- Discussion Card 2
- Big Book, pp. 54–55
- Electronic Art Gallery CD-ROM, Primary

Warm-Up
5 Minutes

Guess Moods Take turns acting out activities that show certain moods. Have children identify the moods, such as happy or sad.

Teach
10-15 Minutes

Discuss Art Concepts Read pages 54–55 with children and have them tell the story the painting shows. Discuss how artists use color to create mood. Display **Art Prints 6** and **17**. Have children identify the mood in each, give reasons why they think so, and compare to *First Steps*. Use Discussion Card 2 for questions. TEKS 2.1A, TEKS 2.3A

Think Critically

1. **(Focus Skill) READING SKILL** What event does the painting show? What is the mood? (a child taking first steps; peaceful, gentle)
   STORY ELEMENTS TEKS 2.3A, TEKS 2.4B; TAKS Reading Objectives 2, 4

2. **How are *First Steps* and Art Print 17 alike?** (Both show loving, happy families.)
   PERCEPTION/COMPARE AND CONTRAST TEKS 2.3B

3. **WRITE** Write about colors that would show your mood today. Explain.
   INDEPENDENT WRITING TAKS Writing Objective 1

STUDENT EDITION OR BIG BOOK

Lesson 9

Vocabulary
mood

Colors Tell Stories

Many artworks tell a story. What story does this painting tell?

Vincent van Gogh, *First Steps, after Millet*

Tell about the setting in the painting. What colors did the artist mostly use? What **mood**, or feeling, do the colors give?

54

Background Information

About the Artist
Vincent van Gogh (VIN•sent van•GOH) (1853–1890) painted over 800 paintings. He sold only one while he was alive, but now his paintings are famous. Van Gogh was very interested in the effect of color. Instead of painting exactly what he saw, he used color to express himself. His favorite color was yellow.

For more information about van Gogh, see pp. R48–R59.

RECOMMENDED READING
In the Garden with Van Gogh by Julie Merberg and Suzanne Bober. Chronicle, 2002. **AVERAGE**

★ **TEKS 2.1A** identify variations in objects and subjects; **TEKS 2.2A** express ideas and feelings; **TEKS 2.2B** create effective compositions; **TEKS 2.2C** identify and practice skills; **TEKS 2.3A** identify stories and constructions; **TEKS 2.3B** compare artworks showing individuals/families; **TEKS 2.4B** identify ideas in artworks by peers and artists; **PDAS Domain I** active participation; *(continued)*

Artist's Workshop

Story Puppet Scene

PLAN

Brainstorm ideas for a story scene. What is the setting and who are the characters? What mood do you want to show?

CREATE

1. **Draw and cut out characters. Glue them onto craft sticks.**

2. **Draw and color the setting. Cut a slit. Move your puppets as you tell a story.**

REFLECT

How did you use colors to show mood in your story?

55

Drama Connection

PDAS Domain IV

Puppets of the World
Tell children that puppets are used in many parts of the world. Indonesia is famous for shadow puppets. With a projector, have children use their puppets and their hands as shadow puppets to perform their stories.

PDAS Domain IV

ESL To encourage **language production**, provide children with various puppets. Recall familiar stories with them. Have them act out the stories and make up new ones. Encourage dialogue.

Challenge Have partners create a new story using their four puppets.

Artist's Workshop

15-25 Minutes

Story Puppet Scene

MATERIALS: construction paper, craft sticks, glue, oil pastels, scissors, crayons, markers

Safety Tips Have children pinch the paper and carefully make a small cut to begin the slit.

PLAN Have children recall familiar stories if they have difficulty thinking of a new one.

CREATE Remind children to use colors that will create a mood that matches their story. Ask them to use color to express their ideas and feelings. TEKS 2.2A, TEKS 2.2B, TEKS 2.2C

REFLECT Ask children to present their stories. Have classmates identify the mood and give reasons for their answers. TEKS 2.4B

Activity Options PDAS Domain IV

Quick Activity Have groups of three work to create two puppets and the picture.

Early Finishers Children can choose from the Idea Wheel, *Teacher Resource Book* pp. 29–30.

Challenge See *Teacher Resource Book* p. 51.

5-10 Minutes

Wrap-Up

Informal Assessment PDAS Domain III

- **How is your scene like *First Steps*? How is it different?** (Responses will vary.)
  PERCEPTION/AESTHETICS TEKS 2.4B

- **How did your classmates use colors to show moods?** (Responses will vary.) ART CRITICISM
  TEKS 2.4B

Extend Through Writing

Interactive "Share the pen" with children to complete a story map for a puppet show.
TAKS Reading Objectives 2, 3; TAKS Writing Objective 3

PDAS Domain II learner-centered instruction; **PDAS Domain III** evaluation and feedback; **PDAS Domain IV** classroom management; **TAKS Reading Objective 2** apply knowledge of literary elements; **TAKS Reading Objective 3** use a variety of strategies; **TAKS Reading Objective 4** apply critical-thinking skills; **TAKS Writing Objective 1** composition; **TAKS Writing Objective 3** organization

LESSON 9 *Colors Tell Stories* **55**

PDAS Domains I, II

Edna Crawford, Animator

CAREERS IN ART

DISCUSS THE ARTWORK

Have children read pages 56–57.

- Have children identify their favorite cartoon characters and tell why they like them.

- Discuss the details that some animators use to make their characters seem real, such as facial expressions, voices and sounds, movements, and clothing.

- Have children look carefully at the series of illustrations from *Apple Surprise* on page 57. Ask: **What story do the pictures tell?** (Responses will vary.) **What do you think the surprise is?** (Possible responses: The balloon pops when the worm bites it; the worm lands in an apple truck.) TEKS 2.3A, TEKS 2.4B

- Ask children to identify Edna Crawford's job and to tell how she uses art as she works. TEKS 2.3C

DISCUSS THE ARTIST

Share background information about the artist.

- Since kindergarten, Edna Crawford has been interested in art. She would finish her work and then spend time creating art.

- Edna attended an art class when she was eleven. In the class, Edna chose a ceramic worm to paint. She painted other objects too, but the worm was her favorite. The worm is the star of *Apple Surprise*.

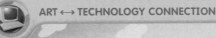
Edna Crawford, Animator

Edna Crawford works on her computer to create cartoon art. She is an **animator**. She makes many pictures of a character until she has one she likes best. It is important to her that her characters seem lifelike.

Background Information

About the Artist

Edna Crawford (1968–) was born in New York City, and her parents are from Colombia, South America. She is an animator and graphic designer. In planning animation, Crawford knows just how the finished work will turn out. She uses her sketchbook to write down her ideas and to draw quick sketches. Then she goes to her computer to try out different ways of animating the characters based on her sketches.

For additional information about Edna Crawford, see pp. R48–R59.

★ TEKS 2.2C identify and practice skills; TEKS 2.3A identify stories and constructions; TEKS 2.3C identify jobs in art; TEKS 2.4B identify ideas in artworks by peers and artists; PDAS Domain I active participation; PDAS Domain II learner-centered instruction; TAKS Reading Objective 4 apply critical-thinking skills

Apple Surprise

1

2

3

4

5

6

DID YOU KNOW?

When she was young, Edna Crawford painted a big red balloon that looked like an apple. Then she painted a worm on it. In college, this became the idea for her story *Apple Surprise*.

Think About Art

How can you use a computer to make pictures?

Multimedia Biographies
Visit *The Learning Site*
www.harcourtschool.com

57

DID YOU KNOW?

Edna Crawford grew up in New York City, a place that is known as "The Big Apple." When she was a girl, she and her sister painted a mural on their bedroom wall that included symbols of New York City, like the Statue of Liberty and a big red apple. Edna painted a string on the apple and changed it into a balloon. Then she painted a picture of her favorite character, the worm, on it. This idea from childhood became the basis for her story *Apple Surprise*.

Ask children to tell what Edna Crawford might draw next in the story *Apple Surprise*.
TAKS Reading Objective 4

Think About Art

How can you use a computer to make pictures?
(Responses will vary, but may include using a drawing program, adding color with a paint tool, using a stamp program, or using a greeting card program to create cards and illustrations.) TEKS 2.3C

ARTIST'S EYE ACTIVITY

Flip-Books Explain that animation is based on showing a series of similar images. Model how to make a flip-book by drawing a series of small images, one on each page. Each image changes slightly to create movement. Children can create their own flip-books, using crayons and markers on paper or a computer drawing program. Provide them with ideas for simple images, such as a face that smiles and frowns or an inchworm that moves across the page. TEKS 2.2C

Multimedia Biographies
Visit *The Learning Site*
www.harcourtschool.com

Technology Connection

Computer Art Explain that animators often create personified animals. Have children use a computer program to create animal characters. Ask them also to create designs and patterns using Copy and Paste.

For additional cross-curricular suggestions, see Art Transparency 6.

TEKS 2.4B; PDAS Domain II
Student Art Show

Display Artworks Have children create an exhibit of their portfolios and finished artworks. Ask children to view and identify ideas in one another's original artworks, portfolios, and the exhibit as a whole. Have them focus on color and value. See also Student Art Exhibitions, page 142.

Lesson 10

PDAS Domains I, II
Colors in Seascapes

OBJECTIVES
- Identify seascapes and horizon lines
- Create an effective seascape
- Identify story elements

RESOURCES
- Art Print 6
- Discussion Card 1
- Big Book, pp. 58–59
- Electronic Art Gallery CD-ROM, Primary

5 Minutes
Warm-Up

Take a Trip to the Beach   Have children imagine a trip to the beach or a lake and then act out what they would see and do there.

10-15 Minutes
Teach

Discuss Art Concepts   Read and discuss pages 58–59 with children. Point out that some boats in the painting are small, to show that they are far away. Use Discussion Card 1 and have children compare the families in *Gloucester Harbor* and in **Art Print 6**. Have children identify the horizon line and tell how the artist made it.
TEKS 2.1A, TEKS 2.2C, TEKS 2.3B

Think Critically

1. (Focus Skill) **READING SKILL** **What is happening in the painting?** (A family is on a relaxing trip in a rowboat.) **STORY ELEMENTS**   TEKS 2.3A

2. **How did the artist use line and color to show movement in the water?** (He used dark wavy lines with light colors to make waves.)
PERCEPTION/COMPARE AND CONTRAST   TEKS 2.1A, TEKS 2.1B

3. **WRITE**   Describe the sky. Tell what time of day you think it is and why.
INDEPENDENT WRITING   TEKS 2.3A; TAKS Writing Objective 1

★ TEKS 2.1A identify variations in objects and subjects; TEKS 2.1B identify elements and principles; TEKS 2.2B create effective compositions; TEKS 2.2C identify and practice skills; TEKS 2.3A identify stories and constructions; TEKS 2.3B compare artworks showing individuals/families; TEKS 2.4B identify ideas in artworks by peers and artists; *(continued)*

Lesson 10

Vocabulary
- seascape
- horizon line

Colors in Seascapes

What is going on in this painting? A **seascape** is an artwork that shows a water setting, like the sea. What colors did the artist use to show water? Why?

Winslow Homer, *Gloucester Harbor*

Can you find the line where the sky and the water meet? This is called the **horizon line**.

58

FYI
Background Information

About the Artist
Winslow Homer (1836–1910) was a self-taught American painter. His first artworks were magazine illustrations and oil paintings of Civil War scenes. In the 1870s, Homer began using watercolors to paint rural scenes. He later lived by the sea in Maine, where he created large-scale seascapes.

For more information about Winslow Homer, see pp. R48–R59.

RECOMMENDED READING
Little Blue and Little Yellow by Leo Lionni. Astor, 1959. **AVERAGE**

Artist's Workshop

Crayon-Resist Seascape

PLAN ....

Think about all the things you can find on the ocean and in the ocean.

CREATE ....

1. **Draw a horizon line. Use crayons to draw boats. Add plants and animals under the water.**

2. **Paint watercolor over the picture. Make it darker at the bottom.**

REFLECT ....

What colors did you use? What does the water look like?

Where can you find a seascape in your town?

59

PDAS Domain IV

Science Connection

Water on Planet Earth
Display a globe or world map. Point out how color designates land and water. Explain that almost 3/4 of the Earth's surface is water. To illustrate this, provide children with a paper plate to fold into fourths and color three sections blue and one brown.

ESL Help children create **oral sentences** about actions related to water, such as swimming, fishing, rowing, or sailing. Provide this sentence frame: _I like ____ at the [beach]._ Have children use a **total physical response** by **pantomiming** each action as they say a sentence.

15-25 Minutes

Artist's Workshop

Crayon-Resist Seascape

MATERIALS: crayons, oil pastels, white paper, watercolor paints, paintbrushes

TECHNIQUE TIP: Tell children to color hard so that pictures will repel the paint better.

PLAN   With children, brainstorm about living and nonliving things in or on the ocean.

CREATE   Encourage children to draw one boat smaller so that it looks farther away. TEKS 2.2B

REFLECT   Ask volunteers to share their pictures. Have classmates identify the horizon line and tell what they like about the artwork.
TEKS 2.2C

Activity Options PDAS Domain IV

Quick Activity   Have children use crayons and omit the watercolor step.

Early Finishers   Have children create a water-themed frame for their picture.

Challenge   See _Teacher Resource Book_ p. 52

5-10 Minutes

Wrap-Up

Informal Assessment PDAS Domain III

- **What ideas did you get from Winslow Homer's painting?** (Responses will vary.)
  PERCEPTION/AESTHETICS   TEKS 2.4B

- **What parts of your classmates' seascapes are most interesting? Why?** (Responses will vary.) **ART CRITICISM**   TEKS 2.4B

Extend Through Writing

Shared   Have children brainstorm titles for seascapes and choose one for their own work. Have them proofread their titles to check for capitalization of important words. TAKS Writing Objective 6

PDAS Domain I active participation; **PDAS Domain II** learner-centered instruction; **PDAS Domain III** evaluation and feedback; **PDAS Domain IV** classroom management; **TAKS Writing Objective 1** composition; **TAKS Writing Objective 6** proofreading

LESSON 10 _Colors in Seascapes_   **59**

Unit 2

PDAS Domains I, III

Review and Reflect

In this unit, children learned about how artists mix and use colors together to show different moods. You may want to use **Art Prints 4–6** and **17–18** and Discussion Cards 1 and 2 to review these concepts.

Vocabulary and Concepts

Review art vocabulary by having children tell which word best goes with each picture. ("Best" responses are shown; accept other reasonable responses.)

1. C **4.** D **7.** G

2. A **5.** H **8.** F

3. B **6.** E

9. Children should mention that the painting is a seascape and tell about the time and place (setting) shown in the painting. They should correctly identify the horizon line. They may describe the mood as calm or peaceful.

Unit 2 Review and Reflect

Vocabulary and Concepts

Tell which picture goes best with each item.

A B C D

1. cool colors   3. primary colors
2. tint   4. value

E F G H

5. shade   7. warm colors
6. seascape   8. secondary colors

9. Tell about the setting of this picture. Point out the horizon line. Tell about the mood.

Winslow Homer, *Gloucester Harbor*

60

TEKS 2.3C

Home and Community Connection

School-Home Connection

Copy and distribute *Teacher Resource Book* pages 79–80 to provide family members with information and activities they can use with children to reinforce concepts taught in this unit.

Community Connection

Ask a local interior designer or window display designer to talk with children about using color to create different moods. You might also invite a painter or hardware store employee to talk about mixing paints to create different shades and tints. Afterward, have children identify the different kinds of jobs in art. **CAREERS IN ART**

★ TEKS 2.1B identify elements and principles; TEKS 2.3A identify stories and constructions; TEKS 2.3C identify jobs in art; TEKS 2.4A define reasons for preferences in personal artworks; TEKS 2.4B identify ideas in artworks by peers and artists; PDAS Domain I active participation; PDAS Domain III evaluation and feedback; *(continued)*

Story Elements

Reread about Edna
Crawford on pages
56–57. Think about the
story her artwork shows.
Fill in the story map.

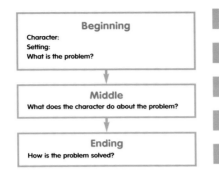

Beginning
Character:
Setting:
What is the problem?

↓

Middle
What does the character do about the problem?

↓

Ending
How is the problem solved?

Write About Art

Write a story about the painting *Balloons for a Dime*.

My friends and I
were playing in the
park on Saturday.

Jonathan Green, *Balloons for a Dime*

61

TEKS 2.4A; PDAS Domain III

Assessment

Portfolio Assessment

Have children choose one artwork from this unit to include in their port-folios. Ask them to review each Artist's Workshop activity and select the piece they like the best. Have children define their reasons for preferring this particular piece. See also Portfolio Recording Form, p. R32.

Additional Assessment Options

- Progress Recording Form, p. R33
- Artist's Workshop Rubrics (Self/Teacher and Peer), pp. R30–R31
- Unit Test, *Teacher Resource Book*, p. 92

Story Elements

Have children reread pages 56–57 and complete a story map to tell about *Apple Surprise*.
TAKS Reading Objectives 1, 2, 3; TAKS Writing Objective 3

Beginning
Character: caterpillar
Setting: outside by a house during the day
What is the problem? The caterpillar wants the apple.

↓

Middle
What does the character do about the problem? It climbs up onto the porch and bites the apple.

↓

Ending
How is the problem solved? The caterpillar is carried away by the balloon it thought was an apple. The caterpillar lands in an apple truck and finds an apple to eat.

Write About Art

Story Encourage children to create a story map before they write about events in *Balloons for a Dime*. Guide them to use appropriate word choices in their writing. TAKS Writing Objectives 1, 3, 5

Critic's Corner

RESPONSE/EVALUATION Have children choose a favorite artwork from this unit.

Describe Have children identify art elements, such as color and value, and story elements.
TEKS 2.1B, TEKS 2.3A

Analyze Ask children to apply unit vocabulary in discussing the artwork.

Interpret Invite children to tell how the colors make them feel and identify the mood. TEKS 2.4B

Evaluate Ask children to give specific reasons for choosing the artwork.

 TAKS Test Preparation: Reading and Writing Through Art, p. 12

TAKS Reading Objective 1 demonstrate understanding of texts; TAKS Reading Objective 2 apply knowledge of literary elements; TAKS Reading Objective 3 use a variety of strategies; TAKS Writing Objective 1 composition; TAKS Writing Objective 3 organization; TAKS Writing Objective 5 usage

UNIT 2 *Review and Reflect* **61**

Unit 3

Pattern, Rhythm, and Texture

Nature's Way

From earliest times, artists have been inspired by their natural environments. In this unit, children learn how artists incorporate patterns, rhythms, and textures from nature into their art.

Resources

- Unit 3 Art Prints (7–9)
- Additional Art Prints (4, 16)
- Art Transparencies 7–9
- Test Preparation: Reading and Writing Through Art, p. 13
- Artist's Workshop Activities: English and Spanish, pp. 21–30
- Encyclopedia of Artists and Art History, pp. R48–R59
- Picture Cards Collection, Cards 29, 40, 53, 67, 69, 72, 75, 95, 111, 122

Using the Art Prints

- Discussion Cards, pp. R34–R42
- Teaching Suggestions, backs of Art Prints
- Art Print Teaching Suggestions: Spanish

Teacher Resource Book

- Vocabulary Cards in English and Spanish, pp. 13–14
- Reading Skill Card 3, p. 25
- Copying Masters, pp. 29, 30, 31, 42
- Challenge Activities, pp. 53–57
- School-Home Connection: English/Spanish, pp. 81–82
- Unit Test, p. 93

Technology Resources

 Electronic Art Gallery CD-ROM, Primary

Picture Card Bank CD-ROM

 Visit *The Learning Site* www.harcourtschool.com

- Multimedia Art Glossary
- Multimedia Biographies
- Reading Skills and Activities

ART PRINT 7

Harmony in Red
by Henri Matisse

ART PRINT 8

Fall Plowing
by Grant Wood

ART PRINT 16

Cosecha (Harvest)
by Women's Co-op, Lima, Peru

ART PRINT 9

Morning Still Life
by Jacob Lawrence

ART PRINT 4

Girl with Sunflowers
by Diego Rivera

Planning Guide
PDAS Domain IV

Lesson	Objectives and Vocabulary	Art Images	Production/Materials
Important Details, pp. 64–65			
11 SHAPES MAKE PATTERNS pp. 66–67 — 30–60 minutes	• Identify pattern and repetition • Create a frame, using shape patterns • *Focus Skill* Identify important details **Vocabulary: pattern, repetition**	• **Star of Bethlehem quilt** by Unknown artist • **Three Flags** by Jasper Johns	**Patterned Picture Frame** ❏ ruler ❏ construction paper ❏ crayons, markers ❏ paints, brushes ❏ found objects ❏ glue
12 COLORS MAKE PATTERNS pp. 68–69 — 30–60 minutes	• Identify principles, such as patterns • Create color patterns using prints • *Focus Skill* Identify important details **Vocabulary: print**	• **Guaymí necklace** by Unknown artist • **Fish Print** by Heather, grade 2	**Patterned Stand-Up Animal** ❏ construction paper ❏ scissors ❏ sponges or cardboard ❏ tempera paints ❏ clothespins
Art ←→ Math Connection: Egyptian Art, pp. 70–71			
13 PATTERNS SHOW RHYTHM pp. 72–73 — 30–60 minutes	• Identify principles such as rhythm • Create pictures showing rhythm • *Focus Skill* Identify important details **Vocabulary: rhythm**	• **Exotic Landscape** by Henri Rousseau • **Peruvian textile** by Unknown artist	**Rain Forest Scene** ❏ construction paper (neutral colors: gray, light brown) ❏ oil pastels ❏ pencils
14 PATTERNS AND TEXTURES IN WEAVINGS pp. 74–75 — 30–60 minutes	• Identify patterns and textures • Construct a weaving • *Focus Skill* Identify important details **Vocabulary: texture, weaving**	• **Riverdance** by Nancy Curry	**Found Object Weaving** ❏ cardboard ❏ yarn ❏ tape ❏ paper strips ❏ found objects
Art ←→ Social Studies Connection: Jacob Lawrence's Patterns, pp. 76–77			
15 PATTERNS SHOW TEXTURE pp. 78–79 — 30–60 minutes	• Understand that patterns can show texture • Create a textured rubbing • *Focus Skill* Identify important details **Vocabulary: visual texture**	• **Dancing Lizard Couple** by Ann Hanson • **Hare** by Albrecht Dürer	**Textured Animal Rubbing** ❏ butcher paper ❏ scissors ❏ crayons ❏ found objects ❏ stapler or tape
Review and Reflect, pp. 80–81			

 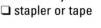

Important Details, pp. 64–65
Opportunities for application of the skill are provided on pp. 66, 68, 72, 74, 78, 81.

Art Puzzlers

Resources and Technology	Suggested Literature	Across the Curriculum
• Art Prints 7–9, 16 • Reading Skill Card 3 • Big Book, pp. 66–67 ⏺ Electronic Art Gallery CD-ROM, Primary	*Lots and Lots of Zebra Stripes: Patterns in Nature* by Stephen R. Swinburne **Easy**	**Math/Social Studies** Flag Patterns, p. 67 **Reading** Important Details, p. 66 **Writing** Independent, p. 67
• Art Prints 4, 7, 16 • Reading Skill Card 3 • Big Book, pp. 68–69 ⏺ Electronic Art Gallery CD-ROM, Primary	*Chameleon's Colors* by Chisato Tashiro **Challenging**	**Science** Pattern Camouflage, p. 69 **Reading** Important Details, p. 68 **Writing** Independent, p. 69
• Art Prints 8, 9 • Discussion Card 9, p. R41 • Reading Skill Card 3 • Big Book, pp. 72–73 ⏺ Electronic Art Gallery CD-ROM, Primary	*Pattern Fish* by Trudy Harris **Challenging**	**Science** Rain Forest Web, p. 73 **Reading** Important Details, p. 72 **Writing** Independent, p. 73
• Art Prints 7, 16 • Discussion Card 2, p. R34 • Reading Skill Card 3 • Big Book, pp. 74–75 ⏺ Electronic Art Gallery CD-ROM, Primary	*Charlie Needs a Cloak* by Tomie dePaola **Easy**	**Science** Water Cycle, p. 75 **Reading** Important Details, p. 74 **Writing** Independent, p. 75
• Art Prints 4, 8, 16 • Discussion Cards 3, 4, 9, pp. R35, R36, R41 • Reading Skill Card 3 • Big Book, pp. 78–79 ⏺ Electronic Art Gallery CD-ROM, Primary	*How Artists Use Pattern and Texture* by Paul Flux **Read-Aloud**	**Science** Survival Traits, p. 79 **Reading** Important Details, p. 78 **Writing** Independent, p. 79

Present these art puzzlers to children at the beginning or end of a class or when children finish an assignment early.

• Look at the **designs** in clothing around you. What **patterns** of lines and shapes do you see repeated? TEKS 2.1A, TEKS 2.1B

• Name something with a bumpy **texture**. Name something with a soft texture. TEKS 2.1A, TEKS 2.1B

• Continue this **shape pattern**: square-square-circle-triangle, square-square-circle-triangle.

• Look outside. Tell what repeating colors, lines, and shapes create a **rhythm** that your eyes follow. TEKS 2.1A, TEKS 2.1B

• Arrange some crayons in a **color pattern**. Tell what you did. TEKS 2.1B, TEKS 2.2C

 School-Home Connection
The activities above are included in the School-Home Connection for this unit. See *Teacher Resource Book,* pp. 81–82.

Assessment Options
• Rubrics and Recording Forms, pp. R28–R33
• Unit 3 Test, *Teacher Resource Book,* p. 93

 Visit *The Learning Site*:
www.harcourtschool.com

Artist's Workshops PREVIEW

PDAS Domain IV

Use these pages to help you gather and organize materials for the Artist's Workshop in each lesson.

LESSON	MATERIALS

11 Patterned Picture Frame p. 67

Objective: To have children use the repetition of shapes to create patterns on a picture frame they make

🕐 15–25 minutes

Challenge Activity: See *Teacher Resource Book,* p. 53.

- ruler
- construction paper
- crayons
- markers
- paints
- paintbrushes
- found objects— buttons, seashells, pom-poms, scraps
- glue

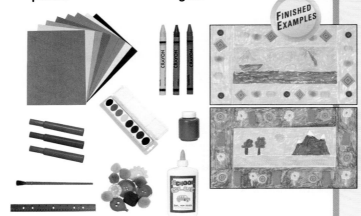

FINISHED EXAMPLES

LESSON

12 Patterned Stand-Up Animal p. 69

Objective: To have children make and use prints to create a pattern of colors on an animal shape that stands up

🕐 15–25 minutes

Challenge Activity: See *Teacher Resource Book,* p. 54.

- construction paper
- scissors
- sponges (or cardboard)
- tempera paints
- clothespins

FINISHED EXAMPLES

Safety Tips

For safety information, see Art Safety, page R4; the Art Safety Poster; or Big Book page 148.

For information on media and techniques, see pages R15–R23.

LESSON	MATERIALS

13 Rain Forest Scene
p. 73

Objective: To have children draw a scene, using patterns of colors, lines, and shapes to create rhythm

🕐 15–25 minutes

Challenge Activity: See *Teacher Resource Book,* p. 55.

- construction paper (neutral colors: gray, light brown)
- oil pastels
- pencils

FINISHED EXAMPLE

---

14 Found Object Weaving p. 75

Objective: To have children explore texture as they create a pattern in a weaving, and add found objects to give it additional texture

🕐 15–25 minutes

Challenge Activity: See *Teacher Resource Book,* p. 56.

- cardboard, yarn
- tissue paper
- tape
- paper strips
- found objects— vines, grass, pine needles, cloth, ribbon, seashells

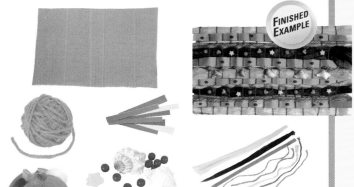

FINISHED EXAMPLE

---

15 Textured Animal Rubbing p. 79

Objective: To have children explore visual textures created by patterns made from rubbings of found objects on the cut-out shape of an animal

🕐 15–25 minutes

Challenge Activity: See *Teacher Resource Book,* p. 57.

- butcher paper
- scissors
- crayons
- found objects—bubble wrap, leaves, cardboard scraps, craft sticks, buttons
- stapler or tape

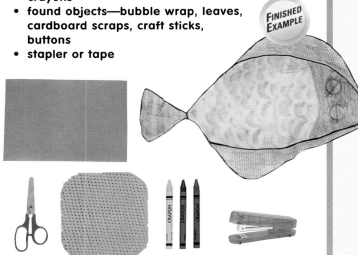

FINISHED EXAMPLE

Unit 3

PDAS Domains I, II

Nature's Way

PREVIEW THE UNIT

Do a Walk-Through   Have children use the Contents to find the page on which Unit 3 begins and turn to it. Tell children that they will explore ways that artists use ideas from the natural environment. Have children look at the lesson titles, art captions, and Artist's Workshop activities.

Explore the Environment   Help children develop and organize ideas from the environment. Take a brief walk outside or have children observe nature through a window, by viewing images, or by handling natural objects. Have them identify variations in objects and subjects from the environment, using their senses. Ask them to identify art elements, such as color, line, and shape.   TEKS 2.1A, TEKS 2.1B

SHARE THE SONG

Have children read the song, and then sing it together. Discuss how the song and painting are similar. Then ask:

What might the trail riders see when they go around the mountain? DRAW CONCLUSIONS
TAKS Reading Objective 4

STEP INTO THE ART

Read the title of the painting. Have children look closely at the painting and describe it. Then ask:

How might you feel if you were one of the trail riders? PERSONAL RESPONSE   TAKS Reading Objectives 1, 4

SHARE BACKGROUND INFORMATION

Explain that Benton is best known for his paintings of people and places in the American South and Midwest. Share Background Information.

LOCATE IT   See *Using the Maps of Museums and Art Sites*, pp. R2–R3.

STUDENT EDITION **OR** BIG BOOK

▲ Thomas Hart Benton, *Trail Riders*

LOCATE IT

This painting is in the National Gallery of Art in Washington, D.C.

See Maps of Museums and Art Sites, pages 144–147.

62

FYI ## Background Information

About the Artist

Thomas Hart Benton (1889–1975) was born in Missouri but lived much of his childhood in Washington, D.C. He saw art there, murals in particular. These influenced his paintings, along with the work of muralist Diego Rivera, whom he met. Benton made sculptures as studies for some of his paintings. This work helped to give his paintings a three-dimensional quality.

For more information about Thomas Hart Benton, see pp. R48–R59.

  For related images, see **Electronic Art Gallery CD-ROM, Primary**.

★ **TEKS 2.1A** identify variations in objects and subjects; **TEKS 2.1B** identify elements and principles; **TEKS 2.2C** identify and practice skills; **PDAS Domain I** active participation; **PDAS Domain II** learner-centered instruction; **PDAS Domain IV** classroom management; **TAKS Reading Objective 1** demonstrate understanding of texts; *(continued)*

3

Nature's Way

She'll Be Coming 'Round the Mountain

She'll be coming 'round the mountain
    when she comes,
She'll be coming 'round the mountain
    when she comes,
She'll be coming 'round the mountain,
She'll be coming 'round the mountain,
She'll be coming 'round the mountain
    when she comes.

Traditional Song

ABOUT THE ARTIST

See Gallery of Artists,
pages 182–191.

Unit Vocabulary

pattern   texture
repetition   weaving
print   visual texture
rhythm

 Multimedia Art Glossary
Visit *The Learning Site*
www.harcourtschool.com

63

Unit Vocabulary

Write the vocabulary words on cards and display them. Point to each word and read it aloud with children. Then put the cards in a pile and hold them up one at a time. Ask children to read aloud the word, and have volunteers tell the meaning and point to an example of the concept in the painting or in the classroom. Tell children that they will learn more about these words in this unit.

pattern a group of repeating lines, shapes, or colors

repetition the act of being repeated, or appearing again and again

print a copy of an artwork; artwork created by transferring color or ink from one surface to another

rhythm patterns of color, lines, or shapes that your eye follows that create a feeling of movement

texture the way a surface feels

weaving fabric or artwork made by interlacing materials

visual texture texture that can be seen rather than felt

Vocabulary Resources

- Vocabulary Cards in English and Spanish: *Teacher Resource Book*, pp. 13–14
- Student Edition Glossary, pp. 192–201

 Multimedia Art Glossary
Visit *The Learning Site*
www.harcourtschool.com

Sketchbook

 Have children use their sketchbooks to practice the skills necessary for producing a variety of artwork, including sketching, planning, and writing ideas, as well as for recording new concepts. Encourage children to sketch indoors as well as outdoors. TEKS 2.2C

TEKS 2.1B, TEKS 2.2C; PDAS Domain IV

 ## Art Center

Materials various fabrics, objects for printing, stamp pads, computer

Ongoing Activity Have children print, collect, or create on a computer patterns, rhythms, and textures. Have them identify and practice print-making skills.

Big Book Place the *Big Book* in the Art Center.

PDAS Domain IV

 ## Classroom Management

Organize children into small groups. Children take turns being the group's leader in charge of handing out and collecting materials.

Display Discussion Cards 3 and 4, pp. R35–R36, and the Idea Wheel, *Teacher Resource Book*, pp. 29–30, for early finishers.

Unit 3

Focus Skill **READING SKILL**

PDAS Domains I, II

Important Details

SKILL TRACE	
IMPORTANT DETAILS	
Introduce	pp. 64–65
Review	pp. 66, 68, 72, 74, 78, 81

DISCUSS THE SKILL

Access Prior Knowledge Explain that **details** are pieces of information that may answer *who*, *what*, *when*, *where*, *how*, and *why* questions. Help children develop and organize ideas from the environment. Ask them to use their senses to look around the classroom and out a window to observe details in their environment. Have children identify variations in subjects and objects, including details about how things look, sound, feel, and smell. Tell them to identify art elements they notice in subjects and objects, such as color, line, and shape. Explain that paying attention to important details will help them better understand the artworks and the information they read in this unit. TEKS 2.1A, TEKS 2.1B; TAKS Reading Objective 1

APPLY TO ART

Important Details in Art Have volunteers read page 64 as classmates follow along in their books. Explain that if they look closely, many art-works have important details that will help them understand the artwork better. Have children tell about the important details in this artwork. (A boy and his mother are standing in the wind. Things from different seasons blow by, such as fall leaves, flowers, and snowflakes.)
TEKS 2.1A; TAKS Reading Objectives 1, 4

Focus Skill **READING SKILL**

Important Details

What is happening in this picture? What things are blowing in the wind?

Stefano Vitale, cover illustration from *When the Wind Stops*, by Charlotte Zolotow **LITERATURE LINK**

When you look closely at a picture, you see **details**, or small parts. Some details are important for showing what a picture is mainly about.

64

Background Information

About the Artist
Stefano Vitale (stay•FAHN•oh vee•TAHL•ee) (1958–) is an artist and children's book illustrator. When asked what he liked most about painting the pictures for this book, he said, "I liked using my imagination to picture the story in my mind."

For more information about Stefano Vitale, see pp. R48–R59.

LITERATURE LINK Share other illustrations from *When the Wind Stops* by Charlotte Zolotow. HarperCollins, 1995.
AVERAGE

★ TEKS 2.1A identify variations in objects and subjects; TEKS 2.1B identify elements and principles; PDAS Domain I active participation; PDAS Domain II learner-centered instruction; PDAS Domain IV classroom management; TAKS Reading Objective 1 demonstrate understanding of texts; *(continued)*

Read about the **important details** in the picture on page 64. Add details to the web.

The seasons are changing quickly for a boy and his mother. Spring flowers and fall leaves blow by in the wind. Snowflakes and raindrops do, too. The sun, the moon, and stars float by in the sky.

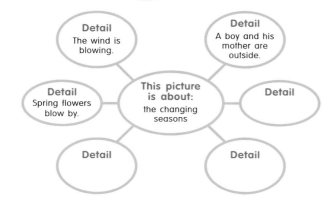

On Your Own

Look again at pages 62–63. What details do you see? Make a web that shows the important details.

65

Important Details   Tell children that paying attention to important details will also help them better understand and enjoy what they read.

Have children read the paragraph on page 65 silently, and then ask a volunteer to read it aloud. Have children identify important details. Then work together to make and complete the web, showing the important details from the paragraph.
TAKS Reading Objectives 1, 3, 4

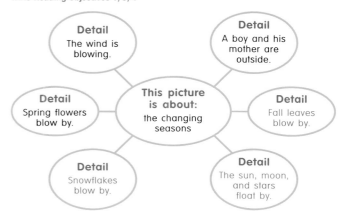

ON YOUR OWN

Have children revisit the painting *Trail Riders* on pages 62–63. They can work individually or with a partner to create a web, identifying and discussing important details in the painting.
TAKS Reading Objectives 3, 4

PDAS Domain IV; TAKS Reading Objective 1

(Focus Skill)

Reading Skill Card

Distribute Reading Skill Card 3, *Teacher Resource Book* p. 25.
Use the web to help discuss important details in artworks.

Extend the Skill   For additional teaching suggestions, see **Art Transparency 7**.

PDAS Domain IV

MEETING INDIVIDUAL NEEDS

ESL   Use **visuals** to support **comprehensible input** for concepts related to seasons.

Display *Picture Cards Collection* cards 29, 95, and 111 for children to discuss and use as a reference. See also *Picture Card Bank CD-ROM*, Category: Weather.

snow

GO ONLINE

Reading Skills and Activities
Visit *The Learning Site*
www.harcourtschool.com

Lesson 11

PDAS Domains I, II
Shapes Make Patterns

OBJECTIVES
- Identify pattern and repetition
- Create a frame, using shape patterns
- Identify important details

RESOURCES
- Art Prints 7–9, 16
- Big Book, pp. 66–67
- Electronic Art Gallery CD-ROM, Primary

5 Minutes
Warm-Up

Recognize a Pattern Display visuals of various flags, including the American flag. Ask children to tell how our flag is different. TEKS 2.1A

10-15 Minutes
Teach

Discuss Art Concepts Have volunteers read aloud pages 66–67. Explain that patterns can be repeating geometric or free-form shapes. Draw simple patterns on the board. Then display **Art Prints 7–9** and **16**, and ask children to identify the patterns. TEKS 2.1B

Think Critically

1. **(Focus Skill) READING SKILL** **Describe the patterns in the quilt.** (One pattern is made of triangles (geometric shapes) and flowers (organic shapes.) **NOTE IMPORTANT DETAILS** TAKS Reading Objectives 1, 4

2. **What patterns do you see on the flag painting?** (alternating stripes; lines of stars; three flags) **PERCEPTION** TEKS 2.1B

3. **WRITE** **Draw the pattern you like best and write reasons why.** INDEPENDENT WRITING TEKS 2.4A; TAKS Writing Objective 1

Lesson 11

Vocabulary
pattern
repetition

Shapes Make Patterns

What does each artwork show? What shapes make up the big star in the quilt?

Unknown artist,
Star of
Bethlehem quilt

Point to the arms of the star and to the flowers. Name the shapes—*triangle, flower, triangle, flower*. Repeating shapes, lines, or colors make a **pattern**.

66

Background Information

About the Artist
Jasper Johns (1930–) was an early leader in American **Pop Art**. He used repeated images in his artworks so that, he explained, "You can see more than one thing at a time."

For more information about Johns and Pop Art, see pp. R48–R59.

RECOMMENDED READING
Lots and Lots of Zebra Stripes by Stephen R. Swinburne. Boyds Mills, 1998. **EASY**

★ TEKS 2.1A identify variations in objects and subjects; TEKS 2.1B identify elements and principles; TEKS 2.2B create effective compositions; TEKS 2.2C identify and practice skills; TEKS 2.4A define reasons for preferences in personal artworks; TEKS 2.4B identify ideas in artworks by peers and artists; PDAS Domain I active participation; *(continued)*

Every pattern has **repetition**, or repeating parts. What repetition does this art show? What comes next in the flag pattern?

 Jasper Johns,
Three Flags

Artist's Workshop

Patterned Picture Frame

Fold up and glue the edges of your paper to make a frame. Decorate with a pattern of shapes.

67

Patterned Picture Frame

MATERIALS: ruler, construction paper, crayons, markers, found objects, glue, paints, paintbrushes

TECHNIQUE TIP: Children can use a computer's copy and paste tools to experiment with repeating designs and patterns.

PLAN Have children identify the skills necessary for making a patterned frame. TEKS 2.2C

CREATE Encourage children to create interesting shape patterns using different media. TEKS 2.2B

REFLECT Have children share their frames and ask classmates to identify the patterns. TEKS 2.1B

Activity Options PDAS Domain IV

Quick Activity Have children use only their crayons or markers to make shape patterns.

Early Finishers Children can paint a picture with shape patterns to insert into the frame.

Challenge See *Teacher Resource Book* p. 53.

 5-10 Minutes

Wrap-Up

Informal Assessment PDAS Domain III

- **What ideas did the art give you about patterns?** (Responses will vary.)
  PERCEPTION/AESTHETICS TEKS 2.1B, TEKS 2.4B

- **Which pattern do you like best? Why?** (Responses will vary.) ART CRITICISM TEKS 2.4A

Extend Through Writing

Independent Have children write a description of shape patterns they made. Remind them to check their spelling. TEKS 2.1B; TAKS Writing Objectives 1, 2

➕➖ Math/Social Studies Connection

Flag Patterns Explain to children that there are 48 stars because there were only 48 states when Johns painted his flags. Have each child design a flag by using a pattern of shapes based on a number pattern such as 2–3–2–3.

MEETING INDIVIDUAL NEEDS
PDAS Domain IV

ESL To help **less-fluent speakers** develop **oral language**, draw shapes on the board and name them. Have children repeat.

Special Needs Children who have difficulty identifying shapes and patterns in artworks can finger-trace shapes you outline in black on a transparent sheet placed over the artworks.

PDAS Domain II learner-centered instruction; **PDAS Domain III** evaluation and feedback; **PDAS Domain IV** classroom management; **TAKS Reading Objective 1** demonstrate understanding of texts; **TAKS Reading Objective 4** apply critical-thinking skills; **TAKS Writing Objective 1** composition; **TAKS Writing Objective 2** conventions

LESSON 11 *Shapes Make Patterns* **67**

Lesson 12

PDAS Domains I, II

Colors Make Patterns

OBJECTIVES
- Identify principles, such as patterns
- Create color patterns using prints
- Identify important details

RESOURCES
- Art Prints 4, 7, 16
- Big Book, pp. 68–69
- Electronic Art Gallery CD-ROM, Primary

5 Minutes

Warm-Up

Predicting Colors Show children crayons arranged in repeating color patterns, such as red-blue-green/red-blue-green. Ask them to tell which color comes next. **TEKS 2.1B**

10-15 Minutes

Teach

Discuss Art Concepts Have children read page 68. Tell children about the Guaymí necklace. (See Art History.) Have them identify variations in the patterns of the necklace and in *Fish Print*, and then in the patterns in **Art Prints 4, 7**, and **16**. TEKS 2.1A, TEKS 2.1B

Think Critically

1. **Focus Skill READING SKILL** **What important details do you see in the art?** (triangles, color patterns; fish, stripes) **IDENTIFY IMPORTANT DETAILS** TAKS Reading Objectives 1, 4

2. **When would someone wear a Guaymí necklace today? Why do you think so?** (Possible response: to a celebration; it is a reward for doing well) **PERCEPTION/ART HISTORY** TEKS 2.3A

3. **WRITE** **What color pattern would you like on a shirt? Why?** (Responses will vary.) **INDEPENDENT WRITING** TEKS 2.4A; TAKS Writing Objective 1

Lesson 12

Vocabulary
print

Colors Make Patterns

What do the artworks show? Point to and say the colors that make up each pattern.

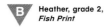

A Unknown artist, Guaymí necklace

B Heather, grade 2, *Fish Print*

Each fish in artwork **B** looks the same. Each is a **print**, or a copy of an artwork. One way to make a print is to cut out a shape. Press the shape into paint and then onto paper over and over.

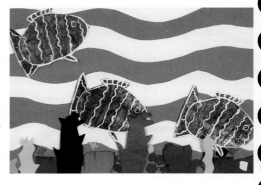

68

Background Information

Art History
The **Guaymí** (wy•MEE) people are the largest native group in Panama. This necklace is a *chaquira* (shah•KEE•rah), a beaded collar worn long ago by men as a treasured ornament for doing well as a warrior. Chaquiras were once made from pieces of bone, seeds, and shells. Today they are worn by men and women.

For more information about the Guaymí people, see pp. R48–R59.

RECOMMENDED READING
Chameleon's Colors by Chisato Tashiro. North-South, 2003. **CHALLENGING**

⭐ TEKS 2.1A identify variations in objects and subjects; TEKS 2.1B identify elements and principles; TEKS 2.2A express ideas and feelings; TEKS 2.2B create effective compositions; TEKS 2.2C identify and practice skills; TEKS 2.3A identify stories and constructions; TEKS 2.4A define reasons for preferences in personal artworks; TEKS 2.4B identify ideas in artworks by peers and artists; PDAS Domain I active participation; PDAS Domain II learner-centered instruction; PDAS Domain III evaluation and feedback; *(continued)*

Artist's Workshop

Patterned Stand-Up Animal

PLAN

Think about the shape of your favorite animal.

CREATE

1. **Fold a large sheet of paper in half. Draw and cut out an animal.**

2. **Cut out one shape a few times from a sponge or cardboard. Print a pattern of colors.**

REFLECT

What patterns did you make?

What color patterns do you see around you?

69

Science Connection

Pattern Camouflage Explain that many animals hide by blending in with the environment. Ask children to create environments for an animal in which its pattern will serve as camouflage. Then have children add a picture of the animal.

 PDAS Domain IV

ESL Display pictures of animals and read the names of each with children.

Use *Picture Cards Collection* cards 40, 53, 67, 69, and 75. See also *Picture Card Bank* **CD-ROM**, Categories: Animals/Pets, Wild, Farm, Water, and Insects.

dog

 15-25 Minutes

Artist's Workshop

Patterned Stand-Up Animal

MATERIALS: construction paper, scissors, sponges (or cardboard), tempera paints, clothespins

TECHNIQUE TIP: Make sure the shapes are entirely covered in paint, but not dripping.

PLAN Have children trace their animal before cutting it out. Tell them not to cut along the fold, so that the animal can stand.

CREATE Direct children to page 160 and model printing techniques. Ask children to identify and practice print-making skills. Have them express their ideas and feelings in their artwork. TEKS 2.2A, TEKS 2.2B, TEKS 2.2C

REFLECT Have children display their animals and describe the patterns they see. TEKS 2.1B

Activity Options PDAS Domain IV

Quick Activity Children can draw the patterns with markers instead of stamping with paint.

Early Finishers Children may create a second animal with a different pattern.

Challenge See *Teacher Resource Book* p. 54.

5-10 Minutes

Wrap-Up

Informal Assessment PDAS Domain III

- **Describe the color pattern you made.** (Responses will vary.) PERCEPTION/AESTHETICS TEKS 2.1B
- **Which patterns look most like those on real animals?** (Responses will vary.) ART CRITICISM TEKS 2.4B

Extend Through Writing

Independent Have children write about color patterns in their environment, using sentences that demonstrate command of punctuation, grammar, and sentence structure. TAKS Writing Objectives 1, 2

PDAS Domains I, II

EGYPTIAN ART

ART AND CULTURE

DISCUSS THE PHOTOGRAPHS

Have volunteers read pages 70–71 as classmates follow along in their books.

- Explain that artists often use materials from nature or show objects from nature in their artworks. Ask: **What things in nature do the ancient Egyptian artworks look like?** (Possible responses: The mask looks like a cobra; the pyramids look like mountains; the statue looks like a hippo in the water.)

- Have children identify a pattern in each artwork and then compare the patterns, noting the variations. Discuss whether each pattern is formed by repeated colors or shapes.
TEKS 2.1A, TEKS 2.1B

DISCUSS EGYPTIAN ART

Share the Background Information. Help children understand the historical and cultural heritage related to these artworks.

- The mask of solid gold and gems from the tomb of King Tutankhamen includes images of a cobra and a vulture, animals thought to protect the king in his afterlife. Ask children why they think these animals are on the mask. Talk about the construction, or the "story" or message one gets from the art. TEKS 2.3A

- Hippopotamuses are plant-eaters that spend their days up to their nostrils in water because they sunburn easily. They were dangerous and feared animals in ancient Egypt because they damaged crops and were a threat to fishermen's boats. Ancient Egyptians placed statues of hippos in tombs to "protect" the people buried there.

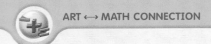
EGYPTIAN ART

Many of Egypt's most famous artworks were made long ago for kings and queens. The gold mask of young King Tutankhamen was found in his tomb in a pyramid. What patterns do you see?

 Gold mask of Tutankhamen

70

 Background Information

Art History

Egyptian Art Of the Seven Wonders of the Ancient World, only the large pyramids at Giza remain. The pyramids were built by three generations of kings to protect deceased rulers and the precious objects buried with them. The pyramid of Khufu, also called the Great Pyramid, may contain more than two million stones and is about 4,500 years old. Many historians think the pyramids were built without machines or iron tools.

For more information about Egyptian art, see pp. R48–R59.

 For related images, see **Electronic Art Gallery CD-ROM, Primary**.

An artist made this hippo long ago. It is decorated with pictures of plants from the Nile River in Egypt where hippos live.

B Statuette of a hippopotamus

THINK ABOUT ART

Why do you think ancient Egyptian artworks are still famous today?

C Pyramids at Giza

71

DID YOU KNOW?

Until this century, the Great Pyramid was the tallest building in the world. As many as 100,000 people at a time may have worked on the Great Pyramid, in shifts lasting about four months. Even though the ancient Egyptians did not have machinery, the Great Pyramid took only about 30 years to complete. Historians are not entirely sure how the builders were able to move millions of stone blocks, many weighing more than two tons.

THINK ABOUT ART

Why do you think ancient Egyptian artworks are still famous? (Possible responses: They are very beautiful. The pyramids are still considered to be very large. It is amazing that the Egyptians could build something so large without machines.) **IMPORTANT DETAILS/DRAW CONCLUSIONS**

EXTEND: ARTIST'S EYE ACTIVITY

Egyptian Masks Help children develop and organize ideas from the environment. Take a short walk outside with children to observe plants and animals in the environ-  ment. As an alternate activity, have them view pictures, videos, or other images of the environment. Ask children to use their senses to identify variations in objects and subjects from the environment. Have them identify art elements, such as color, line, and shape and design principles, such as pattern. Then ask children to draw and color a paper-plate mask of themselves as an Egyptian pharaoh. Ask them to use patterns of animals, plants, or objects from nature that could stand for wisdom, strength, or protection. Have them add details to the masks, using paper scraps and found objects. Then have them share their masks and identify constructions, or the "story" or message behind the symbols in their own and classmates' artworks. TEKS 2.1A, TEKS 2.1B, TEKS 2.2C, TEKS 2.3A

Lesson 13

Patterns Show Rhythm

PDAS Domains I, II

OBJECTIVES
- Identify principles such as rhythm
- Create pictures showing rhythm
- Identify important details

RESOURCES
- Art Prints 8, 9
- Discussion Card 9
- Big Book, pp. 72–73
- Electronic Art Gallery CD-ROM, Primary

5 Minutes

Warm-Up

Clap Rhythms   Clap distinct rhythmic patterns with long and short beats. Ask children to repeat each clapping pattern.

10-15 Minutes

Teach

Discuss Art Concepts   Ask children to read page 72, and discuss it. Have them trace the path that their eyes follow as they look at the artworks. Discuss **rhythm** in the artworks. Then display **Art Prints 8** and **9**. Ask volunteers to choose an artwork and clap to show the rhythm. Discuss how the artists created the rhythms.   TEKS 2.1B

Think Critically

1. **(Focus Skill) READING SKILL**   **What are the important details in Rousseau's painting?** (Monkeys in a rain forest are picking oranges from a tree.)
   IDENTIFY IMPORTANT DETAILS   TAKS Reading Objectives 1, 4

2. **What words describe the rhythm in each artwork?** (Possible responses: jumping; stepping; up, down, up, down)   **PERCEPTION**   TEKS 2.1B

3. **WRITE**   What would you add to *Exotic Landscape* to change the rhythm?
   INDEPENDENT WRITING   TEKS 2.1B; TAKS Writing Objective 1

Lesson 13

Vocabulary
rhythm

Patterns Show Rhythm

What do you see in these artworks? Follow the monkeys' path from the trees to the ground. Can you find the same pattern of movement in artwork **B**?

B Unknown artist, Peruvian textile

A Henri Rousseau, *Exotic Landscape*

In most art, your eyes will follow a pattern of colors, lines, or shapes. This movement that comes from patterns is called **rhythm**.

72

Background Information

About the Artist

Henri Rousseau (ahn•REE roo•SOH) (1844–1910) was a customs worker and did not begin painting until he retired at the age of 49. He became known for jungle scenes full of imagination, images rich in fantasy, and detail. Much of his work was inspired by travel to exotic places and visits to the Paris zoo and botanical gardens.

For more information about Rousseau, see pp. R48–R59.

RECOMMENDED READING
Pattern Fish by Trudy Harris. Millbrook, 2000. **CHALLENGING**

★ TEKS 2.1B identify elements and principles; TEKS 2.2B create effective compositions; TEKS 2.2C identify and practice skills; TEKS 2.3A identify stories and constructions; PDAS Domain I active participation; PDAS Domain II learner-centered instruction; PDAS Domain III evaluation and feedback; *(continued)*

Artist's Workshop

Rain Forest Scene

PLAN

Imagine a rain forest with things moving in it. What patterns could you use to show this?

CREATE

1. Color trees and other plants. Make patterns with things like flowers, leaves, and tree trunks.

2. Add a pattern of animals moving across the picture. Give your picture a strong rhythm.

REFLECT

What patterns did you use? What is the rhythm of your artwork?

73

Science Connection

Rain Forest Web Give examples of the ways living organisms in a rain forest depend on each other and on their environments. Have children draw a web that shows these connections.

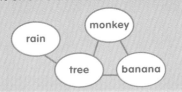

PDAS Domain IV

ESL Use **visuals** to support **comprehensible input** for information related to trees.

Read and display **Picture Cards Collection** cards 72 and 122 for children to use as a reference in talking about *Exotic Landscape.* See also **Picture Card Bank CD-ROM**, Categories: Plants, Parts of Plants.

leaf

Artist's Workshop

15-25 Minutes

Rain Forest Scene

MATERIALS: construction paper, oil pastels

TECHNIQUE TIP: Point out that Rousseau used many shades of green. Invite children to use a pattern of shades and tints of one color to create rhythm.

PLAN Share visuals of rain forests to prompt ideas. Have children sketch their scenes.

CREATE Have children create a pattern that moves the eye across the scene using the principles of pattern and rhythm. TEKS 2.2B

REFLECT Have children point out the patterns and rhythms they created and identify skills they practiced in making their pictures.
TEKS 2.1B, TEKS 2.2C

Activity Options PDAS Domain IV

Quick Activity Have small groups of children work together on large drawing paper.

Early Finishers Ask children to use Discussion Card 9.

Challenge See *Teacher Resource Book* p. 55.

5-10 Minutes

Wrap-Up

Informal Assessment PDAS Domain III

- **How did you show rhythm in your work?**
  (Responses will vary.) **PERCEPTION/AESTHETICS** TEKS 2.1B

- **Which pattern shows the most rhythm?**
  (Responses will vary.) **ART CRITICISM** TEKS 2.1B

Extend Through Writing

Independent Have children write a story about their scenes. Ask them to check that it has a beginning, middle, and ending.
TEKS 2.3A; TAKS Writing Objectives 1, 3

PDAS Domain IV classroom management; **TAKS Reading Objective 1** demonstrate understanding of texts; **TAKS Reading Objective 4** apply critical-thinking skills; **TAKS Writing Objective 1** composition; **TAKS Writing Objective 3** organization

LESSON 13 *Patterns Show Rhythm* **73**

Lesson 14

Patterns and Textures in Weavings

PDAS Domains I, II

OBJECTIVES
- Identify patterns and textures
- Construct a weaving
- Identify important details

RESOURCES
- Art Prints 7, 16
- Discussion Card 2
- Big Book, pp. 74–75
- Electronic Art Gallery CD-ROM, Primary

5 Minutes

Warm-Up

Texture Time Display materials such as wool, corduroy, silk, and fake fur. Ask children to touch each one and describe how it feels.

10-15 Minutes

Teach

Discuss Art Concepts Have children read page 74 and describe the textures and patterns they see. Use Discussion Card 2 for questioning strategies. Then have children compare the patterns and textures in **Art Prints 7** and **16** to those in the weaving. TEKS 2.1B

Think Critically

1. **(Focus Skill) READING SKILL** What are the patterns and textures in the weaving? (blue-black-blue-black; bumpy, rough) **IMPORTANT DETAILS** TEKS 2.1B

2. **How are the textures of the weaving different from a painting?** (It is bumpy; a painting is often flatter and smoother.) **PERCEPTION** TEKS 2.1A

3. **WRITE** Why do you think the artist named this artwork *Riverdance*?

   INDEPENDENT WRITING TEKS 2.4B; TAKS Writing Objective 1

Lesson 14

Vocabulary

texture

weaving

Patterns and Textures in Weavings

How would this artwork feel if you could touch it—soft, scratchy, bumpy? The way something feels is its **texture**.

Nancy Curry, *Riverdance*

This **weaving** is an artwork made by putting paper strips and other things over and under each other. What is the pattern of this weaving?

74

FYI Background Information

About the Artist

Nancy Curry (1961–) uses found objects and enjoys the mix of textures they create in her paper weavings. She says that the weavings allow her to express her individuality and her playful spirit. Curry designs her heavily textured weavings so that they welcome viewers "into the piece."

For more information about Nancy Curry, see pp. R48–R59.

RECOMMENDED READING

Charlie Needs a Cloak by Tomie dePaola. Aladdin, 1973. **EASY**

---

74 UNIT 3 *Nature's Way*   ★ **TEKS 2.1A** identify variations in objects and subjects; **TEKS 2.1B** identify elements and principles; **TEKS 2.2B** create effective compositions; **TEKS 2.2C** identify and practice skills; **TEKS 2.4A** define reasons for preferences in personal artworks; **TEKS 2.4B** identify ideas in artworks by peers and artists; **PDAS Domain I** active participation; *(continued)*

Artist's Workshop

Found Object Weaving

PLAN ....

Think about patterns and textures you would like to put in a weaving.

CREATE ....

1. **Wrap yarn around a piece of cardboard to make a loom.**

2. **Weave things like paper strips, ribbons, vines, and grass. Add found objects.**

REFLECT ....

What patterns and textures does your weaving have?

What different textures are you wearing?

75

Science Connection

Water Cycle Point out that both the weaving on page 74 and **Art Print 16** show artists' interpretations of a river. Discuss the water cycle and display a picture of it. Then guide children in making labeled diagrams of the water cycle.

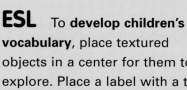

PDAS Domain IV

ESL To develop children's vocabulary, place textured objects in a center for them to explore. Place a label with a texture word on the back of each object. Have children **orally describe** the objects. Ask children to record each texture word in their sketchbook with a picture of something it describes.

15-25 Minutes

Artist's Workshop

Found Object Weaving

MATERIALS: cardboard, yarn, tape, found objects, paper strips

TECHNIQUE TIP: Have children refer to pages 164–165 for help with weaving.

PLAN Have children practice skills by laying out materials in a pattern before weaving. TEKS 2.2C

CREATE Explain that found objects are ordinary things that can be used to provide texture, such as vines, grass, cloth, ribbon, and string.

REFLECT Ask children to share their weavings and tell about textures they used and skills they practiced to create an effective construction. TEKS 2.2B, TEKS 2.2C

Activity Options PDAS Domain IV

Quick Activity Children can weave precut strips of construction paper on a paper loom.

Early Finishers Children choose from the Idea Wheel, *Teacher Resource Book* pp. 29–30.

Challenge See *Teacher Resource Book* p. 56.

5-10 Minutes

Wrap-Up

Informal Assessment PDAS Domain III

- **Describe the textures in your weaving.**
  (Responses will vary.) PERCEPTION/AESTHETICS TEKS 2.1B
- **What do you like best about your weaving?**
  (Responses will vary.) ART CRITICISM TEKS 2.4A

Extend Through Writing

Independent Have children write about the textures in their clothing. Remind them to use conventions of spelling, capitalization, punctuation, grammar, usage, and sentence structure that they have been taught. TAKS Writing Objectives 1, 2, 4, 5

PDAS Domain II learner-centered instruction; PDAS Domain III evaluation and feedback; PDAS Domain IV classroom management; TAKS Writing Objective 1 composition; TAKS Writing Objective 2 conventions; TAKS Writing Objective 4 sentence construction; TAKS Writing Objective 5 usage

LESSON 14 *Patterns and Textures in Weavings* **75**

PDAS Domains I, II

JACOB LAWRENCE'S PATTERNS

ARTIST BIOGRAPHY

DISCUSS THE PAINTINGS

Read pages 76–77 with children.

- Have children tell what each painting is mainly about. Ask them to compare individuals and families in the paintings. Have children describe the patterns they see.
  TEKS 2.1B, TEKS 2.3B, TEKS 2.4B

- Display **Art Print 9**: *Morning Still Life*. Ask children to tell how this painting is like *The Street* and *Vaudeville*. Talk about patterns.
  TEKS 2.1B

- Have children clap the patterns from the artwork. For example, the stripes in the lady's dress in *The Street* can be *clap, stomp, clap, stomp*. Discuss the rhythm of each painting.
  TEKS 2.1B

DISCUSS THE ARTIST

Share the Background Information. Help children understand the historical and cultural heritage Lawrence's artwork represents.

- Ask children to say a sentence to summarize how Lawrence's artwork is an achievement.
  TEKS 2.3A

- Lawrence's artworks appear in more than 200 museums. His paintings tell stories of everyday life, as well as important events in history. In a discussion with children, have them identify the construction, or story or meaning in Jacob Lawrence's artworks.   TEKS 2.3A

- Ask children how they think Jacob Lawrence got the idea for each painting.

JACOB LAWRENCE'S PATTERNS

Jacob Lawrence liked to tell stories through his paintings. He used patterns of shapes to help tell his stories. What are the people here doing? How do your eyes move around each painting? Why?

A *The Street*

76

Background Information

About the Artist

Jacob Lawrence (1917–2000) was born in the South, but grew up in the north. He resisted the trend to paint abstract forms. Instead, his paintings tell about people within the social and cultural events that he experienced: the Great Migration, the Jazz Age, and the Harlem Renaissance. Lawrence also painted busy street scenes, possibly viewed from his neighborhood in New York City.

For more information about Jacob Lawrence, see pp. R48–R59.

 For related images, see **Electronic Art Gallery CD-ROM, Primary**.

★ **TEKS 2.1B** identify elements and principles; **TEKS 2.2A** express ideas and feelings; **TEKS 2.2C** identify and practice skills; **TEKS 2.3A** identify stories and constructions; **TEKS 2.3B** compare artworks showing individuals/families; **TEKS 2.4B** identify ideas in artworks by peers and artists; *(continued)*

What patterns and rhythms can you find in *Vaudeville*?

DID YOU KNOW?

Jacob Lawrence got ideas for patterns from the small, bright rugs that were in his home when he was growing up.

B *Vaudeville*

THINK ABOUT ART

What story do you think Jacob Lawrence is telling in each painting?

Multimedia Biographies
Visit *The Learning Site*
www.harcourtschool.com

77

Social Studies Connection

Museum Visits Jacob Lawrence's paintings may be viewed at:

• *Man with Flowers*, Norton Museum of Art, West Palm Beach, Florida. www.norton.org

For additional cross-curricular suggestions, see Art Transparency 9.

TEKS 2.4B; PDAS Domain II

Visit with an Artist

View Art Arrange for children to visit with an artist either at school or at a museum, gallery, or other location. Ask children to view and identify ideas in original artworks, the portfolio, and an exhibition by the artist. Have them focus on important details and the use of pattern, rhythm, and texture.

DID YOU KNOW?

Even at a young age, Jacob Lawrence noticed patterns and rhythms in the brightly colored designs of the throw rugs that his mother used to decorate their home. He used these patterns in his art, as well as patterns he saw in his neighborhood, such as the shadows of fire escapes, laundry hung on lines strung across yards, and letters on electric signs and on billboards.

Ask children where they think Jacob Lawrence got his ideas for the specific patterns he used in each artwork. TEKS 2.3A

THINK ABOUT ART

What story do you think Jacob Lawrence is telling in each painting? (Possible responses: In *The Street*, neighbors are out for a walk. They stop to talk and to admire one another's children. *Vaudeville* shows two actors in costume on a stage. They are saying hello to one another, but they look sad.) Use Discussion Card 7: Stories, page R39, for more questions. TAKS Reading Objective 2

ARTIST'S EYE ACTIVITY

Paint Like Jacob Lawrence Have children paint a scene of a place they see every day. Encourage them to use large patches of color and to think about the patterns and rhythms of Lawrence's art as they paint. Ask them to use color to express their ideas and feelings through their original artwork. Check to see that children have used a variety of media with appropriate skill. TEKS 2.2A, TEKS 2.2C

Multimedia Biographies
Visit *The Learning Site*
www.harcourtschool.com

TAKS Reading Objective 2 apply knowledge of literary events; PDAS Domain I active participation; PDAS Domain II learner-centered instruction

UNIT 3 *Jacob Lawrence's Patterns* **77**

Lesson 15

PDAS Domains I, II

Patterns Show Texture

OBJECTIVES
- Understand that patterns can show texture
- Create a textured rubbing
- Identify important details

RESOURCES
- Art Prints 4, 8, 16
- Discussion Cards 3, 4, 9
- Big Book, pp. 78–79
- Electronic Art Gallery CD-ROM, Primary

5 Minutes

Warm-Up

Draw Lines   Say words that describe texture, such as *sharp*, *soft*, and *bumpy*, and tell children to illustrate each word with lines only. Then have children compare their line patterns.

10-15 Minutes

Teach

Discuss Art Concepts   Have children read page 78, and discuss the information. Explain that artists can show textures that we can see but not feel. Point out that the pattern on the lizards looks bumpy even though you cannot feel it. Have children describe the textures they see in **Art Prints 4, 8,** and **16**.   TEKS 2.1B

Think Critically

1. **READING SKILL** **What important details are in these artworks?** (a furry rabbit; two bumpy dancing lizards) **IDENTIFY IMPORTANT DETAILS** TEKS 2.1B; TAKS Reading Objectives 1, 4

2. **What patterns did each artist use to show texture?** (circles, triangles, dots, and swirls; many straight lines to show fur) **PERCEPTION** TEKS 2.1B

3. **WRITE**   **Tell which artwork looks more real. Explain.** INDEPENDENT WRITING TAKS Writing Objective 1

Lesson **15**

Vocabulary

visual texture

Patterns Show Texture

How are these artworks alike and different? What do you think each animal feels like?

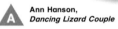 Ann Hanson, *Dancing Lizard Couple*

 Albrecht Dürer, *Hare*

Texture we can see but not touch is called **visual texture**. Patterns of lines, colors, or shapes are used to show how things could feel.

78

FYI Background Information

About the Artists

Albrecht Dürer (AHL•brekt DYUR•er) (1471–1528) may be considered the greatest of all German artists. He made more than 1,000 paintings and was also skilled in printmaking.

Ann Hanson (1959–) says that she has always "been intrigued by nature, in particular, animals." She is interested in their skin and feather patterns.

For more information about the artists and the Renaissance movement, see pp. R48–R59.

★ TEKS 2.1A identify variations in objects and subjects; TEKS 2.1B identify elements and principles; TEKS 2.2B create effective compositions; TEKS 2.4A define reasons for preferences in personal artworks; PDAS Domain I active participation; PDAS Domain II learner-centered instruction; PDAS Domain III evaluation and feedback; *(continued)*

Artist's Workshop

Textured Animal Rubbing

PLAN

Think about textures some animals have, like bumpy skin, smooth scales, and soft wool.

CREATE

1. Use two large pieces of paper. Cut the outline of an animal.

2. Put textures under your paper. Rub with a crayon. Stuff with paper and staple.

REFLECT

What textures did you show? How did you make them?

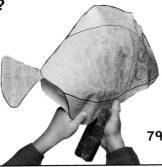

79

Science Connection

Survival Traits Explain that the surface texture of many plants and animals has a purpose: helping them stay alive in their environments. Help children complete a chart like this one.

Animal/ Plant	Surface	Texture	Purpose
cactus	thorns	prickly	protection
rabbit	soft	furry	warmth

PDAS Domain IV

ESL If children have difficulty describing their animals, ask them *yes* or *no* questions such as "Is your animal ___?"

Challenge Provide children with images of animals from the *Picture Cards Collection*. Ask them to classify the animals based on the texture of their body coverings.

Artist's Workshop

Textured Animal Rubbing

15-25 Minutes

MATERIALS: butcher paper, scissors, crayons, stapler or tape, found objects

TECHNIQUE TIP: When rubbing, hold the paper down firmly around the edges of the item.

PLAN Ask children to collect objects inside and outside that have varied textures.

CREATE Have children experiment with textures. The finished product will be an animal shape stuffed with paper scraps. TEKS 2.2B

REFLECT Ask volunteers to share artworks. Classmates can guess what objects were used to produce different textures. TEKS 2.1A

Activity Options PDAS Domain IV

Quick Activity Have each child in a group add a small rubbing to a large animal outline.

Early Finishers Children can use Discussion Card 3, 4, or 9.

Challenge See *Teacher Resource Book* p. 57.

5-10 Minutes

Wrap-Up

Informal Assessment PDAS Domain III

- **What different textures did you show? Why?** (Responses will vary.)
  PERCEPTION/AESTHETICS TEKS 2.1B

- **Did your rubbing turn out the way you planned? Why or why not?** (Responses will vary.) ART CRITICISM TEKS 2.4A

Extend Through Writing

Independent Have children describe how their animals would feel if they could be petted.
TAKS Writing Objective 1

PDAS Domain IV classroom management; TAKS Reading Objective 1 demonstrate understanding of texts;
TAKS Reading Objective 4 apply critical-thinking skills; TAKS Writing Objective 1 composition

LESSON 15 *Patterns Show Texture* **79**

Unit 3

Review and Reflect

In this unit, children have learned about pattern, rhythm, and texture in artworks as well as in the world around them. You may want to use **Art Prints 7–9**, **4**, and **16** and Discussion Cards 1 and 2 to review these elements and principles.

Vocabulary and Concepts

Review art vocabulary by having children use each word to tell about the picture. ("Best" responses are shown; accept other reasonable responses.)

1. B

2. A

3. D

4. C

5. smooth, scaly, bumpy

6. The spool shape is repeated. The spools have a pattern of light and dark stripes.

7. Possible response: Four light lines are followed by a thick dark line five times. Your eyes follow the lines across the page. It seems as if they are winding around something.

STUDENT EDITION OR **BIG BOOK**

Unit 3 Review and Reflect

Vocabulary and Concepts

Tell which picture goes best with each word.

1. weaving
2. print
3. pattern
4. visual texture

 A
 B
 C
 D

....

5. Describe the textures you would feel if you could touch this animal.

6. Tell about the repetition you see in this picture.

7. Tell about the rhythm in the picture.

80

TEKS 2.3C

Home and Community Connection

School-Home Connection

Copy and distribute *Teacher Resource Book* pp. 81–82 to provide family members with ideas for reinforcing art concepts taught in this unit.

Community Connection

You may wish to contact a local wallpaper store for discarded books of wallpaper samples. Have children flip through the books to see the variety of patterns and textures. Explain that some people have jobs designing patterns like these as well as the patterns used for bed linens and clothing. Have children identify similar jobs involving designing patterns and objects we use every day. **CAREERS IN ART**

★ **TEKS 2.1B** identify elements and principles; **TEKS 2.3A** identify stories and constructions; **TEKS 2.3C** identify jobs in art; **TEKS 2.4A** define reasons for preferences in personal artworks; **TEKS 2.4B** identify ideas in artworks by peers and artists; **PDAS Domain I** active participation; **PDAS Domain III** evaluation and feedback; *(continued)*

READING SKILL

Important Details

Reread about the Egyptian hippo on page 71. Write important details in a web.

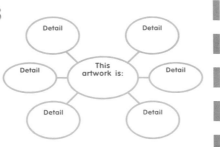

Detail — Detail — This artwork is: — Detail — Detail — Detail

Write About Art

Write a paragraph to describe important details about the lizards. Tell about the colors, shapes, patterns, and textures they have.

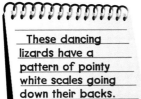

These dancing lizards have a pattern of pointy white scales going down their backs.

Ann Hanson, *Dancing Lizard Couple*

81

TEKS 2.4A, TEKS 2.4B; PDAS Domain III

Assessment

Portfolio Assessment

Work with children to choose one artwork from this unit to add to their portfolios. Have them review each Artist's Workshop activity, select the piece they like best, and explain why they chose it. Provide feedback about children's use of elements, principles, and techniques. See also Portfolio Recording Form, p. R32.

Additional Assessment Options

- Progress Recording Form, p. R33
- Artist's Workshop Rubrics (Self/Teacher and Peer), pp. R30–R31
- Unit Test, *Teacher Resource Book*, p. 93

READING SKILL

Important Details

Draw the web on the board. Have children reread the text about the Egyptian hippopotamus on page 71. Ask children to identify important details in the text and the art and to record them on a web.
TAKS Reading Objectives 1, 3, 4

Detail — Hippos live in the Nile River.
Detail — statue is blue
This artwork is: an ancient Egyptian hippo statue.
Detail — black outlines of plants
Detail — lily pads and other plants in hippos' habitat
Detail — walking
Detail — under water because it's blue

Write About Art

Descriptive Paragraph Review with children the important details they notice in *Dancing Lizard Couple*. Have them include the details in their descriptive paragraph about the lizards. Guide them to recognize and use effective sentence construction and organization.
TAKS Writing Objectives 1, 2, 3, 4

Critic's Corner

RESPONSE/EVALUATION Have children choose the artwork they like best from this unit. Use these steps to discuss their selections.

Describe Have children describe the art and identify patterns, rhythms, and textures. TEKS 2.1B

Analyze Ask children what type of patterns are used and how they affect the artwork. TEKS 2.1B

Interpret Have children identify the "story" behind the artwork. TEKS 2.3A

Evaluate Have children tell whether they would like to have this artwork and why. TEKS 2.4B

TAKS Test Preparation: Reading and Writing Through Art, p. 13

TAKS Reading Objective 1 demonstrate understanding of texts; TAKS Reading Objective 3 use a variety of strategies; TAKS Reading Objective 4 apply critical-thinking skills; TAKS Writing Objective 1 composition; TAKS Writing Objective 2 conventions; TAKS Writing Objective 3 organization; TAKS Writing Objective 4 sentence construction

UNIT 3 *Review and Reflect* **81**

Unit 4 Form and Space

Surprises Everywhere

In this unit, children discover that useful items can be made beautiful, becoming works of art. Artists use form and space to create works that reflect and enrich our surroundings.

Resources

- Unit 4 Art Prints (10–12)
- Additional Art Prints (6, 13)
- Art Transparencies 10–12
- Test Preparation: Reading and Writing Through Art, pp. 14–24
- Artist's Workshop Activities: English and Spanish, pp. 31–40
- Encyclopedia of Artists and Art History, pp. R48–R59
- Picture Cards Collection, Cards 14, 17, 48, 67, 68, 99, 103

Using the Art Prints

- Discussion Cards, pp. R34–R42
- Teaching Suggestions, backs of Art Prints
- Art Print Teaching Suggestions: Spanish

Teacher Resource Book

- Vocabulary Cards in English and Spanish, pp. 15–18
- Reading Skill Card 4, p. 26
- Copying Masters, pp. 29, 30, 31, 37, 38
- Challenge Activities, pp. 58–62
- School-Home Connection: English/Spanish, pp. 83–84
- Unit Test, p. 94

Technology Resources

 Electronic Art Gallery CD-ROM, Primary
Picture Card Bank CD-ROM

 Visit *The Learning Site*
www.harcourtschool.com

- Multimedia Art Glossary
- Multimedia Biographies
- Reading Skills and Activities

ART PRINT 6

Breezing Up (A Fair Wind)
by Winslow Homer

ART PRINT 10

Grandfather Storyteller
by Helen Cordero

ART PRINT 13

Wheat Field and Cypress Trees
by Vincent van Gogh

Art Prints for This Unit

ART PRINT 11

Statue of Abraham Lincoln, Lincoln Memorial
by Daniel Chester French

ART PRINT 12

Interior of the Guggenheim Museum
designed by Frank Lloyd Wright

Planning Guide
PDAS Domain IV

Lesson	Objectives and Vocabulary	Art Images	Production/Materials

Focus Skill: Compare and Contrast, pp. 84–85

Lesson	Objectives and Vocabulary	Art Images	Production/Materials
16 SHAPES AND FORMS pp. 86–87 ⏱ 30–60 minutes	• Identify shape and form • Express ideas and feelings in artworks—clay pinch pot • Make and identify patterns *(Focus Skill)* Compare and contrast **Vocabulary: form**	• **Hopi olla** by Miriam Tewaguna Nampeyo • **Through** by Phillip King	**Decorated Clay Bowl** ❏ clay ❏ objects for making patterns, textures ❏ tempera paints ❏ paintbrushes
17 SCULPTED FORMS pp. 88–89 ⏱ 30–60 minutes	• Identify elements such as space • Express ideas using forms *(Focus Skill)* Compare and contrast **Vocabulary: sculpture, space**	• **The Bremen Town Musicians** by Gerhard Marcks • **Aluminum Horse #5** by Deborah Butterfield	**Foil Sculpture** ❏ aluminum foil ❏ scissors

Art ←→ Social Studies Connection: Cowboys and Cowgirls in Art, pp. 90–91

Lesson	Objectives and Vocabulary	Art Images	Production/Materials
18 RELIEF SCULPTURE pp. 92–93 ⏱ 30–60 minutes	• Identify relief sculptures • Create an effective relief sculpture *(Focus Skill)* Compare and contrast **Vocabulary: relief sculpture**	• **Scenes from the life of a child** by Unknown artist	**Clay Tile Relief Sculpture** ❏ clay ❏ rolling pin ❏ objects for carving clay
19 ARCHITECTURE pp. 94–95 ⏱ 30–60 minutes	• Identify shape and form • Practice skills necessary for producing modeled forms *(Focus Skill)* Compare and contrast **Vocabulary: architecture, architect**	• **Neuschwanstein Castle, Germany** • **Pyramids at the Louvre** by I. M. Pei	**Amazing School Model** ❏ glue, tape, scissors ❏ boxes, cardboard ❏ paper tubes ❏ construction paper ❏ paints, brushes

Art ←→ Social Studies Connection: Frank Lloyd Wright's Buildings, pp. 96–97

Lesson	Objectives and Vocabulary	Art Images	Production/Materials
20 LANDSCAPES pp. 98–99 ⏱ 30–60 minutes	• Recognize landscapes • Create an effective landscape using elements and principles *(Focus Skill)* Compare and contrast **Vocabulary: landscape, foreground, background**	• **In the Meadow** by Claude Monet • **Student art** by Kacy, grade 2	**3-D Landscape Painting** ❏ construction paper ❏ paints, brushes ❏ glue ❏ scissors ❏ found objects

✓ Review and Reflect, pp. 100–101

★ **TEKS 2.1A** identify variations in objects and subjects; **TEKS 2.1B** identify elements and principles; **TEKS 2.2C** identify and practice skills; **PDAS Domain IV** classroom management

Compare and Contrast, pp. 84–85

Focus Skill

Opportunities for application of the skill are provided on pp. 86, 88, 92, 94, 98, 101.

Art Puzzlers

Present these art puzzlers to children at the beginning or end of a class or when children finish an assignment early.

Resources and Technology	Suggested Literature	Across the Curriculum
• Art Prints 10–12 • Reading Skill Card 4 • Discussion Card 3, p. R35 • Big Book, pp. 86–87 • Electronic Art Gallery CD-ROM, Primary	*Peter's Painting* by Sally Moss **Average** 	**Math** Forms Chart, p. 87 **Reading** Compare and Contrast, p. 86 **Writing** Independent, p. 87
• Art Prints 10, 11 • Reading Skill Card 4 • Big Book, pp. 88–89 • Electronic Art Gallery CD-ROM, Primary	*The Bootmaker and the Elves* by Susan Lowell **Read-Aloud** 	**Science** Metal Work, p. 89 **Reading** Compare and Contrast, p. 88 **Writing** Independent, p. 89
• Art Print 11 • Discussion Card 1, p. R34 • Reading Skill Card 4 • Big Book, pp. 92–93 • Electronic Art Gallery CD-ROM, Primary	*The Story of the Statue of Liberty* by Betsy and Giulio Maestro **Challenging** 	**Social Studies** Create Timelines, p. 93 **Reading** Compare and Contrast, p. 92 **Writing** Independent, p. 93
• Art Print 12 • Reading Skill Card 4 • Big Book, pp. 94–95 • Electronic Art Gallery CD-ROM, Primary	*Roberto: The Insect Architect* by Nina Laden **Read-Aloud** 	**Social Studies/Math** Different Homes, Different Shapes, p. 95 **Reading** Compare and Contrast, p. 94 **Writing** Independent, p. 95
• Art Prints 6, 13 • Discussion Cards 2, 6 pp. R34, R38 • Reading Skill Card 4 • Big Book, pp. 98–99 • Electronic Art Gallery CD-ROM, Primary	*Little Mouse's Painting* by Diane Wolkstein **Read-Aloud** 	**Science** Light Affects Colors, p. 99 **Reading** Compare and Contrast, p. 98 **Writing** Independent, p. 99

- What **forms** do you see that have **space** to walk all around them? TEKS 2.1B

- Find a **form** that is like a **sphere**. Find one like a **cube**. TEKS 2.1A, TEKS 2.1B

- Imagine you are in a toy store. What do you see in the **foreground**? What do you see in the **background**? TEKS 2.2C

- If you were an **architect**, describe how you would use **forms**, **shapes**, and **space**. TEKS 2.1B, TEKS 2.2C

- What do you see in a winter **landscape**? A spring **landscape**? TEKS 2.1B

School-Home Connection
The activities above are included in the School-Home Connection for this unit. See *Teacher Resource Book,* pp. 83–84.

Assessment Options

- Rubrics and Recording Forms, pp. R28–R33
- Unit 4 Test, *Teacher Resource Book*, p. 94

GO ONLINE

Visit *The Learning Site*:
www.harcourtschool.com

Artist's Workshops PREVIEW

Use these pages to help you gather and organize materials for the Artist's Workshop in each lesson.

LESSON	MATERIALS

16 Decorated Clay Bowl p. 87

Objective: To have children explore how clay can be molded into a three-dimensional form by creating and decorating a clay pinch pot

🕐 15–25 minutes

Challenge Activity: See *Teacher Resource Book*, p. 58.

- clay
- objects for creating patterns and textures in clay—paper clip, coffee stirrer, straw, pen cap, twigs, craft sticks, seashells
- tempera paints
- paintbrushes

FINISHED EXAMPLE

LESSON

17 Foil Sculpture p. 89

Objective: To have children make an animal sculpture by molding foil to define the animal's body features

🕐 15–25 minutes

Challenge Activity: See *Teacher Resource Book*, p. 59.

- aluminum foil
- scissors

FINISHED EXAMPLE

For safety information, see Art Safety, page R4; the Art Safety Poster; or Big Book page 148.

For information on media and techniques, see pages R15–R23.

LESSON	MATERIALS

18 Clay Tile Relief Sculpture p. 93

Objective: To have children create a relief sculpture of an object that represents something interesting about themselves

🕐 15–25 minutes

Challenge Activity: See *Teacher Resource Book*, p. 60.

- clay
- rolling pin
- objects for carving clay—paper clip, non-serrated plastic knife, coffee stirrer, straw, pen cap, twigs, craft stick

FINISHED EXAMPLE

LESSON

19 Amazing School Model p. 95

Objective: To have children explore form and space as they plan a building and construct a model of their design

🕐 15–25 minutes

Challenge Activity: See *Teacher Resource Book*, p. 61.

- cardboard
- tape, glue
- boxes (small milk cartons, shoebox)
- paper tubes
- construction paper
- paints
- brushes
- scissors

FINISHED EXAMPLE

SCHOOL

LESSON

20 3-D Landscape Painting p. 99

Objective: To have children paint a landscape using their knowledge of space, foreground, background, and horizon line, adding found objects to make it three-dimensional

🕐 15–25 minutes

Challenge Activity: See *Teacher Resource Book*, p. 62.

- construction paper or white paper
- tempera paints
- watercolor paints
- paintbrushes
- glue
- scissors
- found objects—yarn, craft sticks, paper, leaves, twigs

FINISHED EXAMPLE

Unit 4

PDAS Domains I, II

Surprises Everywhere

PREVIEW THE UNIT

Do a Walk-Through Have children use the Contents on page 7 to find the page on which Unit 4 begins and turn to that page. Tell them that in this unit, they will learn how artists use form and space when they create buildings and statues and how they make useful objects beautiful. Have children look at the artworks and discuss questions they have about what they see.

SHARE THE POEM

Read the poem aloud as children view the art. Then have children read the poem aloud.

Does the speaker in the poem feel the same as the children in the art? Explain. (Possible response: Yes, the speaker and the children feel happy, strong, and active.) **DRAW CONCLUSIONS**
TAKS Reading Objectives 1, 4

STEP INTO THE ART

Have children look at the artwork again and tell how it is surprising. Then ask children to compare the individuals in the sculpture with those on pages 28, 42–43, 46, and 54. **COMPARE AND CONTRAST**
TEKS 2.3B

SHARE BACKGROUND INFORMATION

Glenna Goodacre got the idea for this sculpture while observing children who were excited about the 1996 Olympics. The five children in the sculpture are each in a different stage of doing a cartwheel. The statue is supported by an invisible base, so the children look separate and lifelike.

LOCATE IT See *Using the Maps of Museums and Art Sites*, pp. R2–R3.

▲ Glenna Goodacre, *Olympic Wannabes*

LOCATE IT

This sculpture is in Selby Five Points Park in Sarasota, Florida.

See Maps of Museums and Art Sites, pages 144–147.

82

 Background Information

About the Artist

Glenna Goodacre (1939–) is a Texas native noted for her sculptures of people. Her portrait of Sacagawea appears on the golden dollar coin that was released into circulation in 2001. Her sculpture for the *Vietnam Women's Memorial*, which stands next to the *Vietnam Veterans Memorial* on the Mall in Washington, D.C., pays tribute to the women who served in the armed forces in that era.

For additional information about Glenna Goodacre, see pp. R48–R59.

 For related images, see **Electronic Art Gallery CD-ROM, Primary**.

★ TEKS 2.2C identify and practice skills; TEKS 2.3B compare artworks showing individuals/families; PDAS Domain I active participation; PDAS Domain II learner-centered instruction; PDAS Domain IV classroom management; TAKS Reading Objective 1 demonstrate understanding of texts; *(continued)*

4

Surprises Everywhere

At the Top of My Voice

When I stamp
The ground thunders,
When I shout
The world rings,
When I sing
The air wonders
How I do such things.

Felice Holman

ABOUT THE ARTIST

See Gallery of Artists, pages 182–191.

Unit Vocabulary

form	architecture
sculpture	architect
space	landscape
relief sculpture	foreground
	background

Multimedia Art Glossary
Visit *The Learning Site*
www.harcourtschool.com

83

TEKS 2.2C; PDAS Domains II, IV

Art Center

Materials clay

Ongoing Activity Have children use clay to sculpt, experimenting with space. Have them identify and practice skills necessary for making modeled forms.

Big Book Put the *Big Book* in the Art Center.

PDAS Domain IV

Classroom Management

Make 3-D Portfolios Have children display their artworks from this unit in boxes that have sections, such as those from grocery stores. Children can decorate the boxes and label the art. At the end of the unit, they can take the artworks home in the box.

Unit Vocabulary

Write the vocabulary words on the board. Point to each word, read it, and have children repeat. Have them write the words on paper and put a check mark beside words they know and circle words they don't know. Guide children in looking up unfamiliar words in the Glossary on *Student Edition* pages 192–201.

form a three-dimensional object; having height, width, and depth

sculpture a carved, cast, constructed, or modeled artwork that you can see from all sides

space the part of an artwork that is not filled in; the area around an artwork

relief sculpture a sculpture meant to be viewed from one side, in which forms stand out from a flat background

architecture the art and science of designing buildings and other structures

architect a person who designs buildings and other structures

landscape an artwork whose subject is an outdoor scene

foreground the part of an artwork that seems nearest to the viewer

background the part of an artwork that seems farthest from the viewer

Vocabulary Resources

● Vocabulary Cards in English and Spanish: *Teacher Resource Book*, pp. 15–18

● Student Edition Glossary, pp. 192–201

Multimedia Art Glossary
English/Spanish
Visit *The Learning Site*
www.harcourtschool.com

Sketchbook

Remind children to use their sketchbooks to practice the skills necessary for producing a variety of artworks, including planning, sketching, and writing ideas. TEKS 2.2C

Unit 4

Focus Skill **READING SKILL**

PDAS Domains I, II

Compare and Contrast

SKILL TRACE	
COMPARE AND CONTRAST	
Introduce	pp. 84–85
Review	pp. 86, 88, 92, 94, 98, 101

DISCUSS THE SKILL

Access Prior Knowledge Help children develop and organize ideas from the environment. Hold up several pairs of similar objects from the classroom or natural environment. Ask children to use their senses to identify art elements and principles, such as color, texture, line, shape, and pattern. Have them tell how the objects are alike and how they are different.

Explain that looking for similarities and differences in two artworks will help them notice many things, such as shape, color, pattern, and texture. It will also help them think of reasons for liking one artwork better than another. Explain that thinking about how things are alike and how they are different can also help them better understand what they read. TEKS 2.1A, TEKS 2.1B; TAKS Reading Objective 4

APPLY TO ART

Compare and Contrast Read the lesson title and the top of page 84 with children. Have them describe the artworks. Then ask children to read the rest of the page silently. Have them tell the similarities and differences in the two artworks. Explain to children how comparing and contrasting can help them understand artworks better by helping them organize how they look at the art— one characteristic at a time, such as color or what the artwork is made of. TEKS 2.1A, TEKS 2.1B

Focus Skill **READING SKILL** ....

Compare and Contrast

When you **compare**, you tell how things are alike. When you **contrast**, you tell how things are different.

A Horus Falcon

B Amos Supuni, *Baby Chick*

Compare and contrast these artworks. How are their shapes, colors, patterns, and textures the same? How are they different?

84

Background Information

About the Artist/Art History

The **Horus Falcon** was a common figure in ancient Egyptian art and represents Horus the Falcon-God. It was a symbol of divine kingship.

Amos Supuni (1970–) was born in Malawi, Africa, but grew up in Zimbabwe, Africa. Supuni learned to sculpt as a teenager while working with a community youth group. Through a cultural exchange program in Tanzania, he learned many other art techniques, but he is most noted for his sculpture. Supuni enjoys teaching other young sculptors. He believes that art can lead young people out of poverty.

For more information about Supuni and Egyptian art, see pp. R48–R59.

★ **TEKS 2.1A** identify variations in objects and subjects; **TEKS 2.1B** identify elements and principles; **PDAS Domain I** active participation; **PDAS Domain II** learner-centered instruction; **PDAS Domain IV** classroom management; *(continued)*

Read the paragraph. Then make a Venn diagram to tell how the artworks are alike and different. Add your own ideas.

Artworks from different places and times may be alike in some ways but different in others. Both of these artworks are birds. Both have patterns of feathers and are made from rock. One difference is that the baby chick from Zimbabwe is flapping its wings. The Egyptian falcon is sitting still.

DIFFERENT
Horus Falcon
sitting still

ALIKE
birds
made from rock

DIFFERENT
Baby Chick
flapping its wings

On Your Own
Fill in a Venn diagram to compare and contrast sculptures of two children on pages 82–83.

85

APPLY TO READING

Compare and Contrast Tell children that comparing and contrasting information as they read will help them remember and understand the information or events.

Read the directions at the top of page 85, and have children read the paragraph silently. Then have children find similarities and differences cited in the text and write them in a Venn diagram like the one on the page. Have them look at the artworks again and add more ideas to the diagram. TAKS Reading Objectives 1, 3, 4

DIFFERENT
Horus Falcon
sitting still, small beak, reddish, many lines make the feathers

ALIKE
birds, made of rock, look proud, have patterns of feathers

DIFFERENT
Baby Chick
flapping its wings, large beak, blackish, shapes make feathers

ON YOUR OWN

Have children revisit the sculpture on pages 82–83. They can work independently, with a partner, or as a group to compare and contrast any two figures in the sculpture and make a Venn diagram based on their observations. TEKS 2.1A

TAKS Reading Objectives 3, 4

Focus Skill

Reading Skill Card

Distribute Reading Skill Card 4, *Teacher Resource Book*, p. 26. Use the graphic to further compare and contrast artworks in this unit.

Extend the Skill
For additional teaching suggestions, see **Art Transparency 10**.

MEETING INDIVIDUAL NEEDS PDAS Domain IV

ESL Help children **associate meaning** when they compare and contrast. Display pairs of similar Picture Cards, such as 14 (bird) and 99 (rooster). Have children talk about the images.

Special Needs
Provide visually impaired children with similar items to hold and compare.

Reading Skills and Activities
Visit *The Learning Site*
www.harcourtschool.com

TAKS Reading Objective 1 demonstrate understanding of texts; TAKS Reading Objective 3 use a variety of strategies; TAKS Reading Objective 4 apply critical-thinking skills

UNIT 4 *Compare and Contrast* **85**

Lesson 16

Lesson 16

PDAS Domains I, II

Shapes and Forms

OBJECTIVES
- Identify shape and form
- Express ideas and feelings in art-works—clay pinch pot
- Make and identify patterns

RESOURCES
- Art Prints 10–12
- Big Book, pp. 86–87
- Electronic Art Gallery CD-ROM, Primary

5 Minutes

Warm-Up

Describe Forms Have children use their senses to examine objects that are cubes, pyramids, or spheres and describe them. TEKS 2.1A

10–15 Minutes

Teach

Discuss Art Concepts Have children identify which form each artwork is most like and tell why. Share Background Information. Read the artworks' titles and ask children to identify a construct, or meaning behind the artwork, that could explain why the artist made the artwork he or she did. Display **Art Prints 10–12**. Have children describe the forms and variations in the forms.
TEKS 2.1A, TEKS 2.1B, TEKS 2.3A, TEKS 2.4B

Think Critically

1. **READING SKILL** **How are the forms of these artworks different?** (Possible response: *Through* is solid and pointy; Hopi *Olla* is hollow and round.) COMPARE AND CONTRAST
   TEKS 2.1A; TAKS Reading Objective 4

2. **How are the lines on these artworks alike?** (Both have curved and straight lines and patterns.) PERCEPTION/COMPARE AND CONTRAST TEKS 2.1B

3. **WRITE** Write a story that the artwork *Through* makes you think of. INDEPENDENT
   TEKS 2.3A; TAKS Writing Objective 1

Lesson 16

Vocabulary

form

Shapes and Forms

How are these artworks alike? How are they different? Each artwork has **form**—or height, width, and depth.

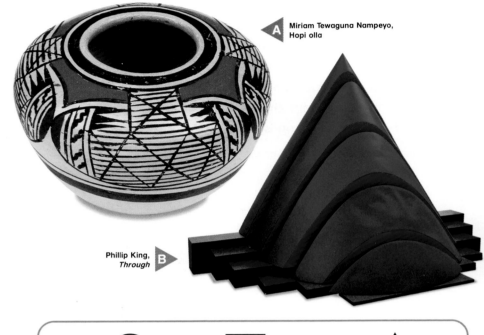

A Miriam Tewaguna Nampeyo, Hopi olla

Phillip King, **B** *Through*

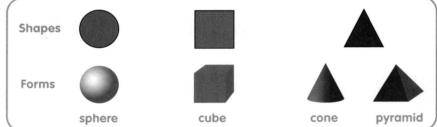

Shapes			
Forms			
sphere	cube	cone	pyramid

86

FYI

Background Information

About the Artists

Miriam Tewaguna Nampeyo (tay•wah•GOO•nuh nahm•PAY•oh) (1956–) is a Native American Hopi potter who made the *olla*, or bowl. Her great-grandmother, Nampeyo of Hano, was famous for reviving prehistoric Southwestern pottery forms.

Phillip King (1934–) is a British sculptor who likes to work with simple forms, painting them in bright colors. King is intrigued by cone shapes.

For additional information about the artists, see pp. R48–R59.

⭐ TEKS 2.1A identify variations in objects and subjects; TEKS 2.1B identify elements and principles; TEKS 2.2A express ideas and feelings; TEKS 2.2B create effective compositions; TEKS 2.2C identify and practice skills; TEKS 2.3A identify stories and constructions; TEKS 2.4B identify ideas in artworks by peers and artists; PDAS Domain I active participation; *(continued)*

Artist's Workshop

Decorated Clay Bowl

PLAN

Think about how to decorate a clay bowl.

CREATE

1. Roll clay into a ball. Push in with your thumbs. Pinch up the sides.

2. Smooth the sides. Make patterns. Paint it when it's dry.

REFLECT

What form was the clay when you started? How did the form change?

What forms do you see in your classroom?

87

PDAS Domain II

Math Connection

Forms Chart Have children make a chart showing the forms from the bottom of page 86. Ask them to look for objects in the classroom that have similar forms and list them.

Forms	Objects
sphere	ball, globe
cube	box, cabinet

PDAS Domain IV

ESL Have children use **total physical response** to distinguish between shapes and forms. Hold up examples of each shape and form on page 86 and say its name. Have children repeat. If the object is a shape, ask children to trace the shape in the air. If the object is a form, have children cup their hands to form a ball (sphere).

15-25 Minutes — Artist's Workshop

Decorated Clay Bowl

MATERIALS: clay, objects for making patterns, tempera paints, brushes

TECHNIQUE TIP: Have children read about clay pots on p. 158. Have them tell the steps to follow and identify skills they need. TEKS 2.2C

PLAN Have children practice necessary skills by forming pinch pots with scraps of clay. TEKS 2.2C

CREATE Encourage children to mix clay of different colors to get the color they want. Have them express their feelings through the bowl. TEKS 2.2A, TEKS 2.2B

REFLECT Have children discuss how their clay was transformed and identify ideas and feelings they and others expressed in the art. TEKS 2.2A

Activity Options PDAS Domain IV

Quick Activity Children can draw and color a picture of a bowl decorated with patterns.

Early Finishers Use Discussion Card 3.

Challenge See *Teacher Resource Book* p. 58.

5-10 Minutes — Wrap-Up

Informal Assessment PDAS Domain III

- **Tell why your bowl is a form rather than a shape.** (Possible response: It has height, width, and depth.) PERCEPTION TEKS 2.1B

- **How are the bowls alike?** (Responses will vary.) ART CRITICISM TEKS 2.1B

Extend Through Writing

Independent Have children write the steps in the correct order for making a clay bowl. Ask them to proofread for correct spelling.
TAKS Writing Objectives 1, 3, 6

PDAS Domain II learner-centered instruction; PDAS Domain III evaluation and feedback; PDAS Domain IV classroom management; TAKS Reading Objective 4 apply critical-thinking skills; TAKS Writing Objective 1 composition; TAKS Writing Objective 3 organization; TAKS Writing Objective 6 proofreading

LESSON 16 *Shapes and Forms* 87

Lesson 17

PDAS Domains I, II
Sculpted Forms

OBJECTIVES
- Identify elements such as space
- Express ideas using forms
- Compare and contrast

RESOURCES
- Art Prints 10, 11
- Big Book, pp. 88–89
- Electronic Art Gallery CD-ROM, Primary

5 Minutes

Warm-Up

Play Statues Tell children to move around until you say *Freeze!* Walk around the group, pointing out the space around the "statues."

10-15 Minutes

Teach

Discuss Art Concepts Have children read page 88 and tell the story they think each artwork shows. Explain that people can walk around sculptures and that these forms are *organic*. Display **Art Prints 10** and **11**. Have children use their senses to identify variations in the subjects of these images and those on page 88.
TEKS 2.1A, TEKS 2.1B, TEKS 2.3A

Think Critically

1. **(Focus Skill) READING SKILL** How is the space around the two sculptures different? (Possible response: You can see through the metal wires of *Aluminum Horse #5*; the other has space between the animals.) **COMPARE AND CONTRAST** TEKS 2.1A, TEKS 2.1B

2. **How are the forms alike?** (Possible response: Both are metal, and both are shaped like animals.) **PERCEPTION** TEKS 2.1B

3. **WRITE** Write a story about one of the sculptures. Check that it has a beginning, middle, and ending. **INDEPENDENT WRITING** TEKS 2.3A; TAKS Writing Objectives 1, 3

★ **TEKS 2.1A** identify variations in objects and subjects; **TEKS 2.1B** identify elements and principles; **TEKS 2.2C** identify and practice skills; **TEKS 2.3A** identify stories and constructions; **TEKS 2.4B** identify ideas in artworks by peers and artists; **PDAS Domain I** active participation; *(continued)*

Lesson 17

Sculpted Forms

Vocabulary
sculpture
space

What forms do these artworks show? Each of these artworks is a **sculpture**, an artwork that you can see from all sides.

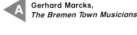
A Gerhard Marcks, *The Bremen Town Musicians*

B Deborah Butterfield, *Aluminum Horse #5*

The part of an artwork that is not filled in is called **space**. Find the space around, through, and between the animals in the sculptures.

88

Background Information

About the Artists
Gerhard Marcks (1889–1981) was a German sculptor. The sculpture on this page is based on a folktale by the Brothers Grimm, in which animals use their unmusical voices to scare away thieves and gain a better life.

Deborah Butterfield (1949–) lives on a ranch in Montana. She often uses "junk" items such as chicken wire and wood fencing when sculpting horses.

For additional information about the artists, see pp. R48–R59.

Foil Sculpture

PLAN

Think of an animal sculpture you want to make.

CREATE

1. **Crumple, pinch, and pull foil to make the body and the head.**

2. **Crumple more foil onto the body. Add legs, a tail, ears, or wings.**

REFLECT

Where do you find space in your sculpture?

Tell about space in your classroom.

89

Science Connection

Metal Work Point out that both sculptures are made of metal. Explain that metals are minerals that come from the earth. Have children list other objects that are made of metal.

Things That Are Metal	
car	can of food
refrigerator	doorknob

PDAS Domain IV

ESL Use **visuals** to support **comprehensible input** for names of farm animals pictured in the sculptures as well as other farm animals.

Use *Picture Cards Collection* cards 48, 67, and 99. See also *Picture Card Bank* **CD-ROM**, Category: Farm Animals.

farm

15-25 Minutes

Artist's Workshop

Foil Sculpture

MATERIALS: aluminum foil, scissors

TECHNIQUE TIP: Have children draw cut lines on the foil to make a basic animal shape.

(head)
(leg) (leg)
(leg) (leg)

PLAN Have children sketch their animal in their sketchbook before sculpting. TEKS 2.2C

CREATE Have children identify and practice skills necessary for making foil sculptures. Encourage them to pose their sculptures to show movement. TEKS 2.2C

REFLECT Have children exhibit their animals. Ask them to identify space in one another's artworks and ideas the artworks show. TEKS 2.1B, TEKS 2.4B

Activity Options PDAS Domain IV

Quick Activity Have children make foil "snakes" in various poses.

Early Finishers Children can do an Idea Wheel activity, *Teacher Resource Book*, pp. 29–30.

Challenge See *Teacher Resource Book* p. 59.

5-10 Minutes

Wrap-Up

Informal Assessment PDAS Domain III

- **Are there any spaces in your sculpture that you didn't expect?** (Responses will vary.)
  PERCEPTION/AESTHETICS TEKS 2.1B

- **What different forms do you see in your classmates' work?** (Responses will vary.)
  ART CRITICISM TEKS 2.1B

Extend Through Writing

Independent Have children write sentences to describe their sculptures. TAKS Writing Objective 1

PDAS Domain II learner-centered instruction; PDAS Domain III evaluation and feedback; PDAS Domain IV classroom management; TAKS Writing Objective 1 composition; TAKS Writing Objective 3 organization

LESSON 17 *Sculpted Forms* **89**

PDAS Domains I, II

Cowboys and Cowgirls in Art

ART AND CULTURE

DISCUSS THE ARTWORKS

Have children read pages 90–91.

- Help children say *charro* [CHAH•roh].

- Explain that the push toy is made of wood and is designed to bob up and down to imitate a bucking horse. Ask children to tell about the form and spaces they see in this artwork and in the others. TEKS 2.1B

DISCUSS ART HISTORY

Share the background information.

- Tell children that Buckeye Blake taught himself to paint. For a while, he painted scenery for Hollywood movies. Now he lives in Montana, where he creates art about Western life.

- Have children demonstrate an understanding of art history and culture as records of human achievment. Discuss with them how the artworks show what the past was like. Tell children that Fanny Sperry Steele won many rodeo events long ago at a time when only a few women competed in rodeos. She specialized in relay racing and bronco riding. Have children identify the story this artwork tells. Then ask: **What was Fanny Sperry Steele's achievement? Why did Buckeye Blake make a statue of her?** TEKS 2.3A

- Explain that Sam Garrett was a western performer in California. He had these boots custom-made in about 1945.

Cowboys and Cowgirls in Art

Push toy **A**

Cowboys and cowgirls are known for riding horses well. This toy shows a Mexican cowboy, or *charro*. What shapes and forms did the toymaker use? What colors and patterns do you see?

90

FYI

Background Information

About the Artist/Art History

Buckeye Blake (1946–) was born in Fullerton, California. His father was a rodeo rider, and his mother was an artist. He uses subjects he knows well as his inspiration—rodeos and ranches.

Cowgirl **Fanny Sperry Steele** (1887–1983) competed in rodeos long ago and won the bronco-riding championships in 1912 and 1913. She has been inducted into the Cowgirl Hall of Fame.

For additional information about Blake, see pp. R48–R59.

For related images, see **Electronic Art Gallery CD-ROM, Primary.**

★ TEKS 2.1B identify elements and principles; TEKS 2.2A express ideas and feelings; TEKS 2.2B create effective compositions; TEKS 2.2C identify and practice skills; TEKS 2.3A identify stories and constructions; TEKS 2.4B identify ideas in artworks by peers and artists; PDAS Domain I active participation; *(continued)*

Artists made these things. How are they works of art? How might each one be used?

Buckeye Blake,
Fanny Sperry Steele

Sam Garrett's
Western boots **C**

Think About Art

What does this art tell you about the life of cowboys and cowgirls?

91

Think About Art

What does this art tell you about the lives of cowboys and cowgirls? (Possible responses: They like to ride horses and are good at it; they wear special clothing.) TEKS 2.4B

ARTIST'S EYE ACTIVITY

Found Object Constructions Have children make a construction related to cowboys and cowgirls, using found objects and everyday objects such as recyclables, things from nature, and classroom scrap materials. Ask them to identify skills necessary for producing constructions and to practice these skills by experimenting with different ways to assemble the pieces of the construction. Have them use design elements and principles they have learned to create effective constructions that express their ideas and feelings. You can help children spray paint their constructions or have them finish them another way. Afterward, have children view one another's constructions and identify ideas and feelings the artworks show and ways form and space were used.
TEKS 2.2A, TEKS 2.2B, TEKS 2.2C, TEKS 2.4B

Multimedia Biographies
Visit *The Learning Site*
www.harcourtschool.com

Social Studies Connection

Museum Visits Other examples of cowgirls in art may be viewed at:

• *National Cowgirl Museum and Hall of Fame,* Fort Worth, Texas. www.cowgirl.net

For additional cross-curricular suggestions, see Art Transparency 11.

TEKS 2.4B; PDAS Domain II
Student Art Show

Display Artworks During this unit, have children display their portfolios and finished artworks. Ask children to view and identify ideas in one another's original artworks, portfolios, and in the exhibit as a whole. Have them focus on form and space. See also Student Art Exhibitions, page 142.

Lesson 18

PDAS Domains I, II
Relief Sculpture

OBJECTIVES
- Identify relief sculptures
- Create an effective relief sculpture
- Compare and contrast

RESOURCES
- Art Print 11
- Discussion Card 1
- Big Book, pp. 92–93
- Electronic Art Gallery CD-ROM, Primary

5 Minutes

Warm-Up

Coin Relief   Place a penny in each child's hand. Before children look at it, have them feel and describe the raised surface.

10-15 Minutes

Teach

Discuss Art Concepts   Read the lesson title on page 92, and have children read the page. Use questions from Discussion Card 1 to discuss the relief sculpture with them. Display **Art Print 11**. Have children compare and contrast the individual in **Art Print 11** with the family on page 92.
TEKS 2.3B

Think Critically

1. **(Focus Skill) READING SKILL** Is the sculpture on page 92 more like the coin or the sculpture on Art Print 11? (Possible response: the coin; it is only partly raised.) **COMPARE AND CONTRAST**   TEKS 2.1A

2. **If the relief sculpture were a scene in real life, what else might be in the spaces?** (Responses will vary.) **PERCEPTION**   TEKS 2.1B

3. **WRITE**   How is the family in the portrait on page 38 like the one in the relief sculpture? How is it different? **INDEPENDENT WRITING**
TEKS 2.3B; TAKS Writing Objective 1

Lesson 18

Vocabulary
relief sculpture

Relief Sculpture

In a **relief sculpture**, forms stand out from a flat surface. What do you see happening in this relief sculpture?

Unknown artist, Scenes from the life of a child

This artwork shows important times in a child's life. How do you think the artist made the forms stand out? Tell where you see space.

92

Background Information

Art History
This relief sculpture from ancient **Rome** is part of a larger sculpture that depicts memorable events in the life of a child from infancy to his schooling with a tutor. Roman reliefs were mainly used to record and celebrate rulers and important historical events.

For more information about ancient Roman art, see pp. R48–R59.

RECOMMENDED READING
The Story of the Statue of Liberty by Betsy and Giulio Maestro. Mulberry, 1986. **CHALLENGING**

★ **TEKS 2.1A** identify variations in objects and subjects; **TEKS 2.1B** identify elements and principles; **TEKS 2.2A** express ideas and feelings; **TEKS 2.2B** create effective compositions; **TEKS 2.2C** identify and practice skills; **TEKS 2.3B** compare artworks showing individuals/families; *(continued)*

Artist's Workshop

Clay Tile Relief Sculpture

PLAN ....

What is something interesting about you? Think of a picture to show it, such as a fish if you like fishing.

CREATE ....

1. Make your clay flat. Draw your picture on the clay.

2. Make the picture stand out. Use tools to carve and take away parts.

 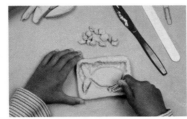

REFLECT ....

What forms did you show in your artwork? Why? How did you use space?

Look at a coin. How is it like your relief sculpture?

93

Artist's Workshop

15-25 Minutes

Clay Tile Relief Sculpture

MATERIALS: clay, rolling pin, objects for carving

TECHNIQUE TIP: Have children use a slab of clay that is thick enough to carve into.

PLAN Brainstorm symbols with children.

CREATE Have children express their feelings and ideas in the form they are creating. Have them identify and practice skills necessary for making a relief sculpture by using objects and their hands to scrape away clay and model a raised form. TEKS 2.2A, TEKS 2.2B, TEKS 2.2C

REFLECT Exhibit the sculptures. Have children identify ideas in their classmates' finished tiles. TEKS 2.4B

Activity Options PDAS Domain IV

Quick Activity Children can press foil onto an arrangement of objects to create a relief sculpture. TEKS 2.2B

Early Finishers Children can use the Idea Wheel, *Teacher Resource Book* pp. 29–30.

Challenge See *Teacher Resource Book* p. 60.

Wrap-Up

5-10 Minutes

Informal Assessment PDAS Domain III

- **What does your sculpture tell about you?**
  (Responses will vary.) PERCEPTION/AESTHETICS

- **Describe how a classmate's tile made good use of space.** ART CRITICISM TEKS 2.4B

Extend Through Writing

Independent Have children write about another tile that would tell something about them.
TAKS Writing Objective 1

Social Studies Connection

Create Timelines Explain to children that the relief shown on page 92 is part of a timeline of one person's life. The timeline shows important events in the order in which they happened. Have children create their own timelines by drawing important events from their lives.

  PDAS Domain IV

ESL Have children draw themselves doing something they like and then talk about it. Help them pick one part of the picture to represent the whole.

Extra Support Help children draw an outline of their picture, cut it out, place it on the clay, and trace around it to make a deep outline.

TEKS 2.4B identify ideas in artworks by peers and artists; PDAS Domain I active participation; PDAS Domain II learner-centered instruction; PDAS Domain III evaluation and feedback; PDAS Domain IV classroom management; TAKS Writing Objective 1 composition

LESSON 18 *Relief Sculpture* **93**

Lesson 19

PDAS Domains I, II

Architecture

OBJECTIVES
- Identify shape and form
- Practice skills necessary for producing modeled forms
- Compare and contrast

RESOURCES
- Art Print 12
- Big Book pp. 94–95
- Electronic Art Gallery CD-ROM, Primary

5 Minutes

Warm-Up

Building Plans Ask children to describe the layout of the school as you sketch a simple "blueprint" on the board. Explain that a plan was drawn before the school was built.

10-15 Minutes

Teach

Discuss Art Concepts Have children read pages 94–95. Explain that an architect uses imagination and science to plan, or **design**, buildings. Review Egyptian Art on pages 70–71. Ask children to identify a possible construct, or meaning behind the art, that led I.M. Pei to design his buildings as he did. Have children compare **Art Print 12** to the buildings on pages 94–95.
TEKS 2.1A, TEKS 2.3A

Think Critically

1. **READING SKILL** **How are the forms in the buildings alike?** (pointy cone-shaped towers look like the pyramids) **COMPARE AND CONTRAST** TEKS 2.1A

2. **Which building has a newer design? How can you tell?** (the pyramid, because it is made of metal and glass) **PERCEPTION** TEKS 2.1A

3. **WRITE** Which building would you rather visit? Why? **INDEPENDENT** TEKS 2.4B; TAKS Writing Objective 1

Lesson 19

Vocabulary
architecture
architect

Architecture

How are the buildings alike and different? **Architecture** is the art and science of planning buildings and other structures. An **architect** is a person who plans what they will look like.

A *Neuschwanstein Castle*, Germany

FYI Background Information

About the Artist/Art History

Neuschwanstein Castle (noy·SHVAHN·shtyn) is a fairly modern castle, designed and built for Prince Ludwig II of Bavaria in the mid-1800s. It has running water, heating, and electricity. It has inspired many movie castles.

I. M. Pei (PAY) (1917–) was born in China but lives in New York City. Pei has designed many famous buildings around the world.

For more information on I. M. Pei and architecture, see pp. R48–R59.

⭐ **TEKS 2.1A** identify variations in objects and subjects; **TEKS 2.1B** identify elements and principles; **TEKS 2.2A** express ideas and feelings; **TEKS 2.2B** create effective compositions; **TEKS 2.2C** identify and practice skills; **TEKS 2.3A** identify stories and constructions; *(continued)*

What lines, shapes, and forms did the architects use in these buildings? How do they look like things in nature?

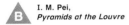 I. M. Pei,
Pyramids at the Louvre

 **Artist's Workshop**

Amazing School Model

1. **Make a model of an amazing school.**

2. **Decorate it. Add a sign.**

95

 **Artist's Workshop**

Amazing School Model

MATERIALS: glue, tape, boxes, paper tubes, construction paper, paints, paintbrushes, cardboard, scissors

PLAN Have children select materials and experiment with constructing buildings.

CREATE Ask children to experiment and practice with forms and spaces to express ideas and feelings. They might use the Pyramid Pattern, *Teacher Resource Book* p. 37. TEKS 2.2A, TEKS 2.2B

REFLECT Ask children to share their models. Have children identify the skills used to produce an effective model of a school. TEKS 2.2C

Activity Options PDAS Domain IV

Quick Activity Have pairs or small groups work together to build one structure.

Early Finishers Children may draw designs for a classroom in the amazing school.

Challenge See *Teacher Resource Book* p. 61.

 Wrap-Up

Informal Assessment PDAS Domain III

- **Identify the lines, shapes, and forms you used in your model.** (Responses will vary.)
  PERCEPTION/AESTHETICS TEKS 2.1B

- **What do you like about your school model? Why?** (Responses will vary.) ART CRITICISM
  TEKS 2.4A

Extend Through Writing

Independent Have children describe the shapes and forms in their school models that they have seen in real buildings. Have them check their spelling, punctuation, and capitalization.
TAKS Writing Objectives 1, 6

 Social Studies Connection

Different Homes, Different Shapes Provide small groups with a picture of a dwelling, such as a teepee, a high-rise, or a one-story house. Have each group model the home using blocks or geometric paper shapes.

PDAS Domain IV

ESL Use **visuals** to support **comprehensible input** for names of buildings and their parts to help children share and describe their school models.

Use *Picture Card Collection* cards 17, 68, and 103. See also *Picture Card Bank* CD-ROM, Categories: My House, Places People Go.

building

TEKS 2.4A define reasons for preferences in personal artworks; TEKS 2.4B identify ideas in artworks by peers and artists; PDAS Domain I active participation; PDAS Domain II learner-centered instruction; PDAS Domain III evaluation and feedback; PDAS Domain IV classroom management; TAKS Writing Objective 1 composition; TAKS Writing Objective 6 proofreading

LESSON 19 *Architecture* **95**

PDAS Domains I, II

Frank Lloyd Wright's Buildings

ARTIST BIOGRAPHY

DISCUSS THE BUILDINGS

Have children read pages 96–97.

- Take a brief nature walk with children, or have them observe nature in another way, such as by handling natural objects or by viewing pictures or videos. Have children identify variations in objects and subjects from the environment, using their senses. Ask them to look for natural objects with interesting forms and describe them. Help children make a chart to record their information. TEKS 2.1A

- Explain that Frank Lloyd Wright is known for designing buildings that fit naturally into their surroundings. Tell children that *Fallingwater* is in the woods in Pennsylvania. Ask children to tell how *Fallingwater* fits with the environment and why its name is appropriate. TEKS 2.4B

- Display **Art Print 12**, and explain that it shows the inside of the Guggenheim Museum, which Wright designed. Explain that it is for modern art. Have children look at the outside of the museum on page 97 and compare it to **Art Print 12**. Talk about how the inside has a spiral walkway that mirrors the outside form.

DISCUSS THE ARTIST

Share background information about the architect.

- Wright told his students to "study nature, love nature, stay close to nature." Ask children how his designs showed his beliefs. TEKS 2.3A, TEKS 2.4B

 ART ⟷ SOCIAL STUDIES CONNECTION

Frank Lloyd Wright's

Frank Lloyd Wright was a famous architect. He designed buildings so they would blend in with the land around them. *Fallingwater* is a house he designed to let a stream and waterfall flow under it.

A ▼ Exterior of *Fallingwater*

96

Background Information

About the Architect

Architect **Frank Lloyd Wright** (1867–1959), who is considered one of the greatest architects of the 20th century, was born in rural Wisconsin. He is known for incorporating natural forms into his building designs. Wright changed the way Americans live by creating open floor plans in which one space flows into the next.

For more information about Frank Lloyd Wright, see pp. R48–R59.

For related images, see **Electronic Art Gallery CD-ROM, Primary**.

★ TEKS 2.1A identify variations in objects and subjects; TEKS 2.1B identify elements and principles; TEKS 2.2A express ideas and feelings; TEKS 2.2B create effective compositions; TEKS 2.3A identify stories and constructions; TEKS 2.4B identify ideas in artworks by peers and artists; *(continued)*

Buildings

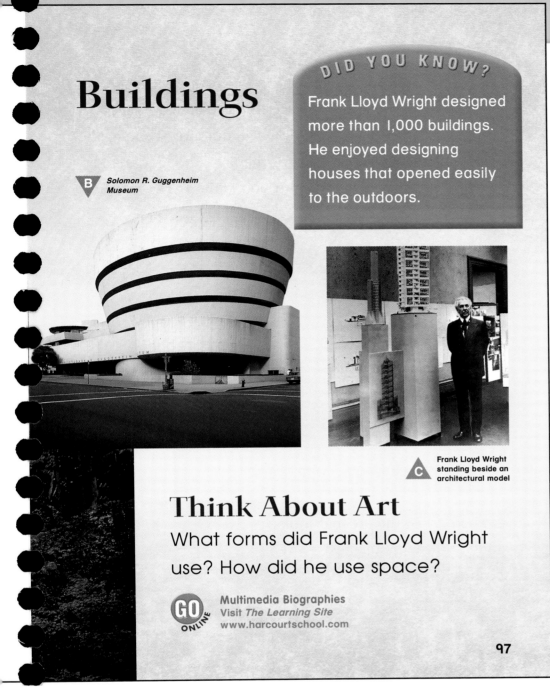

B Solomon R. Guggenheim Museum

C Frank Lloyd Wright standing beside an architectural model

Think About Art

What forms did Frank Lloyd Wright use? How did he use space?

GO ONLINE Multimedia Biographies
Visit *The Learning Site*
www.harcourtschool.com

97

Social Studies Connection

Museum Visits Wright's buildings may be viewed at:

- *Fallingwater*, Mill Run, Pennsylvania.
  www.wpconline.org/fallingwaterhome.htm

For additional cross-curricular suggestions, see Art Transparency 12.

TEKS 2.4B

Visit with an Artist

View Artworks Arrange for children to visit with an architect either at school, at a workplace, or at another location. Ask children to view and identify ideas in the original designs, the portfolio, and an exhibition by the architect. Have them focus on concepts from this unit, such as form and space.

DID YOU KNOW?

Frank Lloyd Wright designed many interesting and famous public buildings, but he concentrated mainly on designing houses. During the early part of his career in the Midwest, he developed a new kind of house style called the Prairie house. These houses were long and low, made to blend with open, flat Midwestern landscapes. This design is still seen today in one-story ranch-style houses. Two of his most famous homes, which also served as his studios and as places for architects to study, are Taliesin in Wisconsin and Taliesin West in Arizona. Frank Lloyd Wright also designed stained-glass windows and furniture to go inside his homes and commercial buildings.

Think About Art

What forms did Frank Lloyd Wright use?
How did he use space? (Possible responses: Most of his forms are geometric and reflect the natural shapes of the land around the buildings or other shapes from nature. The inside spaces of his buildings are interesting.) TEKS 2.1B

ARTIST'S EYE ACTIVITY

Sketch a Building Have children observe the natural environment by looking out a window or by going outdoors. Also provide pictures of unique landscapes, such as mountains, canyons, rivers, valleys, and deserts. Have children identify variations in objects and subjects from the environment, using the senses. Then ask children to choose a natural landscape and sketch a building that harmonizes with the surroundings. Ask them to use a variety of lines to express their ideas and feelings. TEKS 2.1A, TEKS 2.2A, TEKS 2.2B

GO ONLINE Multimedia Biographies
Visit *The Learning Site*
www.harcourtschool.com

Lesson 20

PDAS Domains I, II
Landscapes

OBJECTIVES
- Recognize landscapes
- Create an effective landscape using elements and principles
- Compare and contrast

RESOURCES
- Art Prints 6, 13
- Discussion Cards 2, 6
- Big Book, pp. 98–99
- Electronic Art Gallery CD-ROM, Primary

5 Minutes
Warm-Up

Near and Far One volunteer stands near the group; another stands far away. Have them both hold up a sheet of paper. Talk about which sheet looks bigger. Repeat with other objects. TEKS 2.1A

10-15 Minutes
Teach

Discuss Art Concepts Have children read page 98. Use Discussion Card 2 to analyze the art. Talk about space. Then display **Art Prints 6** and **13**. Have children identify the landscape and recall what a *seascape* is. Have children locate the horizon line in each painting and tell why some objects appear larger than others. TEKS 2.1A, TEKS 2.1B

Think Critically

1. (Focus Skill) **READING SKILL** **How are the two paintings alike and different?** (Possible responses: Both are outdoor scenes. One shows summer, one shows winter.) COMPARE AND CONTRAST TEKS 2.1A

2. **How do you think the artists want you to feel when you see their paintings?** (Possible responses: calm, cool, happy) PERCEPTION TEKS 2.4B

3. **WRITE** Tell how landscapes are like seascapes. INDEPENDENT WRITING TAKS Writing Objective 1

Lesson 20

Vocabulary
landscape
foreground
background

Landscapes

What do you see in these artworks? A **landscape** shows an outdoor scene of the land. The part of the art that is large and seems nearest to you is the **foreground**.

A Claude Monet, *In the Meadow*

The part of the art that looks small and seems farthest away is the **background**.

Kacy, grade 2, Student art B

98

 Background Information

Art History

The name **Impressionism** is from the artwork *Impression: Sunrise* by **Claude Monet** (KLOHD moh•NAY) (1840–1926). In this style, artists focused on creative brushwork rather than realistic subjects. Impressionists often worked outdoors.

For more information about Impressionism and Monet, see pp. R48–R59.

RECOMMENDED READING
Little Mouse's Painting by Diane Wolkstein. Sea Star, 1992. READ-ALOUD

★ TEKS 2.1A identify variations in objects and subjects; **TEKS 2.1B** identify elements and principles; **TEKS 2.2B** create effective compositions; **TEKS 2.2C** identify and practice skills; **TEKS 2.4B** identify ideas in artworks by peers and artists; **PDAS Domain I** active participation; *(continued)*

Artist's Workshop

3-D Landscape Painting

PLAN

Imagine a beautiful landscape scene.

CREATE

1. Paint a landscape with a clear horizon line.

2. Make things large in the foreground and small in the background.

REFLECT

What is in the foreground of your landscape? How do you know? Where is the horizon line?

99

15-25 Minutes — Artist's Workshop

3-D Landscape Painting

MATERIALS: construction paper, paints, paint-brushes, glue, scissors, found objects

TECHNIQUE TIP: Have children practice a necessary skill by beginning their painting with the horizon line. TEKS 2.2C

PLAN After children imagine a scene, have them tell the skills they will need to be able to create a good landscape and then practice those skills as they paint. TEKS 2.2C

CREATE Have children use found objects to make their scenes three-dimensional. Remind them to add larger details to the foreground. Children might use the Near and Far Pictures, *Teacher Resource Book* p. 38. TEKS 2.2B, TEKS 2.2C

REFLECT Exhibit the paintings. Have children identify horizon lines and classmates' ideas. TEKS 2.1B, TEKS 2.4B

Activity Options PDAS Domain IV

Quick Activity Use crayons instead of paints.

Early Finishers Use Discussion Card 6.

Challenge See *Teacher Resource Book* p. 62.

5-10 Minutes — Wrap-Up

PDAS Domain III

Informal Assessment

- **How are the objects in your foreground and background different?** (Things in the foreground are larger.) PERCEPTION/AESTHETICS TEKS 2.1B

- **How is your landscape like Monet's? How is it different?** (Responses will vary.) ART CRITICISM

Extend Through Writing

Independent Have children write a story about spending a day in their landscape. TAKS Writing Objective 1

Science Connection

Light Affects Colors Shine a light on a toy animal. Have children sketch and color it. Then shine the light from another angle and have children draw it again. Discuss how the colors and shading changed, relating this to the way objects look different as the day passes.

PDAS Domain IV

ESL Help children **understand the concept** of a horizon by showing them visuals of landscapes and seascapes. Ask volunteers to finger-trace the horizon and say *horizon*.

Challenge Have children add themselves to their landscape painting and then tell a story about it.

PDAS Domain II learner-centered instruction; PDAS Domain III evaluation and feedback; PDAS Domain IV classroom management; TAKS Writing Objective 1 composition

LESSON 20 *Landscapes* 99

Unit 4

PDAS Domains I, III

Review and Reflect

In this unit, children have learned how artists use form and space in artworks. You may wish to use **Art Prints 6** and **10–13** and Discussion Cards 1 and 2 to review how artists use these elements.

Vocabulary and Concepts

Review art vocabulary by having children choose the best word to complete each sentence. ("Best" responses are shown; accept other reasonable responses.)

1. D

2. B

3. space

4. background

5. sculpture

6. form

7. relief sculpture

8. foreground

9. architecture

Unit 4 Review and Reflect

Vocabulary and Concepts

Choose the best answer to finish each sentence.

1. A picture of the outdoors is a _____.
   A architecture
   B form
   C sculpture
   D landscape

2. An _____ plans buildings.
   A background
   B architect
   C foreground
   D architecture

Choose the word from the box that best completes each sentence.

architecture
background
foreground
form
relief sculpture
sculpture
space

3. The part of an artwork that is empty is called _____.

4. The part of a picture that seems farthest from you is the _____.

5. You can walk all around a _____.

6. A cube is not flat. It is a _____.

7. A sculpture that stands out from a flat surface is a _____.

8. The part of a picture that seems closest to you is the _____.

9. The art of planning buildings is _____.

100

TEKS 2.3C, TEKS 2.4B

Home and Community Connection

School-Home Connection

Distribute *Teacher Resource Book* pp. 83–84 to provide family members with information and activities to reinforce unit concepts.

Community Connection

Invite architects, sculptors, or builders to talk about their work and discuss form and space. Then have children identify different kinds of jobs in art that they have learned about. **CAREERS IN ART**

Visit a community art site. Have children identify ideas in the art and tell how the art enriches their community. Use Discussion Card 10.
COMMUNITY ART

Compare and Contrast

Reread about Frank Lloyd Wright's buildings on pages 96–97. Make a Venn diagram to compare and contrast *Fallingwater* and the Guggenheim Museum.

DIFFERENT   ALIKE   DIFFERENT

Write About Art

Write a paragraph to compare and contrast two animals from *The Bremen Town Musicians*. First tell how they are alike. Then tell how they are different.

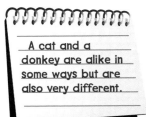

A cat and a donkey are alike in some ways but are also very different.

Gerhard Marcks, *The Bremen Town Musicians*

101

TEKS 2.4A; PDAS Domain III

Assessment

Portfolio Assessment

Have children choose one artwork from this unit to include in their portfolios. Ask them to review each Artist's Workshop activity, select their favorite piece, and tell why they chose it. Provide feedback about children's use of elements, principles, and techniques. See also Portfolio Recording Form, page R32.

Additional Assessment Options

- Progress Recording Form, p. R33
- Artist's Workshop Rubric (Self/Teacher and Peer), pp. R30–R31
- Unit Test, *Teacher Resource Book*, p. 94

Compare and Contrast

Help children to compare and contrast *Fallingwater* and the Guggenheim Museum and to record their observations on a Venn diagram.

DIFFERENT **Fallingwater** in woods, house, rectangular form

ALIKE building designed by Frank Lloyd Wright

DIFFERENT **Guggenheim Museum** in city, museum, rounded spiral form

Write About Art

Compare and Contrast Paragraph Discuss the similarities and differences among the animals in *The Bremen Town Musicians*. Have each child write a paragraph to compare and contrast two of the animals. Ask children to check their writing for clear descriptive words and the paragraph indent. TEKS 2.1A; TAKS Writing Objectives 1, 5, 6

Critic's Corner

RESPONSE/EVALUATION Have children discuss their favorite artwork in the unit. Use these steps.

Describe Ask children to identify and describe the form and space in the artwork. TEKS 2.1B

Analyze Remind them to use words such as *shape*, *form*, and *space* in their discussion.

Interpret Ask children to tell about ideas they have from viewing the artwork. TEKS 2.4B

Evaluate Ask children to discuss the feeling(s) they think the artist wanted to show.

 TAKS Test Preparation: Reading and Writing Through Art, pp. 14–24

PDAS Domain I active participation; PDAS Domain III evaluation and feedback; TAKS Writing Objective 1 composition; TAKS Writing Objective 5 usage; TAKS Writing Objective 6 proofreading

UNIT 4 *Review and Reflect* 101

Unit 5

Emphasis and Balance

Good Neighbors

Art provides ways to express what we think, feel, and believe about our communities. Children will discover how artists use emphasis and balance when they express what is important to them.

Resources

- Unit 5 Art Prints (13–15)
- Additional Art Prints (2, 5)
- Art Transparencies 13–15
- Test Preparation: Reading and Writing Through Art, p. 25
- Artist's Workshop Activities: English and Spanish, pp. 41–50
- Encyclopedia of Artists and Art History, pp. R48–R59
- Picture Card Collection, Cards 17, 26, 30, 41, 42, 50, 59, 66, 73, 82, 87, 89, 108, 109

Using the Art Prints

- Discussion Cards, pp. R34–R42
- Teaching Suggestions, backs of Art Prints
- Art Print Teaching Suggestions: Spanish

Teacher Resource Book

- Vocabulary Cards in English and Spanish, pp. 19–20
- Reading Skill Card 5, p. 27
- Copying Masters, pp. 29, 30, 31, 41
- Challenge Activities, pp. 63–67
- School-Home Connection: English/Spanish, pp. 85–86
- Unit Test, p. 95

Technology Resources

 Electronic Art Gallery CD-ROM, Primary Picture Card Bank CD-ROM

 Visit *The Learning Site* www.harcourtschool.com

- Multimedia Art Glossary
- Multimedia Biographies
- Reading Skills and Activities

Art Prints for This Unit

ART PRINT 13

Wheat Field and Cypress Trees
by Vincent van Gogh

ART PRINT 14

White Breeze
by Jonathan Green

ART PRINT 5

Poppy
by Georgia O'Keeffe

ART PRINT 15

Fulang-Chang and I
by Frida Kahlo

ART PRINT 2

People and Dog in Front of the Sun
by Joan Miró

Planning Guide PDAS Domain IV

Lesson	Objectives and Vocabulary	Art Images	Production/ Materials
Main Idea, pp. 104–105 (Focus Skill)			
21 **EMPHASIS USING COLOR** pp. 106–107 🕐 30–60 minutes	• Identify principles such as emphasis • Create effective compositions with emphasis using color • (Focus Skill) Identify main idea **Vocabulary: emphasis**	• **Goldfish** by Henri Matisse • **Macaw on a Pine Branch** by Ichiryusai Hiroshige	**"Around the Town" Painting** ❑ construction paper ❑ scissors ❑ pencils ❑ paints ❑ paintbrushes
22 **EMPHASIS USING SIZE** pp. 108–109 🕐 30–60 minutes	• Identify principles such as emphasis • Create a collage with emphasis • (Focus Skill) Identify main idea **Vocabulary: subject**	• **The Great Wave off Kanagawa** by Katsushika Hokusai • **The Rainbow** by Tori, grade 2	**Found Object Collage** ❑ heavy paper ❑ glue ❑ scissors ❑ found objects ❑ crayons, markers ❑ oil pastels, paints
Art ↔ Science Connection: Famous Photographers, pp. 110–111			
23 **BALANCE USING SHAPES** pp. 112–113 🕐 30–60 minutes	• Identify balance and symmetry • Produce a balanced sun print • (Focus Skill) Identify main idea **Vocabulary: balance, symmetry**	• **Ancient Greek black-figure hydria with women running** • **Turkish plate decorated with flame motif**	**Sun Print** ❑ dark construction paper ❑ scissors ❑ crayons, oil pastels ❑ glue ❑ yarn
24 **BALANCE USING COLOR** pp. 114–115 🕐 30–60 minutes	• Identify principles such as balance • Create effective portraits • (Focus Skill) Identify main idea **Vocabulary: contrast**	• **Two Dancers in Blue Costumes** by Edgar Degas • **Members of the Drapers Club (Staalmeesters)** by Rembrandt van Rijn	**Famous-Person Portrait** ❑ pencils ❑ oil pastels ❑ construction paper
Art ↔ Social Studies Connection: Frida Kahlo's Portraits, pp. 116–117			
25 **ART TO WEAR** pp. 118–119 🕐 30–60 minutes	• Identify pattern and balance • Create a celebration vest • (Focus Skill) Identify main idea **Vocabulary: textiles, designs**	• **Ceremonial clothing of King Mbop Mbine** • **Child's blouse with geometric mola**	**Celebration Vest** ❑ paper bag ❑ scissors ❑ paints, brushes ❑ glue ❑ found objects ❑ hole punch
Review and Reflect, pp. 120–121			

⭐ TEKS 2.1A identify variations in objects and subjects; TEKS 2.1B identify elements and principles; TEKS 2.2C identify and practice skills; PDAS Domain IV classroom management

Focus Skill

Main Idea, pp. 104–105
Opportunities for application of the skill are provided on pp. 106, 108, 112, 114, 118, 121.

Art Puzzlers

Resources and Technology	Suggested Literature	Across the Curriculum
• Art Prints 5, 13, 14 • Reading Skill Card 5 • Big Book, pp. 106–107 • Electronic Art Gallery CD-ROM, Primary	*How Artists See Animals* by Colleen Carroll **Read-Aloud** 	**Science** Animal Colors, p. 107 **Reading** Main Idea, p. 106 **Writing** Independent, p. 107
• Art Prints 5, 13, 14 • Reading Skill Card 5 • Big Book, pp. 108–109 • Electronic Art Gallery CD-ROM, Primary	*Hokusai: The Man Who Painted a Mountain* by Deborah Kogan Ray **Read-Aloud** 	**Science** Tsunami!, p. 109 **Reading** Main Idea, p. 108 **Writing** Independent, p. 109
• Art Prints 2, 5, 14, 15 • Discussion Card 4, p. R36 • Reading Skill Card 5 • Big Book, pp. 112–113 • Electronic Art Gallery CD-ROM, Primary	*Lunchtime for a Purple Snake* by Harriet Ziefert **Challenging** 	**Math** Use a Balance, p. 113 **Reading** Main Idea, p. 112 **Writing** Independent, p. 113
• Art Prints 5, 14, 15 • Discussion Card 5, p. R37 • Reading Skill Card 5 • Big Book, pp. 114–115 • Electronic Art Gallery CD-ROM, Primary	*Degas and the Little Dancer: A Story About Edgar Degas* by Laurence Anholt **Read-Aloud** 	**Social Studies** Flags with Balance, p. 115 **Reading** Main Idea, p. 114 **Writing** Independent, p. 115
• Art Print 14 • Discussion Cards 1, 2, p. R34 • Reading Skill Card 5 • Big Book, pp. 118–119 • Electronic Art Gallery CD-ROM, Primary	*Abuela's Weave* by Omar S. Casteñeda **Read-Aloud** 	**Social Studies** Where in the World?, p. 119 **Reading** Main Idea, p. 118 **Writing** Independent, p. 119

Present these art puzzlers to children at the beginning or end of a class or when children finish an assignment early.

- What things on both sides of your face and your body give it **balance**? TEKS 2.1A

- Point to an object that has **symmetry**. Use your finger to trace an imaginary line down the middle of the object. TEKS 2.1A

- Look around. Tell what object you notice first. What gives it **emphasis**—its color or size? TEKS 2.1A, TEKS 2.1B

- Arrange objects to show **balance**. Tell what you did and why. TEKS 2.1A, TEKS 2.2C

- Look at the art on a book cover or a poster. What is the **subject**? TEKS 2.1A

 School-Home Connection
The activities above are included in the School-Home Connection for this unit. See *Teacher Resource Book*, pp. 85–86.

Assessment Options
- Rubrics and Recording Forms, pp. R28–R33
- Unit 5 Test, *Teacher Resource Book*, p. 95

 GO ONLINE
Visit *The Learning Site*: **www.harcourtschool.com**

Artist's Workshops PREVIEW

Use these pages to help you gather and organize materials for the Artist's Workshop in each lesson.

LESSON	MATERIALS

21 "Around the Town" Painting p. 107

Objective: To have children paint building shapes to resemble places in their neighborhood, using color to emphasize their favorite place

🕐 15–25 minutes

Challenge Activity: See *Teacher Resource Book,* p. 63.

- pencils
- construction paper
- scissors
- tempera paints
- watercolor paints
- paintbrushes

LESSON

22 Found Object Collage p. 109

Objective: To have children use color, shape, pattern, and texture from found objects to create a collage, using size to emphasize the subject

🕐 15–25 minutes

Challenge Activity: See *Teacher Resource Book,* p. 64.

- cardboard or construction paper
- glue
- scissors
- found objects—bubble wrap, twigs, pine needles, cloth scraps, recyclables
- tempera paints
- paintbrushes
- crayons
- markers
- oil pastels

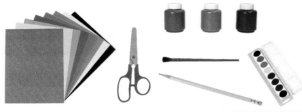

 Safety Tips For safety information, see Art Safety, page R4; the Art Safety Poster; or Big Book page 148.

For information on media and techniques, see pages R15–R23.

LESSON	MATERIALS

23 Sun Print p. 113

Objective: To have children cut a shape from nature that has symmetry, make a print using sunlight, and decorate the print to create a balanced design

🕐 15–25 minutes

Challenge Activity: See *Teacher Resource Book,* p. 65.

- dark construction paper
- scissors
- crayons
- oil pastels
- glue
- yarn

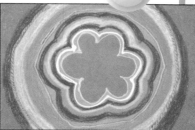
FINISHED EXAMPLE

LESSON

24 Famous-Person Portrait p. 115

Objective: To have children utilize their knowledge of color, balance, and contrast to draw and color a portrait of a famous person

🕐 15–25 minutes

Challenge Activity: See *Teacher Resource Book,* p. 66.

- pencils
- oil pastels
- construction paper

FINISHED EXAMPLE

LESSON

25 Celebration Vest p. 119

Objective: To have children create a celebration vest and decorate it with a balanced design that incorporates line, color, shape, pattern, and weaving

🕐 15–25 minutes

Challenge Activity: See *Teacher Resource Book,* p. 67.

- paper bag
- scissors
- paints
- paintbrushes
- glue
- found objects— buttons, yarn, seashells, feathers
- hole punch

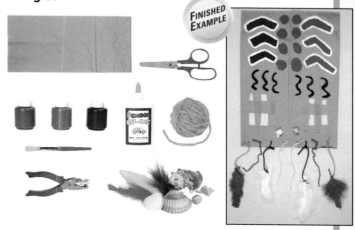
FINISHED EXAMPLE

Unit 5

PDAS Domains I, II

Good Neighbors

PREVIEW THE UNIT

Do a Walk-Through Have children use the Contents and turn to the correct page for Unit 5. Tell children that in this unit they will learn how artists use emphasis and balance. Have them look at the art and predict each lesson's focus.

SHARE THE POEM

Have children read the poem and view the art.

Does the poem have the same mood as the painting? Describe the mood. (Possible responses: Both are peaceful. The poem tells about a pasture and trees—a peaceful place. The painting has soft colors and shows a calm, peaceful scene.) DRAW CONCLUSIONS TEKS 2.4B; TAKS Reading Objective 4

STEP INTO THE ART

Have children look closely at the art and tell how they feel about the painting. Then have them identify variations in objects and subjects from the environment, using their senses. Say: **Imagine that you are in this painting. What do you see, hear, and smell? How is this place like where you live? How is it different?** (Responses will vary.) PERSONAL RESPONSE TEKS 2.1A, TEKS 2.4B

SHARE BACKGROUND INFORMATION

Tell children that Pieter Brueghel the Elder lived nearly 500 years ago, yet his paintings are still popular today. Ask children why they think that is so. Then have them tell the story the painting shows. Ask them to also tell how they know this painting shows a time long ago. TEKS 2.3A

LOCATE IT See *Using the Maps of Museums and Art Sites*, pp. R2–R3.

▲ Pieter Brueghel the Elder, *The Hay Harvest*

LOCATE IT

This painting is in the National Gallery in Prague, Czech Republic.

See Maps of Museums and Art Sites, pages 144–147.

Czech Republic

102

 Background Information

About the Artist

Pieter Brueghel the Elder (BROY • guhl) (about 1520–1569) was an influential painter from the Netherlands. He is referred to as "the Elder" because he is part of an important family of artists; his son Pieter is referred to as "the Younger." Pieter the Elder is known for his paintings and drawings of landscapes and the life of everyday people.

For more information about the artist, see pp. R48–R59.

For related images, see **Electronic Art Gallery CD-ROM, Primary.**

★ **TEKS 2.1A** identify variations in objects and subjects; **TEKS 2.2C** identify and practice skills; **TEKS 2.3A** identify stories and constructions; **TEKS 2.4B** identify ideas in artworks by peers and artists; **PDAS Domain I** active participation; **PDAS Domain II** learner-centered instruction; *(continued)*

Good Neighbors

Harvest Breeze

The smell of fresh cut hay
Aloft on the harvest breeze
Sneaking up from field to house
Up the pasture through the trees.

Tim Gallagher

ABOUT THE ARTIST

See Gallery of Artists, pages 182–191.

Unit Vocabulary

emphasis	contrast
subject	textiles
balance	designs
symmetry	

 Multimedia Art Glossary
Visit *The Learning Site*
www.harcourtschool.com

103

Unit Vocabulary

Read aloud each vocabulary word as children point to it in their books. Have children read it aloud chorally. Then have volunteers use the words they know in oral sentences. Tell children they will learn more about the words as they read the unit.

emphasis the use of size, shape, or color to make part of an artwork stand out

subject a person, object, or scene represented in an artwork; what an artwork is mostly about

balance the arrangement of parts of an artwork to give a feeling of stability or equality: symmetrical—one side mirrors the other; asymmetrical—the sides are not identical; or radial—extending in all directions from a circle's center

symmetry balance in which both sides of an artwork are identical or very similar

contrast a noticeable difference between two things to bring attention to certain elements, such as a light and a dark color

textiles works made using fibers or fabrics, such as quilts, weavings, and clothing

designs arrangements of lines, shapes, textures, colors, and other elements

Vocabulary Resources

- Vocabulary Cards in English and Spanish, *Teacher Resource Book*, pp. 19–20
- Student Edition Glossary, pp. 192–201

 Multimedia Art Glossary
English/Spanish
Visit *The Learning Site*
www.harcourtschool.com

Sketchbook

Remind children to use their sketchbooks to practice skills needed to produce a variety of artworks, such as practicing how to emphasize the main idea of an artwork.
TEKS 2.2C

 TEKS 2.2C; PDAS Domain II

Art Center

Materials mural paper, paint, found objects, craft materials

Ongoing Activity Have children create a mural of their community and add to it during the unit, using a variety of art techniques, emphasis, and balance.

Big Book Put the *Big Book* in the Art Center for children to use.

 PDAS Domain IV

Classroom Management

Found Objects from Home
Contact children's families asking for objects to use in art projects such as egg cartons, foam trays, and packing materials.

Display the Idea Wheel (see *Teacher Resource Book*, pp. 29–30) for children who finish early.

Focus Skill READING SKILL

PDAS Domains I, II
Main Idea

SKILL TRACE	
MAIN IDEA	
Introduce	pp. 104–105
Review	pp. 106, 108, 112, 114, 118, 121

DISCUSS THE SKILL

Access Prior Knowledge Have children recall a story the group has read or heard recently. Ask volunteers to tell what the story was mostly about. Explain that what a paragraph or a story is mainly about is the **main idea**. **Details** give more information about the main idea. Explain that artworks can also have a main idea. Tell children that identifying the main idea will help them understand the artworks and the information in this unit. **TAKS Reading Objective 4**

APPLY TO ART

Identify Main Idea in Art Have children read page 104, including the painting's caption. Have children tell the story they see in the painting and then identify the main idea of the painting. (Possible response: Three girls are dancing together.) **TEKS 2.3A; TAKS Reading Objectives 2, 4**

Help children understand the significance of Gauguin's artwork as it relates to art history. Share the Background Information with children. Explain that many artists were influenced by Gauguin's painting style. Tell children that he is considered one of the founders of modern art. Ask them to say one or two sentences to briefly summarize how Gauguin's artwork is an achievement. **TEKS 2.3A**

Focus Skill READING SKILL

Main Idea

The most important idea of a paragraph, a story, or an artwork is the **main idea**.

Paul Gauguin, *Breton Girls Dancing, Pont-Aven*

What is the main idea of this painting? Use details about the people, the place, and the action to figure out what it is mostly about.

104

FYI Background Information

About the Artist
Paul Gauguin (goh•GAN) (1848–1903) was a stockbroker in France before becoming a full-time artist. In 1882, Gauguin lost his job due to a stock market crash. He then devoted himself to art. After struggling for nearly ten years, Gauguin moved to Tahiti. There, he developed a unique style using lush colors and flat shapes, inspired by the place and the people who lived there. Many artists were influenced by his style, and it helped to give rise to modern art.

For more information about Paul Gauguin, see pp. R48–R59.

★ **TEKS 2.3A** identify stories and constructions; **TEKS 2.4B** identify ideas in artworks by peers and artists; **PDAS Domain I** active participation; **PDAS Domain II** learner-centered instruction; **PDAS Domain IV** classroom management; **TAKS Reading Objective 1** demonstrate understanding of texts; *(continued)*

Read the paragraph. Then make a diagram. Use the details to help you figure out the main idea.

Three girls are having fun doing a folk dance. They are in a field, holding hands and doing dance steps. They are wearing long dresses, hats, and wooden shoes. The girls look as if they all know the dance and enjoy doing it.

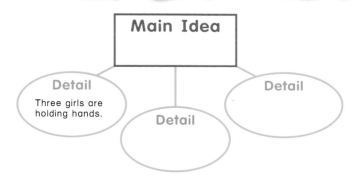

On Your Own

What are the different groups of people doing in the painting on pages 102–103? What is the main idea?

105

APPLY TO READING

Identify Main Idea in Text Have children read the paragraph on page 105. Ask them to identify the main idea and supporting details. (Accept reasonable responses.) Draw a diagram on the board similar to the one shown and fill it in with children's help. TAKS Reading Objectives 1, 3, 4

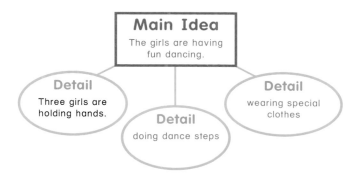

ON YOUR OWN

Have children revisit the painting *The Hay Harvest* on pages 102–103. They can work individually or with a partner to create a main idea and details diagram similar to the one above for this painting. TEKS 2.4B

TAKS Reading Objectives 3, 4

Reading Skill Card

Distribute Reading Skill Card 5, *Teacher Resource Book* p. 27. Use the diagram to help children identify main ideas in artworks in this unit.

Extend the Skill For additional teaching suggestions, see **Art Transparency 13**.

PDAS Domain IV

ESL Invite children to **role-play** the scene in the painting as part of a **total physical response**. Use simple language to describe the main idea, for example, "The girls dance."

Extra Support Copy the paragraph from page 105 on the board. Help children identify and underline the main idea.

Reading Skills and Activities
Visit *The Learning Site*
www.harcourtschool.com

TAKS Reading Objective 2 apply knowledge of literary elements; TAKS Reading Objective 3 use a variety of strategies; TAKS Reading Objective 4 apply critical-thinking skills

UNIT 5 *Main Idea* **105**

Lesson 21

Emphasis Using Color

PDAS Domains I, II

OBJECTIVES
- Identify principles such as emphasis
- Create effective compositions with emphasis using color
- Identify main idea

RESOURCES
- Art Prints 5, 13, 14
- Big Book, pp. 106–107
- Electronic Art Gallery CD-ROM, Primary

Warm-Up
5 Minutes

Which Color? Select books having colorful covers in which one color stands out. Have children identify the color that stands out on each.

Teach
10-15 Minutes

Discuss Art Concepts Ask children to read page 106. Tell them that emphasis can be used to help show the main idea of an artwork. Then display **Art Prints 5**, **13**, and **14**. Ask children to tell which parts are emphasized. TEKS 2.1B

Think Critically

1. **READING SKILL** What is Matisse's painting mostly about? (Possible response: goldfish swimming in a bowl) **MAIN IDEA**
   TEKS 2.4B; TAKS Reading Objective 4

2. **How do both painters use color to emphasize the main idea?** (They both use orange to emphasize the animal the painting is about.)
   PERCEPTION/COMPARE AND CONTRAST TEKS 2.1B

3. **WRITE** How could you emphasize one animal in a painting with many animals?
   INDEPENDENT WRITING TEKS 2.1B; TAKS Writing Objective 1

Lesson 21

Emphasis Using Color

Vocabulary
emphasis

What do you see first in each painting? Why?

A Henri Matisse, *Goldfish*

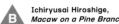
B Ichiryusai Hiroshige, *Macaw on a Pine Branch*

Artists can use color to help you notice a certain part of an artwork. Making things stand out is called **emphasis**.

106

Background Information

About the Artists

Henri Matisse (ahn•REE mah•TEES) (1869–1954) was a leader in the **Fauvist** movement, which was characterized by the use of vivid colors and bold, often distorted forms. Matisse also created large cut-paper figures.

Ichiryusai Hiroshige (hee•roh•shee•gay) (1797–1858), whose first name is really Ando, was a Japanese painter and printmaker famous for his prints of birds, flowers, and landscapes.

For more information about the artists and Fauvism, see pp. R48–R59.

★ TEKS 2.1B identify elements and principles; TEKS 2.2B create effective compositions; TEKS 2.2C identify and practice skills; TEKS 2.4B identify ideas in artworks by peers and artists; PDAS Domain I active participation; PDAS Domain II learner-centered instruction; *(continued)*

Artist's Workshop

"Around the Town" Painting

PLAN

Think of places you like in your neighborhood.

CREATE

1. **Fold your paper two times. Cut a V on the top to make a roof. Unfold.**

2. **Paint places from your neighborhood. Use color to give emphasis to your *favorite* place.**

REFLECT

How did you use color to make your favorite place stand out?

Where do you see color emphasis in your classroom?

107

 ### Science Connection

Animal Colors Explain that the Arctic rabbit grows a white coat to blend in with snow and a brown summer coat to blend in with the ground. Have children put brown and white crayons on white paper. Discuss the colors as they relate to the rabbit.

 PDAS Domain IV

ESL Use **visuals** to support **comprehensible input** of names of buildings and places in the community so children can describe their paintings.

Use *Picture Cards Collection* cards 17, 26, and 89. See also *Picture Card Bank* CD-ROM, Category: Places People Go.

building

Artist's Workshop

15-25 Minutes

"Around the Town" Painting

MATERIALS: construction paper, pencils, scissors, paint, paintbrushes

TECHNIQUE TIP: Remind children not to cut apart the sides of the houses.

PLAN Brainstorm with children places they like to visit in their neighborhoods.

CREATE Have children draw and paint one place on each house shape and use emphasis.
TEKS 2.2B, TEKS 2.2C

REFLECT Ask children to stand up their paintings and discuss how they used color for emphasis.
TEKS 2.1B

Activity Options PDAS Domain IV

Quick Activity Provide pre-cut house shapes.

Early Finishers Children can draw a self-portrait, using color to emphasize feelings.

Challenge See *Teacher Resource Book* p. 63.

5-10 Minutes

Wrap-Up

Informal Assessment PDAS Domain III

- **What place is emphasized? How did you do it?** (Responses will vary.) **PERCEPTION/AESTHETICS**
TEKS 2.1B

- **Which colors worked the best for emphasizing favorite places?** (Responses will vary.)
ART CRITICISM TEKS 2.1B

Extend Through Writing ✏️

Independent Have children write about a place in the community that uses color for emphasis, using sentences that demonstrate command of previously taught conventions of spelling, capitalization, punctuation, grammar, usage, and sentence structure.
TEKS 2.1B; TAKS Writing Objectives 1, 2

PDAS Domain III evaluation and feedback; PDAS Domain IV classroom management; TAKS Reading Objective 4 apply critical-thinking skills; TAKS Writing Objective 1 composition; TAKS Writing Objective 2 conventions

LESSON 21 *Emphasis Using Color* **107**

Lesson 22

PDAS Domains I, II
Emphasis Using Size

OBJECTIVES
- Identify principles such as emphasis
- Create a collage with emphasis
- Identify main idea

RESOURCES
- Art Prints 5, 13, 14
- Big Book, pp. 108–109
- Electronic Art Gallery CD-ROM, Primary

5 Minutes

Warm-Up

What Do You See? Tell children to close their eyes and imagine an elephant and a mouse in the room. Ask: **Which would you see first? Why?**

10-15 Minutes

Teach

Discuss Art Concepts Have children read page 108. Explain that **proportion** is the size of one part compared to the whole. If one part looks larger, it usually has greater importance. Discuss emphasis in **Art Prints 5**, **13**, and **14**. Then share Background Information. Have children identify a construct, or meaning behind the artwork, that may have led Hokusai to paint the scene. (respect for Mt. Fuji and nature) TEKS 2.1B, TEKS 2.3A

Think Critically

1. **READING SKILL** What is the main idea of *The Great Wave off Kanagawa*? (Possible response: People aren't as strong as the sea.)
   MAIN IDEA TEKS 2.4B; TAKS Reading Objective 4

2. **How does each artist emphasize the subject?**
   PERCEPTION/COMPARE AND CONTRAST TEKS 2.1A

3. **WRITE** How could you change *The Rainbow* to emphasize the sun?
   INDEPENDENT WRITING TEKS 2.1B; TAKS Writing Objective 1

Lesson 22

Vocabulary
subject

Emphasis Using Size

What is happening in each artwork? What is the most important thing you see?

A Katsushika Hokusai, *The Great Wave off Kanagawa*

What an artwork is about is called the **subject**. Artists often make the subject large for emphasis.

B Tori, grade 2, *The Rainbow*

108

Background Information

About the Artist
Katsushika Hokusai (kaht•soo•shee•kah hoh•kus•eye) (1760–1849) was an influential Japanese painter and printmaker. This is one of thirty-six paintings Hokusai made of Mt. Fuji. In a traditional Japanese scene, Mt. Fuji would be the focus. Instead, Hokusai drew attention to Mt. Fuji by framing it with the giant wave.

For more information about the artist, see pp. R48–R59.

RECOMMENDED READING
Hokusai: The Man Who Painted a Mountain by Deborah Kogan Ray. Farrar, Straus & Giroux, 2001. **READ-ALOUD**

★ TEKS 2.1A identify variations in objects and subjects; TEKS 2.1B identify elements and principles; TEKS 2.2B create effective compositions; TEKS 2.2C identify and practice skills; TEKS 2.3A identify stories and constructions; TEKS 2.4B identify ideas in artworks by peers and artists; PDAS Domain I active participation; *(continued)*

Artist's Workshop

Found Object Collage

PLAN ....

Think about something real or make-believe you can make with found objects.

CREATE ....

1. Glue objects onto paper. Make one part stand out.

2. Draw, paint, and decorate the background.

REFLECT ....

How did you make the subject of your picture stand out?

Where do you see size emphasis in your classroom?

109

15-25 Minutes

Found Object Collage

MATERIALS: cardboard or construction paper, found objects, glue, scissors, paint, crayons, markers, oil pastels

TECHNIQUE TIP: Have children color first and then glue on bubble wrap.

PLAN Have children identify the skills necessary for constructing the collage. TEKS 2.2C

CREATE Remind children to arrange their objects before gluing them. TEKS 2.2B, TEKS 2.2C

REFLECT Have children identify and discuss emphasis in an exhibit of peers' work. TEKS 2.4B

Activity Options PDAS Domain IV

Quick Activity Have children use crayons to draw a picture that uses size for emphasis.

Early Finishers Children can use the Idea Wheel. See *Teacher Resource Book* pp. 29–30.

Challenge See *Teacher Resource Book* p. 64.

5-10 Minutes

Wrap-Up

Informal Assessment PDAS Domain III

- **What did you emphasize in your collage? How did you create that emphasis?**

  (Responses will vary.) **PERCEPTION/AESTHETICS** TEKS 2.1B, TEKS 2.2C

- **How did your classmates use size?**

  (Responses will vary.) **ART CRITICISM** TEKS 2.4B

Extend Through Writing

Independent Have children write a story about the subject of their collage, using sentences that demonstrate a command of previously taught spelling and grammar conventions. Have them check for a beginning, middle, and ending.
TEKS 2.3A; TAKS Writing Objectives 1, 2, 3

Science Connection

Tsunami! A tsunami (soo•NAH•mee) is a huge wave caused by a storm or an earthquake or volcanic eruption under the sea. It may grow to more than 100 feet tall. To explore waves, have children drop objects into a pan of water. Then, elevate the pan and hit the bottom, forming more waves.

 PDAS Domain IV

ESL
Display objects of varying size. Ask children to identify the largest item with the sentence "___ is the largest."

Challenge
Explain that open space is important in Asian art. The background is emptier than in European art. Have children paint a landscape in this style.

ART ←→ SCIENCE CONNECTION

PDAS Domains I, II

Famous Photographers

CAREERS IN ART

DISCUSS THE PHOTOGRAPHS

Have children read pages 110–111.

- Tell children that *Moon Over Half Dome* is a large work called a **photomural**. It was photographed in Yosemite National Park, California. Ansel Adams used special large cameras with small openings to help show light and texture.

- Explain that Flor Garduño was traveling on a country road in Guatemala and saw a girl wearing the traditional dress of the area. Garduño had the girl pose half in light and half in shadow to create the striking effect in *Basket of Light*.

DISCUSS THE PHOTOGRAPHERS

Share background about the photographers.

- As a child, Adams received a camera while on vacation at Yosemite. His photographs have helped people appreciate the beauty of nature. He once worked as a photographer for the U.S. Department of the Interior, which runs the national parks.

- From an early age, Flor Garduño wanted to become an artist. She worked for the government of Mexico taking pictures of Mexican Indian communities to record their traditions.

- Ask children to identify the jobs Adams and Garduño had and tell whether or not they would like to do those jobs and give reasons for their answers. TEKS 2.3C

ART ←→ SCIENCE CONNECTION

Famous Photographers

A **photographer** is an artist who takes pictures with a camera. Ansel Adams is well known for his black-and-white photographs of landscapes. Where do you see the light in *Moon Over Half Dome*?

Ansel Adams photographing the Big Sur coast

A

Ansel Adams, *Moon Over Half Dome*

B

110

Background Information

About the Photographers

Ansel Adams (1902–1984) believed that it was important to have an idea of the final photograph before taking the picture. Adams is famous for his black-and-white photographs that emphasize texture and vivid detail.

Flor Garduño (gahr•DOO•nyoh) (1957–) was born in Mexico and had a job there as a photographer during which she took pictures of remote villages and native traditions.

For more information about the photographers, see pp. R48–R59.

For related images, see **Electronic Art Gallery CD-ROM, Primary.**

110 UNIT 5 *Good Neighbors* ★ **TEKS 2.1B** identify elements and principles; **TEKS 2.2C** identify and practice skills; **TEKS 2.3C** identify jobs in art; **TEKS 2.4B** identify ideas in artworks by peers and artists; **PDAS Domain I** active participation; **PDAS Domain II** learner-centered instruction; **TAKS Reading Objective 4** apply critical-thinking skills

Flor Garduño is best known for her photographs of people. This photograph shows a celebration of light.

Flor Garduño,
Basket of Light

Flor Garduño
photographing a volcano

Think About Art

How does a photographer use light and size to show emphasis?

111

Think About Art

How does a photographer use light and size to show emphasis? (Possible responses: A subject may be shown larger for emphasis; light shining on part of a picture makes it more noticeable than shadowy parts. Both light and size help to show the main idea of the photograph.) **MAIN IDEA**
TEKS 2.1B; TAKS Reading Objective 4

ARTIST'S EYE ACTIVITY

Art Through a Viewfinder Help children develop and organize ideas from the environment. Take a short walk outside with them, or have them look out of the windows, to observe light and shadows in the environment. Have them identify art elements in the environment, such as form, line, shape, and space and design principles, such as emphasis, pattern, rhythm, and movement. Then discuss how important it is to use a viewfinder in a camera to frame or compose a picture. Model for children how to fold a sheet of paper and cut out a square from its center or have them use the My Viewfinder copying master on *Teacher Resource Book* page 41. Children look through the openings to compose pictures of their environment. Then have them draw the scene they would most like to photograph. TEKS 2.1B, TEKS 2.2C

Social Studies Connection

Museum Visits Photographic works by Ansel Adams may be visited online or in person:

• Museum of Modern Art, New York, NY. www.moma.org

For additional cross-curricular suggestions, see Art Transparency 14.

TEKS 2.4B; PDAS Domain II

Student Art Show

Display Artworks In this unit, have children create an exhibit of their portfolios and artworks. Ask children to identify ideas in one another's original artworks, portfolios, and the exhibit as a whole. Have them focus on unit concepts, such as emphasis and balance. See also Student Art Exhibitions, page 142.

Lesson 23

Balance Using Shapes

PDAS Domains I, II

OBJECTIVES
- Identify balance and symmetry
- Produce a balanced sun print
- Identify main idea

RESOURCES
- Art Prints 2, 5, 14, 15
- Discussion Card 4
- Big Book, pp. 112–113
- Electronic Art Gallery CD-ROM, Primary

5 Minutes

Warm-Up

Balancing Act Have children balance while standing on both feet and on one foot, with one arm out and then both. Ask which was easiest.

10-15 Minutes

Teach

Discuss Art Concepts Have children read page 112. Discuss the emphasis in each artwork and how shapes are used to help them balance. Have children place a pencil across the plate in several ways to discover *radial symmetry*. Point out that many artworks are pleasing because they have balance. Then ask children to identify how **Art Prints 2**, **5**, **14**, and **15** balance. TEKS 2.1B

Think Critically

1. **(Focus Skill) READING SKILL** What is the main idea of the images on the vase? (Women are running a race.) **MAIN IDEA** TEKS 2.4B

2. **What could you add to each artwork and still keep it balanced?** (Responses will vary.) **PERCEPTION**

3. **WRITE** Compare the shapes on the vase to the shapes on the plate. **INDEPENDENT WRITING**
   TEKS 2.1B; TAKS Writing Objective 1

Lesson 23

Balance Using Shapes

Vocabulary
balance
symmetry

What do these artworks show? The artists put the same shapes on both sides. These artworks have **balance**.

A Ancient Greek black-figure hydria with women running

B Turkish plate decorated with flame motif

Lay your pencil on each artwork to divide it in half. Each artwork has **symmetry** since both sides are the same. How is the symmetry in **A** different from **B**?

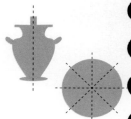

112

Background Information

About Art History

Black-figure vases such as the ancient **Greek** *hydria* shown here were produced during the Archaic Period (700–480 B.C.). During this time, human figures began to be depicted by artists with greater realism than before. *Hydria* were typically used to store water. They were also used as ballot boxes.

For more information about Greek art, see pp. R48–R59.

RECOMMENDED READING

Lunchtime for a Purple Snake by Harriet Ziefert. Houghton Mifflin, 2003. **CHALLENGING**

Lunchtime for a Purple Snake

★ TEKS 2.1B identify elements and principles; TEKS 2.2B create effective compositions; TEKS 2.2C identify and practice skills; TEKS 2.4B identify ideas in artworks by peers and artists; **PDAS Domain I** active participation; **PDAS Domain II** learner-centered instruction; **PDAS Domain III** evaluation and feedback; *(continued)*

Sun Print

PLAN

Think of things from nature that have two sides the same, like a butterfly or a flower.

CREATE

1. **Fold paper. Cut out a shape. Lay it on dark paper. Put it in the sun.**

2. **Take off the shape to see the sun print. Decorate it with a balanced design.**

REFLECT

How did the sun make a print? How does your picture show balance and symmetry?

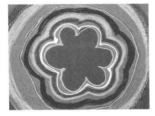

113

Sun Print

Artist's Workshop

15-25 Minutes

MATERIALS: dark construction paper, scissors, crayons, oil pastels, glue, yarn

TECHNIQUE TIP: Put the project in the sun for several hours to make a good print.

PLAN Have children brainstorm objects in nature that are symmetrical.

CREATE Ask children to identify and practice skills for making a sun print. Have them share the sun prints before decorating them. Discuss how the sun made them. Explain that sun prints are like photography—light is used to make an image. TEKS 2.2B, TEKS 2.2C

REFLECT Ask children to finger trace lines of symmetry on one another's artwork and tell about balance.
TEKS 2.1B, TEKS 2.4B

Activity Options PDAS Domain IV

Quick Activity Have children fold paper in half, cut out a symmetrical shape, and decorate it.

Early Finishers Children can use Discussion Card 4.

Challenge See *Teacher Resource Book* p. 65.

Wrap-Up

5-10 Minutes

Informal Assessment PDAS Domain III

- **In what ways is your artwork balanced?**
  (Responses will vary.) **PERCEPTION/AESTHETICS**
  TEKS 2.1B
- **Which designs have symmetry?** (Responses will vary.) **ART CRITICISM** TEKS 2.4B

Extend Through Writing

Independent Have children write a description of something in the classroom that has balance.
TEKS 2.1B; TAKS Writing Objective 1

Math Connection

Use a Balance Provide children with balance scales and small objects. Have them experiment until they balance two groups of objects. Then have them fold paper in half and draw the groups of objects on either side to create a balanced picture.

PDAS Domain IV

ESL Have children use **total physical response** to understand symmetry. Ask partners to face each other. One partner moves and the other acts as a mirror.

Special Needs Cut paper shapes in half. Have children match the halves. Then ask them to trace the whole shape and draw the line of symmetry.

Lesson 24

Balance Using Color

OBJECTIVES
- Identify principles such as balance
- Create effective portraits
- Identify main idea

RESOURCES
- Art Prints 5, 14, 15
- Discussion Card 5
- Big Book, pp. 114–115
- Electronic Art Gallery CD-ROM, Primary

5 Minutes

Warm-Up

Balance a Pattern Have children arrange colored beads or other manipulatives in a line so the colors form a symmetrical pattern.

10-15 Minutes

Teach

Discuss Art Concepts Have children read pages 114–115. Have them lay a pencil along the line of symmetry of each artwork. Talk about how these artworks are not as neatly symmetrical as those in Lesson 23, but are balanced by color. Discuss how contrast provides emphasis and also helps balance the paintings. Display **Art Prints 5, 14,** and **15**. Have children identify balance. TEKS 2.1B

Think Critically

1. **(Focus Skill) READING SKILL** What is the main idea of each painting? (Possible responses: Dancers are resting; men are meeting.) **MAIN IDEA** TEKS 2.4B; TAKS Reading Objective 4

2. **What colors are used for contrast in each painting?** (light pink and blue; white and black) **PERCEPTION/COMPARE AND CONTRAST** TEKS 2.1B

3. **WRITE** How is each painting balanced?
   INDEPENDENT WRITING TEKS 2.1B; TAKS Writing Objective 1

Lesson 24

Vocabulary
contrast

Balance Using Color

What do you see in each painting? How are the two sides of painting **A** alike?

 Edgar Degas,
Two Dancers in Blue Costumes

Artists often put the same color on both sides of an artwork to balance it. Artists also use things that are very different, like light and dark colors, to show **contrast**.

114

Background Information

About the Artists

Edgar Degas (duh•GAH) (1834–1917), a French painter and sculptor, often showed dancers from unusual vantage points.

Rembrandt van Rijn (REM•brant fuhn RYN) (1606–1669) created contrast through *chiaroscuro*, or light and shadow. He painted many portraits of groups of business people, such as the one here.

For more information about the artists, see pp. R48–R59.

RECOMMENDED READING
Degas and the Little Dancer: A Story About Edgar Degas by Laurence Anholt. Barron's, 1996. **READ-ALOUD**

★ **TEKS 2.1B** identify elements and principles; **TEKS 2.2A** express ideas and feelings; **TEKS 2.2B** create effective compositions; **TEKS 2.2C** identify and practice skills; **TEKS 2.4B** identify ideas in artworks by peers and artists; **PDAS Domain I** active participation; **PDAS Domain II** learner-centered instruction; *(continued)*

Rembrandt van Rijn,
Members of the Drapers Club (Staalmeesters)

Contrast helps you notice things like the men's faces. What makes this painting balanced?

Artist's Workshop

Famous-Person Portrait

1. Draw a portrait of a famous person.

2. Color the background so that it shows balance and contrast.

115

PDAS Domain IV

ESL Use **total physical response** and the paintings and other **visuals** to develop vocabulary related to body parts. Play "Simon Says" using names of body parts.

Use **Picture Cards Collection** cards 42, 50, 73, and 82. See also **Picture Card Bank CD-ROM**, Category: My Body.

legs

Artist's Workshop

15-25 Minutes

Famous-Person Portrait

MATERIALS: oil pastels, construction paper, pencil

TECHNIQUE TIP: Model how to use colors opposite on the color wheel for contrast.

PLAN   Have children identify the skills they need in order to make the portrait. TEKS 2.2C

CREATE   Have children use color to express their ideas and feelings about the person. Have them practice skills for drawing and coloring a portrait and adjust their artwork to make it balance. TEKS 2.2A, TEKS 2.2B, TEKS 2.2C

REFLECT   Exhibit portraits, and have children identify the people and ideas shown. TEKS 2.4B

Activity Options   PDAS Domain IV

Quick Activity   Have children sketch a famous person and color the clothing, using balance.

Early Finishers   Children can use Discussion Card 5.

Challenge   See *Teacher Resource Book* p. 66.

5-10 Minutes

Wrap-Up

Informal Assessment   PDAS Domain III

- **What ideas and feelings did you show in your portrait?** (Responses will vary.)
  PERCEPTION/AESTHETICS

- **How did your classmates use color for balance? How did they use contrast?**
  (Responses will vary.) **ART CRITICISM**

Extend Through Writing

Independent   Have children write an informational paragraph about their famous person and check it for a main idea and correct punctuation.
TAKS Writing Objectives 1, 2, 6

PDAS Domain III evaluation and feedback; PDAS Domain IV classroom management; TAKS Reading Objective 4 apply critical-thinking skills; TAKS Writing Objective 1 composition; TAKS Writing Objective 2 conventions; TAKS Writing Objective 6 proofreading

LESSON 24 *Balance Using Color* **115**

ART ←→ SOCIAL STUDIES CONNECTION

 ART ←→ SOCIAL STUDIES CONNECTION

PDAS Domains I, II
Frida Kahlo's Portraits

ARTIST BIOGRAPHY

DISCUSS THE PORTRAITS

Read pages 116–117 with children.

- Explain that many of Frida Kahlo's paintings are self-portraits. Review *self-portrait*. Display **Art Print 15**. Ask children to identify variations in how the artist appears in the self-portraits and the photograph on page 117.
TEKS 2.1A, TEKS 2.3B

- Display **Art Prints 3**, **4**, **6**, **10**, **15**, and **17** and other artworks showing individuals and families. Have children compare the portrayal of families and individuals in the artworks.
TEKS 2.3B, TEKS 2.4B

- Help children understand the cultural significance of Frida Kahlo's artwork. Tell them that Frida Kahlo was proud of her Mexican heritage and culture, and so she often wore traditional Mexican clothing and painted with bright colors and flattened forms, inspired by Mexican folk art. Ask children to describe how Frida Kahlo's paintings reflect this construct, or meaning behind her artwork. Then ask them to identify a story in each painting. TEKS 2.3A

DISCUSS THE ARTIST

Share background information about the artist.

- Explain that Frida Kahlo was born in Mexico. Have a child locate Mexico on a map or globe.

- Point out that Kahlo was married to Diego Rivera, another Mexican artist whose work they studied in Unit 1. Have children compare the styles of the two artists. TEKS 2.4B

- Have children say a sentence or two to summarize how Frida Kahlo's art is an achievement.
TEKS 2.3A

Frida Kahlo's

Frida Kahlo is famous for her self-portraits. As a teenager in Mexico, she was in an accident. While Frida rested in bed, she taught herself to paint. She looked in a mirror and painted many portraits of herself, showing her ideas and feelings.

 A *The Frame, Self-Portrait*

116

 Background Information

About the Artist

Frida Kahlo (FREE•dah KAH•loh) (1907–1954), a polio survivor, was exploring courses in medical illustration as a teen when a life-threatening accident left her bedridden for a year and a half. She turned to painting. Her love of Mexican culture is reflected in her naïve painting, color choice, and subject details. Many of her paintings are self-portraits.

For more information about Frida Kahlo, see pp. R48–R59.

For related images, see **Electronic Art Gallery CD-ROM, Primary.**

★ **TEKS 2.1A** identify variations in objects and subjects; **TEKS 2.1B** identify elements and principles; **TEKS 2.2C** identify and practice skills; **TEKS 2.3A** identify stories and constructions; **TEKS 2.3B** compare artworks showing individuals/families; *(continued)*

Portraits

B ▶ Photograph of Frida Kahlo

C ▶ Frida and Diego Rivera

DID YOU KNOW?

Frida Kahlo liked to include the flowers and animals of Mexico in her art. Tell where she used these things to balance her self-portrait on page 116.

Think About Art

What is special about you that you would put in a self-portrait?

 Multimedia Biographies
Visit *The Learning Site*
www.harcourtschool.com

117

TEKS 2.1B, TEKS 2.4B

Social Studies Connection

Museum Visits Kahlo's paintings may be visited at museums:

- *Self-Portrait with Cropped Hair*, Museum of Modern Art, New York, NY. www.moma.org

For additional cross-curricular suggestions, see Art Transparency 15.

Visit with an Artist

View Art Arrange for children to visit with an artist either at school or at a museum, art gallery, or other location. Ask children to view and identify ideas in original artworks, the portfolio, and an exhibition by the artist. Have them focus on unit concepts, identifying main idea, emphasis, and balance.

DID YOU KNOW?

The bird shapes at the bottom of the painting on page 116 help balance the sides of the painting and also balance with the arch shape over Kahlo's head. Ask children to point out other ways the paintings balance. Then have children identify similarities and differences in the way Frida Kahlo is portrayed in each image. Ask them to also identify variations in objects from her culture that are shown, such as jewelry, clothing, and decorations. TEKS 2.1A

Think About Art

What is special about you that you would put in a self-portrait? (Responses will vary. Children may talk about hobbies or interests.)

PDAS Domain II
ARTIST'S EYE ACTIVITY

Paint Like Frida Kahlo Talk about the colorful plant and animal details in *The Frame, Self-Portrait* and in **Art Print 15**. Tell children that Kahlo often painted plants and animals found in Mexico. Take a short nature walk with children or have them observe nature in another way. Ask them to identify art elements and principles, such as color, texture, pattern, and balance. Also, have them identify variations in objects and subjects from the environment, using their senses. Then, have children brainstorm colorful plants and animals from their environment. Have them paint a self-portrait with a brightly colored, detailed frame that includes selected plants and animals. After children finish, have them describe the construct, or meaning behind their artwork, that led them to include the animals and plants that they did. TEKS 2.1A, TEKS 2.1B, TEKS 2.2C, TEKS 2.3A

 Multimedia Biographies
Visit *The Learning Site*
www.harcourtschool.com

Lesson 25

PDAS Domains I, II

Art to Wear

OBJECTIVES
- Identify pattern and balance
- Create a celebration vest
- Identify main idea

RESOURCES
- Art Print 14
- Discussion Cards 1, 2
- Big Book, pp. 118–119
- Electronic Art Gallery CD-ROM, Primary

5 Minutes

Warm-Up

Textile Display Distribute swatches of textiles and fabrics of various colors and textures. Have children identify variations in the samples. TEKS 2.1A

10-15 Minutes

Teach

Discuss Art Concepts Have children read page 118. Ask children to tell what the clothing is made of and how the designs are balanced. Use Discussion Cards 1 and 2 to ask additional questions. Then display **Art Print 14**, and have children describe the designs on the hat and dress. Talk about balance, emphasis, and contrast. TEKS 2.1B

Think Critically

1. (Focus Skill) **READING SKILL** **What is the main idea of this lesson?** (Possible response: Clothing can be artwork when it has a beautiful design.)
   MAIN IDEA TAKS Reading Objectives 1, 4

2. **Which piece of clothing would you rather wear? Why?** (Responses will vary.)
   PERCEPTION/COMPARE AND CONTRAST TEKS 2.4B

3. **WRITE** Write a story that one of the artworks might tell about the person who wore it. **INDEPENDENT WRITING** TEKS 2.3A; TAKS Writing Objective 1

Lesson 25

Art to Wear

Vocabulary
textiles
designs

What do you notice about these artworks? Some artists use **textiles**, or cloth and other fibers, to make beautiful clothing.

Ceremonial clothing of King Mbop Mbine **A**

B Child's blouse with geometric mola

Pictures and patterns on artworks are called **designs**. What patterns do you see on the clothing? How are the designs balanced?

118

Background Information

Art History

The **Kuba people** (artwork A) live in the Democratic Republic of the Congo. Their decorative raffia textiles are made by people in the same clan. Shells, feathers, and other objects are part of the artwork.

The **Cuna people** (artwork B) live in Panama on islands and in the rainforest. Women make traditional mola blouses with many layers of cloth appliqué.

For more information about Kuba and Cuna cultures, see pp. R48–R59.

RECOMMENDED READING
Abuela's Weave by Omar S. Casteñeda. Lee & Low, 1993. **READ-ALOUD**

★ TEKS 2.1A identify variations in objects and subjects; TEKS 2.1B identify elements and principles; TEKS 2.2B create effective compositions; TEKS 2.2C identify and practice skills; TEKS 2.3A identify stories and constructions; TEKS 2.4A define reasons for preferences in personal artworks; TEKS 2.4B identify ideas in artworks by peers and artists; PDAS Domain I active participation; *(continued)*

Artist's Workshop

Celebration Vest

PLAN

Think about a celebration where you could wear a decorated vest.

CREATE

1. Make a vest from a paper bag. Cut a slit up the front. Cut holes for your head and arms.

2. Decorate your vest. Think about balance and emphasis. Glue on objects. Add some weaving.

REFLECT

How is the design of your vest balanced?

119

Artist's Workshop

15-25 Minutes

Celebration Vest

MATERIALS: paper bag, scissors, paints, brushes, found objects, glue, hole punch, yarn

TECHNIQUE TIP: Model how to pinch the bag to safely cut the armholes.

PLAN Have children identify and practice the skills needed to make a celebration vest.
TEKS 2.2C

CREATE Ask children to use balance and emphasis while designing their constructions.
TEKS 2.2B, TEKS 2.2C

REFLECT Have volunteers wear their vests. Ask classmates to identify balance and emphasis and the kind of celebration it is for.
TEKS 2.1B, TEKS 2.4B

Activity Options PDAS Domain IV

Quick Activity Have children draw and color a design on paper for a celebration vest.

Early Finishers Children can choose an Idea Wheel activity, *Teacher Resource Book*, pp. 29–30.

Challenge See *Teacher Resource Book* p. 67.

5-10 Minutes

Wrap-Up

Informal Assessment PDAS Domain III

- **What is pleasing about your designs?**
  (Responses will vary.) **PERCEPTION/AESTHETICS**
  TEKS 2.4A
- **Which designs were most balanced? Why?**
  (Responses will vary.) **ART CRITICISM** TEKS 2.4B

Extend Through Writing

Independent Have children write a how-to paragraph about making a celebration vest, and check that the sentences are in the correct order.
TEKS 2.2C, TAKS Writing Objectives 1, 3

Social Studies Connection

Where in the World? Explain that the Democratic Republic of the Congo (formerly Zaire) is in Africa and Panama is in Central America. Have children find these countries on a map or globe, and talk about them, using *north*, *south*, *east*, and *west*.

PDAS Domain IV

ESL Use **visuals** to help children **comprehend** words that name clothes. Name each item, and have children repeat as they act out putting it on.

Use *Picture Cards Collection* cards 30, 41, 59, 66, 87, 108, and 109. See also *Picture Card Bank* CD-ROM, Category: Things I Wear.

shirt

PDAS Domain II learner-centered instruction; PDAS Domain III evaluation and feedback; PDAS Domain IV classroom management; TAKS Reading Objective 1 demonstrate understanding of texts; TAKS Reading Objective 4 apply critical-thinking skills; TAKS Writing Objective 1 composition; TAKS Writing Objective 3 organization

LESSON 25 *Art to Wear* **119**

Unit 5

PDAS Domains I, III

Review and Reflect

In this unit, children have learned to express themselves using balance to create pleasing designs and emphasis to show what is important in their artwork. You may want to use **Art Prints 2, 5,** and **13–15** and Discussion Cards 1 and 2 to review these principles.

Vocabulary and Concepts

Review art vocabulary by having children choose the best word to complete each sentence. ("Best" responses are shown; accept other reasonable responses.)

1. C

2. A

3. A

4. D

5. B

6. D

Sort Artworks   Display **Art Prints 1–15,** or have children refer to the artworks in their books from the units they have read so far. For reinforcement of the art principles, have children identify the artworks that best exhibit **balance** and those that clearly show **emphasis**. Have them tell why the artworks are good examples of the art principle. Then ask children to tell why the other artworks do not reflect the art principles as strongly.   TEKS 2.1B, TEKS 2.4B

Afterward, have children choose five Art Prints, put them in order of preference, and explain why.

Unit 5 Review and Reflect

Vocabulary and Concepts

Choose the best answer to finish each sentence.

1. Light and dark colors create _____.

   A textiles
   B symmetry
   C contrast
   D subject

2. Making something stand out in an artwork is _____.

   A emphasis
   B balance
   C textiles
   D designs

3. If both sides are exactly alike, art has _____.

   A symmetry
   B contrast
   C subject
   D emphasis

4. What an artwork is about is the _____.

   A symmetry
   B contrast
   C balance
   D subject

5. An artwork with the same shapes on both sides has _____.

   A textiles
   B balance
   C subject
   D emphasis

6. Cloth and fabric are _____.

   A balance
   B emphasis
   C designs
   D textiles

120

TEKS 2.2A

Home and Community Connection

School-Home Connection

Copy and distribute *Teacher Resource Book* pp. 85–86 to provide family members with information and activities they can use with children to reinforce concepts taught in this unit.

Community Connection

Have children participate in a community art project, or have them create a class mural, quilt, collage, or other type of art to donate to beautify a building in the community. Ask children to express their ideas and feelings in the artwork, using a variety of colors, textures, and materials. They can use Discussion Card 10 to talk about community art.

COMMUNITY ART

★ **TEKS 2.1B** identify elements and principles; **TEKS 2.2A** express ideas and feelings; **TEKS 2.4A** define reasons for preferences in personal artworks; **TEKS 2.4B** identify ideas in artworks by peers and artists; **PDAS Domain I** active participation; **PDAS Domain III** evaluation and feedback; *(continued)*

READING SKILL

Main Idea

Reread about Frida Kahlo on page 116. Look at the art. Then make a diagram to tell the main idea and details.

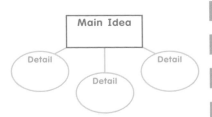

Main Idea

Detail Detail

Detail

Write About Art

Write a paragraph that tells the main idea of the painting. Make a diagram like the one above, and use ideas from it as you write.

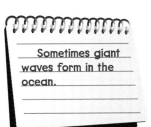

Sometimes giant waves form in the ocean.

Katsushika Hokusai, *The Great Wave off Kanagawa*

121

TEKS 2.4A, TEKS 2.4B; PDAS Domain III

Assessment

Portfolio Assessment

Have children choose an artwork from this unit to include in their portfolios. Ask them to look over all the pieces they created for the Artist's Workshops and select their favorite. Have them tell why they selected the piece. Then have partners share portfolios, choose an interesting artwork, and identify ideas they understand from it. See also Portfolio Recording Form, page R32.

Additional Assessment Options

- Progress Recording Form, p. R33
- Artist's Workshop Rubrics (Self/Teacher and Peer), pp. R30–R31
- Unit Test, *Teacher Resource Book*, p. 95

READING SKILL

Main Idea

Have children make a diagram like the one on page 121. Ask children to reread page 116. Talk about the main idea of the text and the painting. Then have them complete the diagram.
TAKS Reading Objectives 1, 3, 4

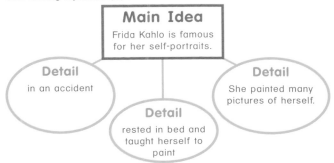

Main Idea
Frida Kahlo is famous for her self-portraits.

Detail
in an accident

Detail
rested in bed and taught herself to paint

Detail
She painted many pictures of herself.

Write About Art

Main Idea Paragraph   Review with children the main idea of *The Great Wave off Kanagawa*. Discuss how artists can use emphasis to show the main idea in an artwork. Have children write a paragraph about the subject of the painting. They can begin by creating a main idea diagram.
TAKS Writing Objectives 1, 3

Critic's Corner

RESPONSE/EVALUATION   Have children select the artwork they liked most in the unit. Use these steps to guide a discussion.

Describe   Have children describe the subject of the artwork.

Analyze   Ask children to use language such as *emphasis* and *balance* to describe the artwork.
TEKS 2.1B

Interpret   Have children share ideas they see and understand from the artwork.   TEKS 2.4B

Evaluate   Ask children if they would like to make artwork like the one they chose.

 TAKS Test Preparation: Reading and Writing Through Art, p. 25

TAKS Reading Objective 1 demonstrate understanding of texts; TAKS Reading Objective 3 use a variety of strategies;
TAKS Reading Objective 4 apply critical-thinking skills; TAKS Writing Objective 1 composition; TAKS Writing Objective 3 organization

Unit 6
Unity and Variety
World Treasures

Artists' experiences and cultures shape the art they create. In this unit, children will discover old and new artworks from around the world that include unity and variety in their designs.

Resources

- Unit 6 Art Prints (16–18)
- Additional Art Prints (9, 11)
- Art Transparencies 16–18
- Test Preparation: Reading and Writing Through Art, pp. 26–36
- Artist's Workshop Activities: English and Spanish, pp. 51–60
- Encyclopedia of Artists and Art History, pp. R48–R59
- Picture Cards Collection, Cards 55, 57, 76, 79, 94

Using the Art Prints

- Discussion Cards, pp. R34–R42
- Teaching suggestions, backs of Art Prints
- Art Print Teaching Suggestions: Spanish

Teacher Resource Book

- Vocabulary Cards in English and Spanish, pp. 21–22
- Reading Skill Card 6, p. 28
- Copying Masters, pp. 29, 30, 36
- Challenge Activities, pp. 68–72
- School-Home Connection: English/Spanish, pp. 87–88
- Unit Test, p. 96

Technology Resources

 Electronic Art Gallery CD-ROM, Primary
Picture Card Bank CD-ROM

 Visit *The Learning Site*
www.harcourtschool.com

- Multimedia Art Glossary
- Multimedia Biographies
- Reading Skills and Activities

Art Prints for This Unit

ART PRINT 16

Cosecha (Harvest)
by Women's Co-op, Lima, Peru

ART PRINT 17

Nurse and Child
by Mary Cassatt

ART PRINT 18

Flowers in a Vase
by Henri Rousseau

ART PRINT 9

Morning Still Life
by Jacob Lawrence

ART PRINT 11

Statue of Abraham Lincoln, Lincoln Memorial
by Daniel Chester French

6 Planning Guide
PDAS Domain IV

Lesson	Objectives and Vocabulary	Art Images	Production/Materials

★ Focus Skill **Cause and Effect, pp. 124–125**

| **26** **MOSAICS** pp. 126–127 🕐 30–60 minutes | • Identify art principles such as unity
• Create an effective mosaic
• (Focus Skill) Recognize cause and effect

Vocabulary: mosaic, unity | • **Rabbit Devouring a Bunch of Grapes** by Unknown artist
• **Student art** by Kaela, grade 2 | **Paper-Plate Mosaic**
❑ paper plate
❑ colored paper
❑ foil, glue
❑ pencils
❑ scissors
❑ markers |
| **27** **DESIGNS OF MONEY** pp. 128–129 🕐 30–60 minutes | • Identify art principles such as unity
• Create effective money designs
• (Focus Skill) Recognize cause and effect

Vocabulary: symbol | • **One-dollar bill, U.S., front**
• **One-dollar bill, U.S., back**
• **Farthings, England**
• **Twenty-peso bill, Mexico**
• **1000-yen bill, Japan**
• **Gold panda coin, China**
• **Gold kangaroo coin, Australia** | **Money Design**
❑ foam plate
❑ pencils, paper
❑ scissors
❑ tempera paints
❑ paintbrushes
❑ paper for printing |

🌐 Art ↔ Social Studies Connection: **Mary Cassatt's Treasures, pp. 130–131**

| **28** **STILL LIFES** pp. 132–133 🕐 30–60 minutes | • Understand how to achieve variety using art elements
• Create an effective still life
• (Focus Skill) Recognize cause and effect

Vocabulary: still life, variety | • **Still Life—Fruit, Bottles** by William H. Johnson
• **A Still Life of Fruit and Flowers in a Basket** by Jacob van Hulsdonck | **Still-Life Painting**
❑ objects
❑ white paper
❑ pencils
❑ tempera paints
❑ paintbrushes
❑ oil pastels |
| **29** **STORIES IN CLOTH ART** pp. 134–135 🕐 30–60 minutes | • Identify stories and constructions in artworks
• Construct a story-cloth collage
• (Focus Skill) Recognize cause and effect

Vocabulary: story cloth | • **Hmong story cloth of village life** by Unknown artist | **Story-Cloth Collage**
❑ pillowcase or paper
❑ glue, scissors
❑ cloth, found objects
❑ fabric paints
❑ tempera paints
❑ markers |

📖 Art ↔ Literature Connection: **Gerald McDermott, Book Illustrator, pp. 136–137**

| **30** **ART ON STAMPS** pp. 138–139 🕐 30–60 minutes | • Identify variety in graphic art
• Design a stamp
• (Focus Skill) Recognize cause and effect

Vocabulary: graphic art | • **Dog Stamp** by Ashley, U.S.
• **Olympic Soccer**—Ghana
• **Beetle**—Nicaragua
• **Greetings from Texas**—U.S.
• **Two Cowboys**—Poland
• **Heroes**—U.S. | **Stamp of the Future**
❑ construction paper
❑ scissors
❑ oil pastels
❑ watercolor paints
❑ paintbrushes
❑ pencils |

✓ Review and Reflect, pp. 140–141

★ **TEKS 2.1A** identify variations in objects and subjects; **TEKS 2.1B** identify elements and principles; **TEKS 2.2C** identify and practice skills; **PDAS Domain IV** classroom management

Cause and Effect, pp. 124–125

Focus Skill

Opportunities for application of the skill are provided on pp. 126, 128, 132, 134, 138, 141.

Art Puzzlers

Present these art puzzlers to children at the beginning or end of a class or when children finish an assignment early.

Resources and Technology	Suggested Literature	Across the Curriculum
• Art Print 16 • Discussion Cards 1, 4 pp. R34, R36 • Reading Skill Card 6 • Big Book, pp. 126–127 • Electronic Art Gallery CD-ROM, Primary	*Lunch* by Denise Fleming **Easy** 	**Science** Mosaics from Nature, p. 127 **Reading** Cause and Effect, p. 126 **Writing** Independent, p. 127
• Art Print 11 • Reading Skill Card 6 • Big Book, pp. 128–129 • Electronic Art Gallery CD-ROM, Primary	*Round and Round the Money Goes: What Money Is and How We Use It* by Melvin and Gilda Berger **Read-Aloud** 	**Math** Classroom Store, p. 129 **Reading** Cause and Effect, p. 128 **Writing** Independent, p. 129
• Art Prints 9, 18 • Discussion Card 2, p. R34 • Reading Skill Card 6 • Big Book, pp. 132–133 • Electronic Art Gallery CD-ROM, Primary	*The Jumbo Book of Art* by Irene Luxbacher **Read-Aloud** 	**Science** Seeds, p. 133 **Reading** Cause and Effect, p. 132 **Writing** Independent, p. 133
• Art Print 16 • Discussion Card 7, p. R39 • Reading Skill Card 6 • Big Book, pp. 134–135 • Electronic Art Gallery CD-ROM, Primary	*Nine-in-One GRR! GRR!* by Blia Xiong (adapted by Cathy Spagnoli) **Average** 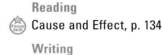	**Social Studies** Locate Countries, p. 135 **Reading** Cause and Effect, p. 134 **Writing** Independent, p. 135
• Art Print 11 • Reading Skill Card 6 • Big Book, pp. 138–139 • Electronic Art Gallery CD-ROM, Primary	*Mailing May* by Michael O. Tunnell **Read-Aloud** 	**Social Studies** Stamps from Around the World, p. 139 **Reading** Cause and Effect, p. 138 **Writing** Independent, p. 139

- A tree with leaves has **unity**. All parts look like they belong together. Name other things in nature that show unity. TEKS 2.1A, TEKS 2.1B

- Describe a meal with a **variety** of food and a toy store with a variety of toys. TEKS 2.1A, TEKS 2.1B

- What **symbol** on your paper means "good work"? What are symbols for our country? For sports teams? TEKS 2.1A

- Place things on a table to show **variety**. Arrange them to be an interesting **still life**. TEKS 2.1A, TEKS 2.1B, TEKS 2.2C

- Describe **graphic art** you have seen on food packages, such as cereal boxes and fruit juices. TEKS 2.1A

School-Home Connection
The activities above are included in the School-Home Connection for this unit. See *Teacher Resource Book,* pp. 87–88.

Assessment Options
- Rubrics and Recording Forms, pp. R28–R33
- Unit 6 Test, *Teacher Resource Book*, p. 96

Visit *The Learning Site*:
www.harcourtschool.com

Artist's Workshops PREVIEW

Use these pages to help you gather and organize materials for the Artist's Workshop in each lesson.

LESSON	MATERIALS

26 Paper-Plate Mosaic

p. 127

Objective: To have children make a mosaic by cutting and gluing small pieces of paper and foil onto a paper plate to create patterns or a subject that shows unity

 15–25 minutes

Challenge Activity: See *Teacher Resource Book,* p. 68.

- paper plate
- colored paper
- foil
- glue
- scissors
- pencils or markers

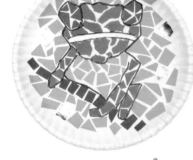

LESSON

27 Money Design p. 129

Objective: To have children design a coin or a bill that has a symbol that represents their city or state, and make prints with it

 15–25 minutes

Challenge Activity: See *Teacher Resource Book,* p. 69.

- foam plate
- pencils, paper
- scissors
- tempera paints
- paintbrushes
- paper for printing

Safety Tips For safety information, see Art Safety, page R4; the Art Safety Poster; or Big Book page 148.

For information on media and techniques, see pages R15–R23.

LESSON	MATERIALS

㉘ Still-Life Painting
p. 133

- pencils
- items for still life (example: stuffed animals)
- white paper
- tempera paints
- brushes
- oil pastels

Objective: To have children arrange and paint a still life that has unity and variety, using objects of different shapes, sizes, colors, and textures

🕐 **15–25 minutes**

Challenge Activity: See *Teacher Resource Book*, p. 70.

㉙ Story-Cloth Collage
p. 135

- pillowcase or paper
- glue
- fabric paints
- tempera paints
- paintbrushes
- scissors
- markers
- found objects— yarn, buttons, ribbon, pieces of fabric

Objective: To have children use multi-media and found objects to construct a collage to tell a story about a favorite memory

🕐 **15–25 minutes**

Challenge Activity: See *Teacher Resource Book*, p. 71.

㉚ Stamp of the Future
p. 139

- construction paper
- scissors
- oil pastels
- watercolor paints
- brushes
- pencils

Objective: To have children draw a stamp using art elements and principles of design to show a subject in the future

🕐 **15–25 minutes**

Challenge Activity: See *Teacher Resource Book*, p. 72.

Unit 6

World Treasures

PREVIEW THE UNIT

Do a Walk Through   Have children use the Contents and turn to the correct page for Unit 6. Explain that in this unit they will look at artworks that have unique styles from cultures around the world. Have children read the lesson titles and look at the artworks. Ask them to choose a favorite artwork and tell why it interests them.

SHARE THE POEM

Read the poem aloud as children view the art. Then have children choral-read the poem.

What do you think the poet would like about the headdress? Why? (Possible responses: He might feel like a king if he were wearing it. It is so beautiful it would make him happy.) **DRAW CONCLUSIONS**   TAKS Reading Objectives 1, 4

STEP INTO THE ART

Have children carefully observe and describe the object in the picture. Then ask: **How would you feel if you were wearing this headdress?** (Responses will vary.) **PERSONAL RESPONSE**

SHARE BACKGROUND INFORMATION

Explain that Aztec people most likely made this headdress. Point out on a map or globe where the Aztecs lived (Mexico). Share Art History.

This headdress includes over 450 feathers from the quetzal (ket•SAHL) bird. The name *quetzal* is taken from the Aztec word *quetzalli*, meaning "precious" or "beautiful." The Aztec people prized this bird for its feathers, which served as symbols of wealth and social status.

LOCATE IT   See *Using the Maps of Museums and Art Sites*, pp. R2–R3.

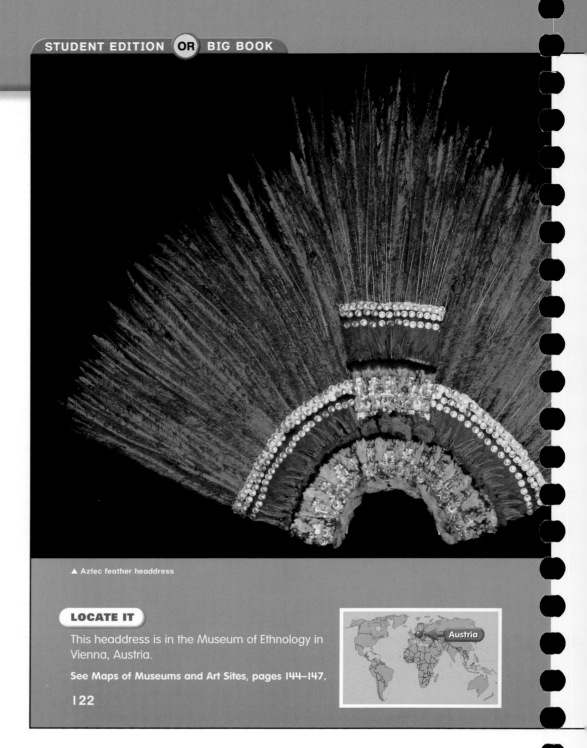

STUDENT EDITION **OR** BIG BOOK

▲ Aztec feather headdress

LOCATE IT

This headdress is in the Museum of Ethnology in Vienna, Austria.

See Maps of Museums and Art Sites, pages 144–147.

122

Background Information

Art History

The Aztecs, a people who ruled what is now central and southern Mexico from the 14th through 16th centuries, likely made this headdress. The Aztecs had an advanced civilization and were superb artisans. They revered a plumed serpent god called Quetzalcoatl, who was shown wearing a quetzal headdress. This particular quetzal headdress became famous because of the theory that it once belonged to the last Aztec ruler of Mexico—Motecuhzoma, also known as Montezuma.

For more information about Aztec art, see pp. R48–R59.

World Treasures

Happy Thought

The world is so full of a
number of things,
I'm sure we should all be
as happy as kings.

Robert Louis Stevenson

Unit Vocabulary

mosaic variety
unity   story cloth
symbol graphic art
still life

 Multimedia Art Glossary
Visit *The Learning Site*
www.harcourtschool.com

123

Unit Vocabulary

Have volunteers read aloud the vocabulary words. Then ask children to sort the words into two groups: words they know and words they don't know. Have volunteers share the meanings of the words they know. Discuss the words they do not know.

mosaic an artwork in which small pieces of tile, glass, stones, paper, or other materials are adhered to a background in order to create a pattern or image

unity a principle of art in which parts of an artwork look like they belong together, creating a sense of wholeness

symbol an image that stands for a word, message, or idea

still life an artwork composed of an arrangement of objects

variety a principle of art in which different design elements, such as line, shape, and color, are used to create interest

story cloth a textile artwork designed to tell a story that often has textile figures and objects attached and hand-sewn designs

graphic art artworks designed and produced for commercial purposes, such as signs, posters, and computer software

Vocabulary Resources

- Vocabulary Cards in English and Spanish, *Teacher Resource Book*, pp. 21–22
- Student Edition Glossary, pp. 192–201

 Multimedia Art Glossary
English/Spanish
Visit *The Learning Site*
www.harcourtschool.com

Sketchbook

 Remind children to use their sketchbooks to help them practice the skills needed to produce a variety of artworks. Encourage children to experiment with different styles from around the world. TEKS 2.2C

 PDAS Domains II, IV

Art Center

Materials butcher paper, tape

Ongoing Activity On a large sheet of butcher paper, draw the outline of a treasure chest. Invite children to attach a variety of pictures, notes, and symbols related to the artworks, such as a feather or a cancelled stamp.

Big Book Put the *Big Book* in the Art Center.

PDAS Domain IV

Classroom Management

Organize materials cafeteria-style when multiple supplies are needed for a project. Place each type of material in its own container. Place the containers in a "cafeteria" (on a long table). Provide children with trays or box lids and have them pick up and return their materials in a single-file line.

Unit 6

Focus Skill READING SKILL

PDAS Domains I, II

Cause and Effect

SKILL TRACE	
CAUSE AND EFFECT	
Introduce	pp. 124–125
Review	pp. 126, 128, 132, 134, 138, 141

DISCUSS THE SKILL

Access Prior Knowledge   Drop a pencil and ask children what happened. (The pencil dropped.) Ask them what **caused** the pencil to drop. (You let it go.) Ask them what happened because you let the pencil go. (It fell to the floor.) Explain that this is called the **effect**. Invite children to describe or demonstrate other cause-and-effect relationships. Explain that understanding cause and effect will help them to better understand the artworks and the information in this unit.
TAKS Reading Objective 4

APPLY TO ART

Recognize Cause and Effect in Art   Have children read page 124 and discuss the story the picture shows. Ask them to tell what caused the girl to cover her ears. (Her brother is singing loudly; the dog is barking.)

Tell children that thinking about causes and effects can help them better understand the story an artwork tells. Have children tell more about the story and the cause-and-effect relationships they see in the painting.   TEKS 2.3A; TAKS Reading Objective 4

Help children understand the cultural significance of Rockwell's art. Share the Background Information with children. Explain that his artwork showed scenes of American life as it was in the 20th century. Ask children to say one or two sentences to summarize how they think Rockwell's art is an achievement.

STUDENT EDITION **OR** BIG BOOK

Focus Skill READING SKILL

Cause and Effect

What is happening to make the girl cover her ears in this painting? The **cause** is the reason something happens. The **effect** is what happens.

Norman Rockwell, *The Music Man*

124

Background Information

About the Artist

Norman Rockwell (1894–1978) was an American painter and illustrator. He is best known for his magazine covers and illustrations in publications such as the *Saturday Evening Post*. Rockwell took art lessons from the age of thirteen and had published his first illustrations by the time he was seventeen. His most popular works feature families and everyday small-town life depicted in humorous detail. Some of his most famous subjects include Rosie the Riveter, the integration of public schools, and holidays.

For more information about Norman Rockwell, see pp. R48–R59.

★ TEKS 2.3A identify stories and constructions; TEKS 2.4B identify ideas in artworks by peers and artists; PDAS Domain I active participation;
PDAS Domain II learner-centered instruction; PDAS Domain IV classroom management; TAKS Reading Objective 1 demonstrate understanding of texts; *(continued)*

Read. Then make a chart. Tell the cause and the effects that happen because of it.

My brother loves to sing cowboy songs, but he sings them too loudly. He sings so hard and so loudly that his feet come off the ground. Our dog starts to howl, and I have to cover my ears.

Cause
The girl's brother is singing too loudly.

Effect The dog howls.

Effect

Effect

On Your Own

Choose one of the stamps on pages 138–139. Make a cause-and-effect chart to tell about it.

125

APPLY TO READING

Cause and Effect in Text Have children read the paragraph on page 125. Then make a cause-and-effect chart. Explain that one thing can cause several other things to happen. Have children tell what the paragraph is about, and ask them to identify cause-and-effect relationships from the paragraph and the painting. TAKS Reading Objectives 1, 3, 4

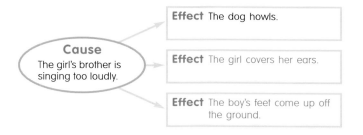

Cause
The girl's brother is singing too loudly.

Effect The dog howls.

Effect The girl covers her ears.

Effect The boy's feet come up off the ground.

ON YOUR OWN

Have children look at the postage stamps on pages 138–139. Ask them to choose one stamp and to fill in a cause-and-effect chart to tell about the "story" in the picture or why they think the particular image was chosen to be on that stamp. TEKS 2.3A, TEKS 2.4B

PDAS Domain IV;
TAKS Reading Objectives 3, 4

Focus Skill

Reading Skill Card

Distribute Reading Skill Card 6, *Teacher Resource Book* page 28. Use the chart to further discuss cause-and-effect relationships in this unit.

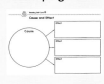

Extend the Skill For additional teaching suggestions, see **Art Transparency 16**.

PDAS Domain IV

MEETING INDIVIDUAL NEEDS

ESL Have small groups **role-play** the scene in the artwork to **develop vocabulary** and related **language concepts**. Then review causes and effects in the art.

Extra Support Review cause-and-effect relationships relevant to children during the school day, such as what happens when the bell rings.

Reading Skills and Activities
Visit *The Learning Site*
www.harcourtschool.com

Lesson 26

PDAS Domains I, II
Mosaics

OBJECTIVES
- Identify art principles such as unity
- Create an effective mosaic
- Recognize cause and effect

RESOURCES
- Art Print 16
- Discussion Cards 1, 4
- Big Book, pp. 126–127
- Electronic Art Gallery CD-ROM, Primary

5 Minutes
Warm-Up

Smiley Design Give small yellow and black paper squares to children. Have children arrange them to form a smiley face. Discuss how each piece was needed.

10-15 Minutes
Teach

Discuss Art Concepts Ask volunteers to read page 126, and use Discussion Card 1 to analyze the mosaics. Share Art History. Explain that a mosaic has *unity* because the parts look like they belong together. Display **Art Print 16**. Have children compare it with the mosaics.

Think Critically

1. (Focus Skill) **READING SKILL** The artists used small pieces to make the mosaics. Describe the effects on the art. CAUSE AND EFFECT
   TAKS Reading Objective 4

2. **How did the artist use color to create unity in the rabbit mosaic?** (The border has the same colors as the picture.)
   PERCEPTION/COMPARE AND CONTRAST   TEKS 2.1B

3. **WRITE** Why do you think the artist made a rabbit mosaic? INDEPENDENT WRITING
   TAKS Writing Objective 1

⭐ **TEKS 2.1A** identify variations in objects and subjects; **TEKS 2.1B** identify elements and principles; **TEKS 2.2B** create effective compositions; **TEKS 2.2C** identify and practice skills; **TEKS 2.4A** define reasons for preferences in personal artworks; **TEKS 2.4B** identify ideas in artworks by peers and artists; *(continued)*

Lesson 26

Vocabulary
mosaic
unity

Mosaics

What do these pictures show? A **mosaic** is an artwork made with small pieces of things like stone, tile, glass, or paper.

 Unknown artist, *Rabbit Devouring a Bunch of Grapes*

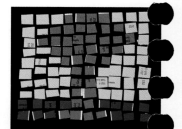 **B** Kaela, grade 2, Student art

When all parts look as if they belong together, the artwork has **unity**. How does each mosaic show unity?

126

Background Information

Art History
The earliest **mosaics** were made from pebbles. Later, cut or shaped pieces of materials such as marble, hard stone, glass, and mother of pearl were used. The pieces, called *tesserae*, were embedded in mortar using various techniques. Mosaic design was very common in ancient Roman art. The designs were often copied from the patterns in rugs made in Asia.

For more information about Roman art, see pp. R48–R59.

Artist's Workshop

Paper-Plate Mosaic

PLAN

Think of a mosaic design for a plate. What patterns or subject will you show?

CREATE

1. Draw a picture. Cut or tear paper and foil into small pieces.

2. Glue the pieces onto the plate to make shapes and patterns.

REFLECT

How does your mosaic show unity?

Where have you seen a mosaic? Tell about it.

127

15-25 Minutes Artist's Workshop

Paper-Plate Mosaic

MATERIALS: paper plate, colored paper, foil, scissors, glue, pencils or markers

TECHNIQUE TIP: Refer children to page 167 for help making a mosaic.

PLAN Suggest that children draw one item large enough to fill most of the plate.

CREATE Have children create a patterned border or use color to help unify their mosaic.
TEKS 2.2B, TEKS 2.2C

REFLECT Have children identify ideas in one another's mosaics, such as variations in the subject and how the mosaic shows unity.
TEKS 2.1A, TEKS 2.4B

Activity Options PDAS Domain IV

Quick Activity Have children outline a design on graph paper and then color the squares.

Early Finishers Children may use Discussion Card 4, p. R36.

Challenge See *Teacher Resource Book*, p. 68.

5-10 Minutes Wrap-Up

Informal Assessment PDAS Domain III

- **In what different ways did your classmates give their mosaics unity?** (Responses will vary.) PERCEPTION/AESTHETICS TEKS 2.1B

- **What do you like best about your mosaic? Why?** (Responses will vary.) ART CRITICISM TEKS 2.4A

Extend Through Writing

Independent Have children write a paragraph describing the subject of their mosaic. Ask them to check that their sentences have describing words that make the description clear.
TAKS Writing Objectives 1, 5

Science Connection

Mosaics from Nature Have children collect small, natural objects, such as pebbles, shells, and seeds and then sort them by color. Have each child sketch a subject. Then have them make mosaics by gluing the objects onto cardboard or putting them into plaster of Paris, clay, or a similar substance.

PDAS Domain IV

ESL Reinforce the meaning of *unity* with a **total physical response** activity. Have children walk randomly around the room. Then call out "unity" and have children join hands in a circle.

Special Needs Have children draw a picture on their plate with colored pencils. Provide pre-cut paper and foil squares.

PDAS Domain I active participation; PDAS Domain II learner-centered instruction; PDAS Domain III evaluation and feedback; PDAS Domain IV classroom management; TAKS Reading Objective 4 apply critical-thinking skills; TAKS Writing Objective 1 composition; TAKS Writing Objective 5 usage

LESSON 26 *Mosaics* 127

Lesson 27

PDAS Domains I, II

Designs of Money

OBJECTIVES
- Identify art principles such as unity
- Create effective money designs
- Recognize cause and effect

RESOURCES
- Art Print 11
- Big Book, pp. 128–129
- Electronic Art Gallery CD-ROM, Primary

5 Minutes

Warm-Up

Sports Symbols   Display sport team names with symbols and discuss with children how some represent strength, swiftness, and so on.

10-15 Minutes

Teach

Discuss Art Concepts   Have children read and discuss pages 128–129. Explain that many countries use **symbols** on their money to represent people and things that are important to the country's culture, history, and location. Display **Art Print 11**. Have children tell where this image appears on U.S. money (penny) and what this image means to them.   TEKS 2.3A

Think Critically

1. **(Focus Skill) READING SKILL**   Why do you think we have pictures of Presidents on our money? (They helped the country.) **Have children compare the individuals.** CAUSE AND EFFECT
   TEKS 2.3B; TAKS Reading Objective 4

2. **How does our one-dollar bill show unity?**
   (Responses will vary.) **PERCEPTION**   TEKS 2.1B

3. **WRITE**   Why do you think these animals are shown on the money? INDEPENDENT WRITING
   TEKS 2.3A; TAKS Writing Objective 1

Lesson 27

Vocabulary
symbol

Designs of Money

A **symbol** is a person or thing that stands for something else. Who is George Washington? What does he stand for?

A One-dollar bill, U.S., front

B One-dollar bill, U.S., back

C Farthings, England

D Twenty peso bill, Mexico

What pictures and symbols do you see on the money? What do you think the symbols tell about the countries?

128

Background Information

Art History

Coins have been used for about 2,500 years. Historians study coins because their symbols provide information about the political history, religion, and culture of the time in which they were made.

The English farthings shown here were issued by King Edward, who reigned from A.D. 1042–1066. Rather than make smaller coins for lower values, coins were cut into fourths. *Farthing* literally meant "a fourth."

For more information about Symbols in art, see pp. R48–R59.

★ **TEKS 2.1B** identify elements and principles; **TEKS 2.2A** express ideas and feelings; **TEKS 2.2B** create effective compositions; **TEKS 2.2C** identify and practice skills; **TEKS 2.3A** identify stories and constructions; **TEKS 2.3B** compare artworks showing individuals/families; **PDAS Domain I** active participation; *(continued)*

How do the coins and bills show unity? Where do you see balance? Emphasis?

 E 1000-yen bill, Japan

F Gold panda coin, China

Gold kangaroo coin, Australia **G**

Artist's Workshop

Money Design

1. **Choose a symbol for your city or state.**

2. **Design a coin or a bill. Make prints.**

129

Artist's Workshop

15-25 Minutes

Money Design

MATERIALS: foam plate, pencil, tempera paints, paintbrushes, paper for printing, scissors

TECHNIQUE TIP: Refer children to page 162 for directions on making prints.

PLAN Have children list and sketch ideas for their symbols. Have them identify the skills necessary to make a print. TEKS 2.2C

CREATE Ask children to create a design with varied lines to express their feelings and ideas about their city or state. Have them practice their print-making skills. TEKS 2.2A, TEKS 2.2B, TEKS 2.2C

REFLECT Have volunteers share their designs and discuss each symbol's meaning. TEKS 2.3A

Activity Options PDAS Domain IV

Quick Activity Children draw and color their coins on round paper or a paper plate.

Early Finishers Ask children to make both a bill and a coin.

Challenge See *Teacher Resource Book*, p. 69.

Wrap-Up

5-10 Minutes

Informal Assessment PDAS Domain III

- **Which symbol did you emphasize? How?**
  (Responses will vary.) ART CRITICISM TEKS 2.1B

- **Which money designs showed unity?**
  (Responses will vary.) PERCEPTION/AESTHETICS TEKS 2.1B

Extend Through Writing ✏

Independent Have children write about why their coins should be used in their city or state. Have them check that their sentences give good reasons and are constructed correctly.
TAKS Writing Objectives 1, 4

 PDAS Domain II

Math Connection

Classroom Store Help children set up a classroom store. Assign roles such as shelf stocker, cashier, and customer. First, have the shelf stockers use self-stick notes to assign a price of a dollar or less to each product. Then have the customers use play money to "shop" in the store.

 PDAS Domain IV

MEETING INDIVIDUAL NEEDS

ESL Use **visuals** to **support comprehension**. Distribute copies of the back of *Picture Cards Collection* Card 79, and have children cut the page into eight separate cards. Partners flip over two cards at a time, matching a label with a coin. See also *Picture Card Bank* CD-ROM, Category: Time/Money.

 money

PDAS Domain II learner-centered instruction; PDAS Domain III evaluation and feedback; PDAS Domain IV classroom management;
TAKS Reading Objective 4 apply critical-thinking skills; TAKS Writing Objective 1 composition; TAKS Writing Objective 4 sentence construction

LESSON 27 *Designs of Money* **129**

PDAS Domains I, II

Mary Cassatt's Treasures

ARTIST BIOGRAPHY

DISCUSS THE PAINTINGS

Have children read pages 130–131.

- Have children describe how Cassatt achieves unity in *Women Admiring a Child*.

- Help children understand the significance of Cassatt's work as it relates to art history. Explain that Mary Cassatt painted in the Impressionist style, experimenting with light, color, and brushstrokes to create impressions of her subjects, not exact images. Ask children what ideas and feelings Cassatt expresses with colors and forms. **TEKS 2.1B**

- Display **Art Print 17**, and have children compare and contrast the way individuals and families are portrayed in this painting and in those on pages 38, 54, 76, 130, and 131. Ask: **What is the subject of the painting? How do you think the people feel about one other? What mood do these paintings have?** **TEKS 2.3B, TEKS 2.4B**

DISCUSS THE ARTIST

Share background information about the artist.

- Explain that when Mary Cassatt was a young girl, she traveled to Europe with her parents and was inspired by the art she saw there. Later, she moved to Paris, France to escape American resistance to both women painters and to new ideas about painting.

- Tell children that Cassatt influenced Americans to begin collecting Impressionist artworks.

Mary Cassatt's Treasures

Mary Cassatt was an American artist who lived most of her life in France. She is best known for her paintings of mothers and children. Cassatt liked to show people in everyday activities. She used light, bright colors in her art.

A *Women Admiring a Child*

130

FYI **Background Information**

About the Artist

Mary Cassatt (kuh•SAT) (1844–1926) was an American painter who spent most of her career living and working in France. She began to study at the Pennsylvania Academy of the Fine Arts when she was sixteen. She later moved to Paris and was invited by her friend Edgar Degas to join the Impressionists. She first exhibited with them in 1879. Mary Cassatt was one of only two women and the only American to join the Impressionists. Most of her works show women and children involved in daily activities.

For more information about Mary Cassatt, see pp. R48–R59.

★ **TEKS 2.1B** identify elements and principles; **TEKS 2.2A** express ideas and feelings; **TEKS 2.2B** create effective compositions; **TEKS 2.3A** identify stories and constructions; **TEKS 2.3B** compare artworks showing individuals/families; **TEKS 2.4B** identify ideas in artworks by peers and artists; *(continued)*

How did Cassatt use lines, shapes, and colors to unify her art?

DID YOU KNOW?

Mary Cassatt later made prints that showed a change in her style of art. She used stronger lines and patterns, like those in Japanese art.

B *Portrait of the Artist*

GO ONLINE **Multimedia Biographies**
Visit *The Learning Site*
www.harcourtschool.com

Think About Art

What everyday activities would you like to paint? Why?

C *Summertime*

131

Social Studies Connection

Museum Visits Cassatt's paintings may be visited in person or online:

- **The Museum of Fine Arts**, Houston. Houston, Texas www.mfah.org

For additional cross-curricular suggestions, see Art Transparency 17.

TEKS 2.4B
Visit with an Artist

Identify Ideas in Artworks
Arrange for children to visit with an artist either at school or at a museum, gallery, or other location. Ask children to view and identify ideas in original artworks, the portfolio, and an exhibition by the artist. Have them focus on concepts from this unit, such as use of unity and variety.

DID YOU KNOW?

Explain to children that in 1890, Mary Cassatt attended an exhibition of Japanese prints. She then created a series of prints influenced by this style. They had simple shapes, flat colors, and strong outlines. Cassatt's style had changed from emphasizing form to emphasizing line and pattern.

Have children look again at the Japanese prints *Macaw on a Pine Branch* on page 106, and *The Great Wave off Kanagawa* on page 108. Ask children to pick a subject and draw it using Cassatt's Impressionist style, and then draw it again using the Japanese print style. Ask them to compare how using different kinds of lines gives the artworks different moods. TEKS 2.2B, TEKS 2.3A

Think About Art

What everyday activities would you like to paint? Why? (Possible response: playing a game with my family, my favorite sports; these are things I enjoy and do often.)

ARTIST'S EYE ACTIVITY

Family/Group Portrait Cassatt was noted for her portraits of mothers and children. She often used members of her own family as models. Have children use oil pastels to create a family portrait or a portrait of other people important to them. Discuss Cassatt's use of color, and have children focus on using a variety of colors to express their own ideas and feelings. TEKS 2.2A

GO ONLINE **Multimedia Biographies**
Visit *The Learning Site*
www.harcourtschool.com

Lesson 28

PDAS Domains I, II
Still Lifes

OBJECTIVES
- Understand how to achieve variety using art elements
- Create an effective still life
- Recognize cause and effect

RESOURCES
- Art Prints 9, 18
- Discussion Card 2
- Big Book, pp. 132–133
- Electronic Art Gallery CD-ROM, Primary

5 Minutes

Warm-Up

Still-Life Dance Play music and have small groups dance. Tell the dancers to be still when the music stops. One child in each group arranges the members in an interesting still-life pose.

10-15 Minutes

Teach

Discuss Art Concepts Have children read page 132. Use Discussion Card 2 for questioning strategies. Explain that a still life can have both living and nonliving objects. Then display **Art Prints 9** and **18**. Have children identify variations in objects and subjects from the environment in these still lifes and those on page 132. TEKS 2.1A

Think Critically

1. **READING SKILL** **Why did the artists use different shapes and colors?** (for variety)
   CAUSE AND EFFECT TEKS 2.1B; TAKS Reading Objective 4

2. **In what ways are the paintings alike and different?** (Both show fruit; one uses bright colors; the other looks softer and more realistic.) PERCEPTION/COMPARE AND CONTRAST
   TAKS Reading Objective 4

3. **WRITE** **Why do you think the artists painted these objects?** INDEPENDENT WRITING
   TAKS Writing Objective 1

132 UNIT 6 *World Treasures*

Lesson 28

Vocabulary
still life
variety

Still Lifes

What objects are in each painting? A group of objects arranged by an artist and then shown in an artwork is a **still life**.

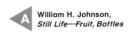
A William H. Johnson, *Still Life—Fruit, Bottles*

Jacob van Hulsdonck, *A Still Life of Fruit and Flowers in a Basket* B

An artwork with different things in it has **variety**. What lines, shapes, colors, and textures are in each still life? How does each show unity?

132

Background Information

About the Artists
William H. Johnson (1901–1970) used an Abstract Expressionist style with rich texture and bright colors inspired by his African American heritage.

Jacob van Hulsdonck (1582–1647) was a Belgian painter noted for his still lifes featuring realistic, textured fruit.

For more information about the artists, see pp. R48–R59.

RECOMMENDED READING
The Jumbo Book of Art by Irene Luxbacher. Kids Can Press, 2003. READ-ALOUD

★ TEKS 2.1A identify variations in objects and subjects; TEKS 2.1B identify elements and principles; TEKS 2.2B create effective compositions; TEKS 2.2C identify and practice skills; TEKS 2.4B identify ideas in artworks by peers and artists; PDAS Domain I active participation; PDAS Domain II learner-centered instruction; *(continued)*

Artist's Workshop

Still-Life Painting

PLAN

Arrange a variety of objects in interesting ways. Put some objects in front of others.

CREATE

1. **Choose the best arrangement and draw it.**

2. **Paint light areas first. Then paint darker areas.**

REFLECT

What lines, shapes, colors, and textures are in your still life?

Away from school, where can you see objects arranged like a still life?

133

 15-25 Minutes

Artist's Workshop

Still-Life Painting

MATERIALS: objects, tempera paints, paintbrushes, white paper, oil pastels, pencils

TECHNIQUE TIP: Arrange objects so they overlap but do not hide one another.

PLAN Have children experiment with different arrangements that have variety and unity. TEKS 2.2C

CREATE Suggest that children first sketch the still life in pencil. TEKS 2.2B, TEKS 2.2C

REFLECT Exhibit the still-life paintings, and have children discuss unity and identify the variety of lines, shapes, colors, and textures. TEKS 2.1B

Activity Options PDAS Domain IV

Quick Activity Arrange a still-life ahead of time for the whole group to draw.

Early Finishers Children can use the Idea Wheel, *Teacher Resource Book*, pp. 29–30.

Challenge See *Teacher Resource Book*, p. 70.

5-10 Minutes

Wrap-Up

Informal Assessment PDAS Domain III

- **Why did you choose the objects you did for your still life?** (Responses will vary.)
  ART CRITICISM

- **What gave the still-life paintings variety?** (Responses will vary.) **PERCEPTION/AESTHETICS**
  TEKS 2.4B

Extend Through Writing ✏️

Independent Have children write a riddle describing their still life. They should check that they used complete sentences with clear describing words and that their sentences are punctuated correctly. TAKS Writing Objectives 1, 2, 5

Science Connection

Seeds Have children identify the living and nonliving objects in the still lifes and describe the characteristics of each. Then cut fruit and have children examine the seeds with a hand lens, plant the seeds, and keep a log of their growth.

PDAS Domain IV

ESL Introduce the names of common fruits and flowers depicted in still-life paintings by using **visuals** to **reinforce new vocabulary**.

Use *Picture Cards Collection* Cards 55 and 57. See also *Picture Card Bank* **CD-ROM**, Categories: Food from Plants, Plants.

fruit

PDAS Domain III evaluation and feedback; **PDAS Domain IV** classroom management; **TAKS Reading Objective 4** apply critical-thinking skills; **TAKS Writing Objective 1** composition; **TAKS Writing Objective 2** conventions; **TAKS Writing Objective 5** usage

LESSON 28 *Still Lifes* **133**

Lesson 29

PDAS Domains I, II
Stories in Cloth Art

OBJECTIVES
- Identify stories and constructions in artworks
- Construct a story-cloth collage
- Recognize cause and effect

RESOURCES
- Art Print 16
- Discussion Card 7
- Big Book, pp. 134–135
- Electronic Art Gallery CD-ROM, Primary

5 Minutes

Warm-Up

Group Story Display an illustration in a story-book without showing the words. Start telling a story about the picture and have children add to it.
TEKS 2.3A

10-15 Minutes

Teach

Discuss Art Concepts Have children read page 134. Then have them tell the story they see in the artwork. Discuss unity and variety. Tell them that threads were sewn on, or **embroidered**, to make the pictures. Then display **Art Print 16**. Ask children how they think this artwork was made and to tell the story they see.
TEKS 2.3A; TAKS Reading Objective 1

Think Critically

1. **READING SKILL** Why might the artist have made this story cloth? (Possible response: to tell others about his or her life)
   CAUSE AND EFFECT TEKS 2.3A; TAKS Reading Objective 4

2. How is the story cloth like other artworks you have seen? (Responses will vary.)
   PERCEPTION/COMPARE AND CONTRAST

3. **WRITE** Write a story about the Hmong village in the story cloth. INDEPENDENT WRITING
   TEKS 2.3A; TAKS Writing Objective 1

Lesson 29

Vocabulary
story cloth

Stories in Cloth Art

What is happening in this piece of art? A **story cloth** is an old form of artwork that tells a story on cloth or other textiles.

Unknown artist, Hmong story cloth of village life

What can you tell about the life of these people from this artwork?

134

Background Information

Art History

The **Hmong people** are originally from China. Political events caused many Hmong people to leave their homeland and live in refugee camps in Vietnam, Laos, and Thailand. While there, the women embroidered beautiful story cloths to record their history and everyday life.

For more information, see Folk art, pp. R48–R59.

RECOMMENDED READING
Nine-in-One GRR! GRR! by Blia Xiong (adapted by Cathy Spagnoli). Children's Book Press, 1989. AVERAGE

---

134 UNIT 6 *World Treasures* ★ TEKS 2.2B create effective compositions; TEKS 2.2C identify and practice skills; TEKS 2.3A identify stories and constructions; TEKS 2.4B identify ideas in artworks by peers and artists; PDAS Domain I active participation; PDAS Domain II learner-centered instruction; PDAS Domain III evaluation and feedback; *(continued)*

Artist's Workshop

Story-Cloth Collage

PLAN

Think about a favorite memory and the story it tells.

CREATE

1. **Draw important parts of your story on cloth or paper.**

2. **Glue cloth and objects onto the picture. Make a border.**

REFLECT

How does your story cloth tell the most important parts of your story?

What other cloth art have you seen? Did it tell a story?

135

Artist's Workshop

15-25 Minutes

Story-Cloth Collage

MATERIALS: pillowcase or paper, glue, fabric paints, tempera paints, brushes, markers, found objects (buttons, ribbon, fabric, yarn), scissors

Safety Tips Remind children to be careful while cutting cloth and other textiles.

PLAN Have children identify and practice the skills necessary for constructing a story-cloth collage. TEKS 2.2C

CREATE Provide various scraps and found objects to add to the story cloth. TEKS 2.2B

REFLECT Have children identify the story shown in each classmate's story collage. TEKS 2.3A

Activity Options   PDAS Domain IV

Quick Activity Children can draw and color the story rather than making a collage.

Early Finishers Have children use Discussion Card 7, p. R39.

Challenge See *Teacher Resource Book*, p. 71.

5-10 Minutes

Wrap-Up

Informal Assessment   PDAS Domain III

- **What ideas for your collage did you get from the Hmong story cloth?** (Responses will vary.) PERCEPTION/AESTHETICS   TEKS 2.4B

- **How did you show what was important?** (Responses will vary.) ART CRITICISM

Extend Through Writing

Independent Ask children to write the story that their collage tells. Have them check that it has a beginning, middle, and ending and that their sentences are constructed correctly.
TEKS 2.3A; TAKS Writing Objectives 1, 3, 4

Social Studies Connection

Locate Countries Tell children that the Hmong moved to Laos, Vietnam, and Thailand. Help children find these countries on a world map. Explain that many Hmong people eventually moved to the United States. Ask volunteers to share experiences of moving.

PDAS Domain IV

ESL Have children **role-play** the scene shown on the Hmong story cloth as you describe what they are doing. Help volunteers to form their own **oral sentences** that describe their actions.

Challenge Have children tape-record a story about the story cloth on page 134 or about the one they made.

PDAS Domain IV classroom management; **TAKS Reading Objective 1** demonstrate understanding of texts; **TAKS Reading Objective 4** apply critical-thinking skills; **TAKS Writing Objective 1** composition; **TAKS Writing Objective 3** organization; **TAKS Writing Objective 4** sentence construction

LESSON 29 *Stories in Cloth Art* **135**

PDAS Domains I, II

Gerald McDermott,
BOOK ILLUSTRATOR

CAREERS IN ART

Have children read pages 136–137.

- Talk about what it means to be a book illustrator. Ask: **What steps do you think an illustrator follows to make pictures for a book? What would you like best about being an illustrator?** TEKS 2.3C

- Have children look again at the characters shown in the illustrations. Ask them to tell what makes the illustrations look as if they were influenced by Native American culture. (Possible responses: The Coyote is blue, the Zuni color for the West; the crow has a Native American necklace; the artwork has patterns that look like those on Native American pottery.) TEKS 2.3A

DISCUSS THE ILLUSTRATOR

Share the background information.

- Tell children that in his job as an illustrator, Gerald McDermott has created over twenty-five books and films. He most often writes and illustrates folk tales that have been passed down by Native Americans and from other cultures around the world. Ask children to describe Gerald McDermott's job in their own words. TEKS 2.3C

- Explain that Gerald McDermott has won the Caldecott Medal, which is an award given each year to a children's book illustrator. Ask children if they have seen it on book covers.

Gerald McDermott,
BOOK ILLUSTRATOR

136

Gerald McDermott is a storyteller and artist for children's books. He began studying art when he was four years old. In *Coyote* he uses bright colors and patterns to tell a trickster tale.

FYI Background Information

About the Artist

Gerald McDermott (1941–) is the author and illustrator of many children's books, including Caldecott Medal winner *Arrow to the Sun* and two Caldecott Honor books, *Raven: A Trickster Tale from the Pacific Northwest* and *Anansi the Spider: A Tale from the Ashanti*. McDermott began studying art at the Detroit Institute of the Arts at the age of four. He is fascinated with mythology, in particular trickster tales from Native American traditions.

For more information about Gerald McDermott, see pp. R48–R59.

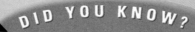

Think About Art

What do you think is happening on this page of the story? Why?

DID YOU KNOW?

The Pueblo people of Zuni use blue as a symbol for the West. That is the reason Gerald McDermott made the character Coyote blue.

137

TEKS 2.2C

Social Studies Connection

The Zuni People Explain that the Zuni people live in the Southwestern United States. Have children research ancient Pueblo homes and construct a model Pueblo village from wood, cardboard, or clay.

For additional cross-curricular suggestions, see Art Transparency 18.

TEKS 2.4B

Student Art Show

Display Artworks Have children create a display of their portfolios and artworks. Ask them to identify ideas in one another's original artworks and portfolios and in the exhibit as a whole. Have them focus on concepts from this unit, such as unity and variety. See also Student Art Exhibitions, page 142.

DID YOU KNOW?

Tell children that the Zuni people of New Mexico believe in six main directions. A certain animal and color represent each direction. The North is the mountain lion (yellow), and the South is the badger (red). The West is the bear (blue), and the East is the wolf (white). Additionally, the mole (black) is the Inner Earth, or down, and the eagle (all colors) is the Sky, or up. Have children identify the Native American colors and symbols in Gerald McDermott's artwork. TEKS 2.3A

Think About Art

What do you think is happening on this page of the story? Why? (Possible responses: Coyote is talking to the crow; he is playing a trick on the crow.) TEKS 2.3A; TAKS Reading Objectives 2, 4

ARTIST'S EYE ACTIVITY

Animal Illustrations Help children develop and organize ideas from the environment. Take a short walk outside to view small animals in the environment or have children view animals in pictures, videos, or in some other way. Ask them to group animals according to art elements such as color, texture, form, line, shape, and space and art principles such as emphasis, pattern, rhythm, and variety.

Discuss Gerald McDermott's illustration style, noting his use of bright colors and geometric shapes to draw things in the environment. Then reread aloud the Did You Know? text from above. Have children create additional illustrations for the story about Coyote. Ask them to color or paint an animal from their environment in one of the symbolic colors, using geometric patterns.
TEKS 2.1B, TEKS 2.2C, TEKS 2.3A

Multimedia Biographies
Visit *The Learning Site*
www.harcourtschool.com

TAKS Reading Objective 2 apply knowledge of literary elements; **TAKS Reading Objective 4** apply critical-thinking skills

UNIT 6 *Gerald McDermott, Book Illustrator* **137**

Lesson 30

PDAS Domains I, II

Art on Stamps

OBJECTIVES
- Identify variety in graphic art
- Design a stamp
- Recognize cause and effect

RESOURCES
- Art Print 11
- Big Book, pp. 138–139
- Electronic Art Gallery CD-ROM, Primary

5 Minutes

Warm-Up

Discuss Stamps Provide small groups with a variety of stamps. Have them study the stamps, comparing and contrasting the designs.

10-15 Minutes

Teach

Discuss Art Concepts Have children read pages 138–139. Tell them that graphic art often includes letters and words as well as pictures. Ask children to discuss the unity and variety shown in these stamps. Share and discuss the Art History information below. Then display **Art Print 11**. Have children decide whether this image would make a good stamp. Tell them that images of President Lincoln have been on many stamps.

Think Critically

1. (Focus Skill) **READING SKILL** Why do countries use art on their stamps? (Responses will vary.)
   CAUSE AND EFFECT TAKS Reading Objective 4

2. **Choose two stamps. How they are alike? How are they different?** (Responses will vary.) PERCEPTION/COMPARE AND CONTRAST TEKS 2.1A

3. **WRITE** Write a story one of these stamps might tell about the country it is from.
   INDEPENDENT WRITING TEKS 2.3A; TAKS Writing Objective 1

Lesson 30

Vocabulary

graphic art

Art on Stamps

Which of these stamps is your favorite? Why? Stamp designs are examples of **graphic art**—art used on products.

A Ashley, *Dog Stamp*—U.S.

B Olympic Soccer—Ghana, Africa

D *Greetings from Texas*—U.S.

C Beetle—Nicaragua

Some people buy or collect stamps because of the art. You can also see graphic art on money, signs, TV ads, and websites.

138

Background Information

Art History

Postage stamps date back to May 6, 1840, when the United Kingdom issued the first government-printed stamp. The stamp cost one penny and depicted Queen Victoria. In 1847, the United States printed its first stamps, a 5-cent stamp picturing Benjamin Franklin and a 10-cent stamp picturing George Washington.

For more information about Graphic arts, see pp. R48–R59.

RECOMMENDED READING
Mailing May by Michael O. Tunnell. Greenwillow, 1997.
READ-ALOUD

⭐ TEKS 2.1A identify variations in objects and subjects; TEKS 2.1B identify elements and principles; TEKS 2.2C identify and practice skills; TEKS 2.3A identify stories and constructions; TEKS 2.4A identify reasons for preferences in personal artworks; PDAS Domain I active participation; *(continued)*

What are the subjects of these stamps? What stories do some of these artworks tell? How do the stamps show unity and variety?

 Two cowboys—Poland

 Heroes—U.S.

Artist's Workshop

Stamp of the Future

1. **Draw a stamp that shows the future.**

2. **Add color. Give your stamp a title.**

139

Artist's Workshop
15-25 Minutes

Stamp of the Future

MATERIALS: construction paper, scissors, oil pastels, watercolor paints, paintbrushes

TECHNIQUE TIP: Have children experiment in their sketchbooks or on a computer with different kinds of lettering and graphic designs. TEKS 2.2C

PLAN Have children brainstorm ideas about what the future may be like.

CREATE Have children glue their finished stamps onto paper cut to look like a stamp's edges. TEKS 2.2C

REFLECT Ask children to share their stamps and tell why they designed them as they did. TEKS 2.4A

Activity Options PDAS Domain IV

Quick Activity Distribute copies of the stamp template from *Teacher Resource Book*, p. 36.

Early Finishers Children can use the Idea Wheel, *Teacher Resource Book*, pp. 29–30.

Challenge See *Teacher Resource Book*, p. 72.

5-10 Minutes

Wrap-Up

Informal Assessment PDAS Domain III

- **Which stamp would you most want for a stamp collection? Tell why.** (Responses will vary.) PERCEPTION/AESTHETICS

- **Which stamps are good examples of unity and variety?** (Responses will vary.) ART CRITICISM

Extend Through Writing

Independent Ask children to explain which art elements and principles they used in their stamp designs. Have them check that they used a variety of sentences and that the sentences are constructed correctly. TEKS 2.1B; TAKS Writing Objectives 1, 4

Social Studies Connection

Stamps from Around the World
Organize children into small groups, and assign each group a stamp from pages 138–139. Have them locate on a map where the stamp is from. Guide them in researching the place.

Suggest that children whose families receive mail from overseas bring in the stamps.

PDAS Domain IV

ESL Use **visuals** to support **comprehensible input** for concepts related to the post office. Then have children **pantomime** writing, addressing, stamping, and mailing letters. **Model** oral sentences describing the activities.

Use *Picture Cards Collection* cards 76 and 94.

postcard

PDAS Domain II learner-centered instruction; PDAS Domain III evaluation and feedback; PDAS Domain IV classroom management; TAKS Reading Objective 4 apply critical-thinking skills; TAKS Writing Objective 1 composition; TAKS Writing Objective 4 sentence construction

LESSON 30 *Art on Stamps* **139**

Unit 6

Review and Reflect

In this unit, children have learned about the principles of unity and variety in art. You may want to use **Art Prints 16–18**, **9**, **11** and Discussion Cards 1 and 2 to review how artists use these principles.

Vocabulary and Concepts

Review art vocabulary by having children choose the best item to complete each sentence.

1. B, symbol

2. B, mosaic

3. D, variety

4. C, still life

5. A, unity

6. C, story cloth

Art Parade   For further review, have children create simple costumes and dress as their favorite **element**, such as line, shape, color, value, form, space, or texture or as their favorite **principle**, such as pattern, rhythm, movement, balance, emphasis, unity, or variety. Encourage children to be creative. Have a parade, and ask children to identify the elements and principles and talk about the different ways the elements and principles were portrayed. TEKS 2.1B

Unit 6 Review and Reflect

Vocabulary and Concepts

Choose the best answer to complete each sentence.

1. A _____ stands for something.
   - **A** graphic art
   - **B** symbol
   - **C** variety
   - **D** still life

2. An artwork with small pieces of paper glued together is a _____.
   - **A** variety
   - **B** mosaic
   - **C** symbol
   - **D** unity

3. An artwork with many different kinds of things in it has _____.
   - **A** mosaic
   - **B** symbol
   - **C** still life
   - **D** variety

4. A painting of flowers in a vase is a _____.
   - **A** story cloth
   - **B** graphic art
   - **C** still life
   - **D** mosaic

5. An artwork with parts that all belong together has _____.
   - **A** unity
   - **B** story cloth
   - **C** graphic art
   - **D** still life

6. Textiles are used to make a _____.
   - **A** still life
   - **B** mosaic
   - **C** story cloth
   - **D** symbol

140

Home and Community Connection

School-Home Connection

Copy and distribute *Teacher Resource Book* pp. 87–88 to provide family members with information and activities they can use with children to reinforce concepts taught in this unit.

Community Connection

You may wish to invite local artists, craftspeople, and other community members to share in a year-end exhibition and celebration of art.

---

140 – **UNIT 6**   *World Treasures*   ★   **TEKS 2.1B** identify elements and principles; **TEKS 2.4A** define reasons for preferences in personal artworks; **TEKS 2.4B** identify ideas in artworks by peers and artists; **PDAS Domain I** active participation; **PDAS Domain III** evaluation and feedback; **TAKS Reading Objective 3** use a variety of strategies; **TAKS Writing Objective 1** composition

Focus Skill READING SKILL

Cause and Effect

Reread page 130. Then look at *Women Admiring a Child*. Make a cause-and-effect chart. Tell what is happening and why.

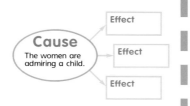

Write About Art

Write a cause-and-effect paragraph about the painting *Summertime*. Tell what the people are doing on the boat and why.

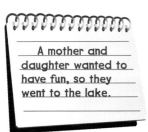

A mother and daughter wanted to have fun, so they went to the lake.

Mary Cassatt, *Summertime*

141

TEKS 2.4A; PDAS Domain III

Assessment

Portfolio Assessment

Have children choose one artwork from this unit to include in their portfolios. Ask them to review each Artist's Workshop activity, select the piece they like best, and tell why they chose it. Provide feedback about children's use of elements, principles, and techniques. See also Portfolio Recording Form, page R32.

Additional Assessment Options

*   Progress Recording Form, p. R33
*   Artist's Workshop Rubrics (Self/Teacher and Peer), pp. R30–R31
*   Unit Test, *Teacher Resource Book*, p. 96

Focus Skill READING SKILL

Cause and Effect

Draw the chart on the board. Then have children reread page 130 and look at *Women Admiring a Child*. Have them complete the chart.
TAKS Reading Objective 3

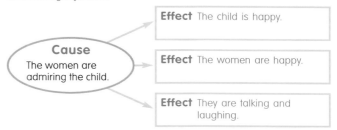

Write About Art

Cause-and-Effect Paragraph Review with children the details of the painting *Summertime*. Tell them to use what they see in the painting and what they know about cause and effect as they write. Children can plan by making a cause-and-effect chart. TAKS Writing Objective 1

Critic's Corner

RESPONSE/EVALUATION Have children select their favorite artwork from this unit. Follow these steps to discuss it.

Describe Ask children to describe the subject of the artwork they chose.

Analyze Tell children to describe how the artist achieved unity and variety. If symbols are present, have children tell what they think they represent.

Interpret Have children tell about the ideas the artist might have been trying to express. TEKS 2.4B

Evaluate Have children tell whether or not they would like to have the artwork displayed in their classroom and give reasons why.

 TAKS Test Preparation: Reading and Writing Through Art, pp. 26–36

Student Art Exhibitions

When children display their work in art exhibitions, they gain confidence in their abilities to create and evaluate artworks.

PREPARATION

- Decide whether to hold an exhibition at the end of the school year as a culminating activity or at intervals throughout the year.
- Decide whether to include the work of several grade levels or groups or just one at a time.
- Help children create and distribute invitations to family members, friends, and classmates.
- Guide children in mounting, framing, and labeling their artworks to prepare them for display. See Displaying Artwork, *Teacher Edition,* page R23, and *Teacher Resource Book,* page 31, for ideas.

John Mendez
My Pet Dino
2005, oil pastels
Mrs. Lew's 2nd Grade Class
Pillit Elementary School

▲ **display card**

DISPLAYS

Two-Dimensional Artworks
- Tack to bulletin boards in the classroom or hallway.
- Clip with clothespins to drying racks or a clothesline.
- Line up along chalk trays.
- Prop up on makeshift easels.

Three-Dimensional Artworks
- Place on a large table, bookcase, or group of desks.
- Cover surfaces with cloth or colored paper.
- Place boxes of varying heights under the cloth.
- Arrange larger artworks behind smaller ones.

RECORDING THE EVENT

- Videotape the art show in progress.
- Take digital photographs before and during the art show. You can use these images to create a slide show or a digital portfolio.

Resources and Correlations

Using the
Student Handbook

Introduce the Student Handbook by having children turn to page 143. Do a walk-through with children, explaining how they can use the sections throughout the year.

USING THE MAPS OF MUSEUMS AND ART SITES

Guide children in looking at the maps on pages 144–147 of the Student Handbook.

- Explain that art comes from all over our country and the world and that these maps show only a small number of the world's art museums and art sites.
- Model how to find one site on the map and the corresponding art in the *Student Edition.*
- Have volunteers locate and discuss art sites.

Use these optional map activities to extend the learning.

PASSPORT TO ART

MATERIALS: *Teacher Resource Book,* page 33; markers; stapler; stamping pad and stamps (optional)

DIRECTIONS:

- Give children a copy of *Teacher Resource Book,* page 33.
- Children staple blank pages inside the cover.
- Have a volunteer select and read aloud a numbered site on the World Map.
- Children turn to the corresponding page in their art books, read the caption, and discuss the art.
- On the blank pages in their passports, children write the name of the art, artist, and place the art is displayed or from.
- Children might also "stamp" their passports to show they have "visited" this country's art.

ARTIST'S TOOLBOX

MATERIALS: photographs or real examples of a paintbrush, camera, pencil, oil pastels, glue, clay tool, and hammer and chisel; paper; small box

DIRECTIONS:

- Display the art tools or pictures of the tools at the front of the room. Discuss how each is used in art.
- Write the city and state or country names from the map sites on slips of paper, and place them in a box.
- Small groups select one slip of paper, locate the site, and then turn to the page where the art appears.
- Children discuss which tool(s) they believe the artist used to make the artwork.

ALL ABOARD

MATERIALS: index cards, markers, small box

DIRECTIONS:

- Write each number and site on the U.S. map on an index card.
- A volunteer is chosen to become Conductor and stands in front of the classroom. Give the Conductor a box containing the complete set of index cards with the site names.
- The Conductor chooses one card from the box and reads it aloud.
- The child who can locate the corresponding art first, name it, and hold up the page for classmates to see becomes the next Conductor.

 Use the **Electronic Art Gallery, CD-ROM, Primary,** for additional images in the United States.

Student Handbook

CONTENTS

142

143

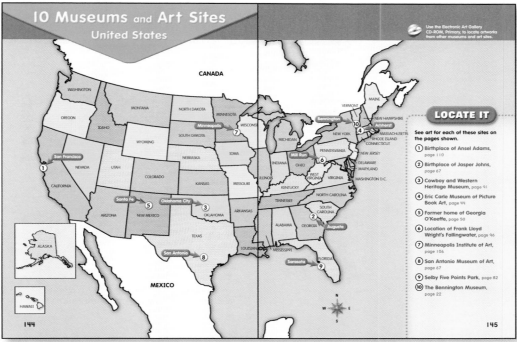

10 Museums and Art Sites
United States

Use the Electronic Art Gallery CD-ROM, Primary, to locate artworks from other museums and art sites.

CANADA

WASHINGTON
OREGON
IDAHO
MONTANA
NORTH DAKOTA
MINNESOTA
WISCONSIN
Minneapolis ⑦
MICHIGAN
VERMONT
MAINE
Bennington
⑩ NEW HAMPSHIRE
④ Amherst
MASSACHUSETTS
RHODE ISLAND
CONNECTICUT
NEW YORK
San Francisco ①
NEVADA
UTAH
WYOMING
SOUTH DAKOTA
NEBRASKA
IOWA
ILLINOIS
INDIANA
OHIO
Mill Run ⑥
PENNSYLVANIA
NEW JERSEY
DELAWARE
MARYLAND
WEST VIRGINIA
VIRGINIA
WASHINGTON D.C.
CALIFORNIA
ARIZONA
NEW MEXICO
Santa Fe ⑤
Oklahoma City ③
OKLAHOMA
COLORADO
KANSAS
MISSOURI
KENTUCKY
TENNESSEE
NORTH CAROLINA
SOUTH CAROLINA
ARKANSAS
MISSISSIPPI
ALABAMA
GEORGIA ②
Augusta
San Antonio ⑧
TEXAS
LOUISIANA
Sarasota ⑨
FLORIDA
ALASKA
HAWAII
MEXICO

LOCATE IT

See art for each of these sites on the pages shown.

① Birthplace of Ansel Adams, page 110
② Birthplace of Jasper Johns, page 67
③ Cowboy and Western Heritage Museum, page 91
④ Eric Carle Museum of Picture Book Art, page 44
⑤ Former home of Georgia O'Keeffe, page 50
⑥ Location of Frank Lloyd Wright's Fallingwater, page 96
⑦ Minneapolis Institute of Art, page 106
⑧ San Antonio Museum of Art, page 67
⑨ Selby Five Points Park, page 82
⑩ The Bennington Museum, page 22

144

145

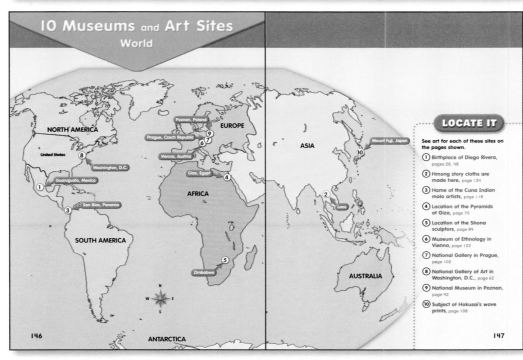

10 Museums and Art Sites
World

NORTH AMERICA
United States ⑧
Washington, D.C.
Guanajuato, Mexico ①
San Blas, Panama ③
SOUTH AMERICA
Poznan, Poland ⑨
Prague, Czech Republic ⑦ ⑥
EUROPE
Vienna, Austria
Giza, Egypt ④
AFRICA
Zimbabwe ⑤
ASIA
Mount Fuji, Japan ⑩
② Laos
AUSTRALIA
ANTARCTICA

LOCATE IT

See art for each of these sites on the pages shown.

① Birthplace of Diego Rivera, pages 26, 48
② Hmong story cloths are made here, page 134
③ Home of the Cuna Indian mola artists, page 118
④ Location of the Pyramids of Giza, page 70
⑤ Location of the Shona sculptors, page 84
⑥ Museum of Ethnology in Vienna, page 122
⑦ National Gallery in Prague, page 102
⑧ National Gallery of Art in Washington, D.C., page 62
⑨ National Museum in Poznan, page 42
⑩ Subject of Hokusai's wave prints, page 108

146

147

Art Safety

Use only materials your teacher says are safe.

Use tools carefully. Keep them away from your face.

Keep art materials out of your mouth.

Clean up spills right away.

Wear a smock when you use messy materials.

Never run with scissors or other sharp objects.

Keep the area around you neat.

Wash your hands after making art.

148

149

Art Techniques

DRAWING
Pencil

Press lightly to make light lines.

Press harder to make dark lines.

Tilt the tip to make thick lines.

Make dots with the tip.

DRAWING
Markers

You can make dots and circles.

Make thin lines with the tip.

Use the side to make thick lines.

Put the cap on when you are done.

150

151

Art Techniques

DRAWING
Crayons

Make thin lines and dots with the tip.

Tilt the tip to make thick lines.

Make big dots with the bottom.

Color big spaces with the side.

DRAWING
Oil Pastels

Make light and dark lines.

Color big spaces with the side.

Blend colors with a paper towel.

Add colors on top of other colors.

152

153

PAINTING
Mixing Colors

1. Dip the brush in a color. Put the paint on a plate or tray.

2. Rinse the brush. Blot. Dip it into another color.

3. Mix the colors. Use the new color.

4. Rinse and blot between colors.

154

PAINTING
Tempera

Use a wide brush for thick lines and big spaces.

Use a thin brush for details.

Try making short, fast strokes.

Try holding your brush different ways. See what kinds of lines you can make.

155

PAINTING
Watercolor

1. Drip water onto each color. Get paint on the brush.

2. Mix colors on a tray or plate.

Press hard to make thick lines. Press lightly to make thin lines.

Paint on wet paper. Make a wash.

156

PAINTING
Crayon Resist

1. Draw with crayons or oil pastels.

2. Color the picture. Press hard.

3. Paint over the drawing with watercolors.

4. The drawing shows through.

157

CLAY
Pinch Pot

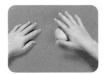

1. Roll clay into a ball.

2. Push down in the middle with your thumbs.

3. Pull up the sides. Try to make them even.

4. Smooth out the sides.

158

CLAY
Sculpture

1. Roll clay into an oval.

2. Pull out a part for the head.

3. Pull out parts for the arms and legs. Make the legs thick.

4. Smooth out the sculpture. Add details.

159

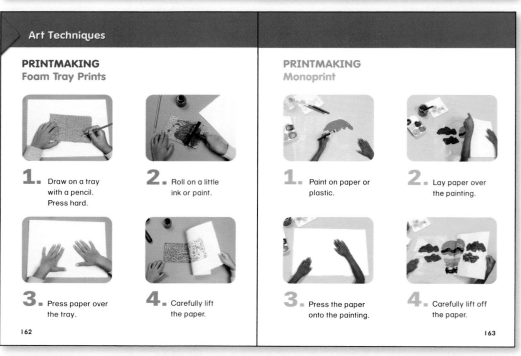

Art Techniques

PRINTMAKING
Sponge Prints

1. Cut shapes from a sponge.

2. Wet the sponge. Dip it in paint.

3. Press onto paper.

4. Use a new sponge for each color.

160

PRINTMAKING
Stencils

1. Draw shapes on thick paper.

2. Cut them out from the inside.

Paint inside the stencil with a brush.

Paint inside the stencil with a sponge.

161

Art Techniques

PRINTMAKING
Foam Tray Prints

1. Draw on a tray with a pencil. Press hard.

2. Roll on a little ink or paint.

3. Press paper over the tray.

4. Carefully lift the paper.

162

PRINTMAKING
Monoprint

1. Paint on paper or plastic.

2. Lay paper over the painting.

3. Press the paper onto the painting.

4. Carefully lift off the paper.

163

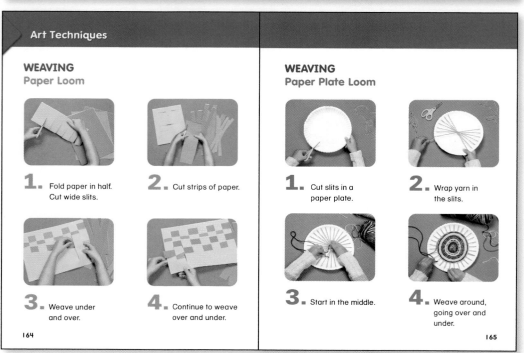

Art Techniques

WEAVING
Paper Loom

1. Fold paper in half. Cut wide slits.

2. Cut strips of paper.

3. Weave under and over.

4. Continue to weave over and under.

164

WEAVING
Paper Plate Loom

1. Cut slits in a paper plate.

2. Wrap yarn in the slits.

3. Start in the middle.

4. Weave around, going over and under.

165

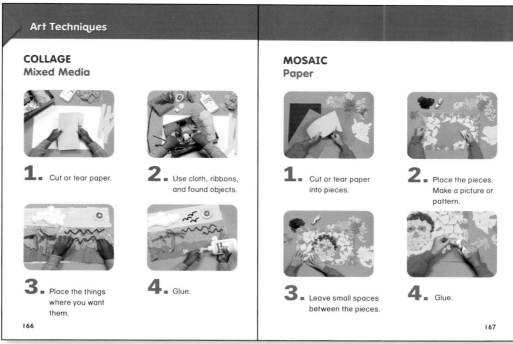

COLLAGE
Mixed Media

1. Cut or tear paper.

2. Use cloth, ribbons, and found objects.

3. Place the things where you want them.

4. Glue.

166

MOSAIC
Paper

1. Cut or tear paper into pieces.

2. Place the pieces. Make a picture or pattern.

3. Leave small spaces between the pieces.

4. Glue.

167

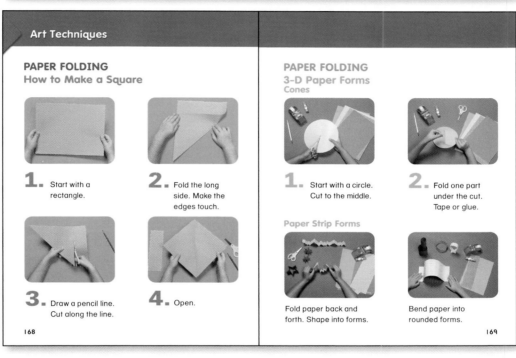

PAPER FOLDING
How to Make a Square

1. Start with a rectangle.

2. Fold the long side. Make the edges touch.

3. Draw a pencil line. Cut along the line.

4. Open.

168

PAPER FOLDING
3-D Paper Forms
Cones

1. Start with a circle. Cut to the middle.

2. Fold one part under the cut. Tape or glue.

Paper Strip Forms

Fold paper back and forth. Shape into forms.

Bend paper into rounded forms.

169

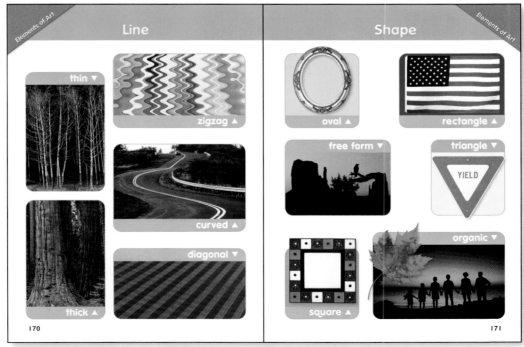

Line

thin ▼

zigzag ▲

curved ▲

diagonal ▼

thick ▲

170

Shape

oval ▲

rectangle ▼

free form ▼

triangle ▼

YIELD

square ▲

organic ▼

171

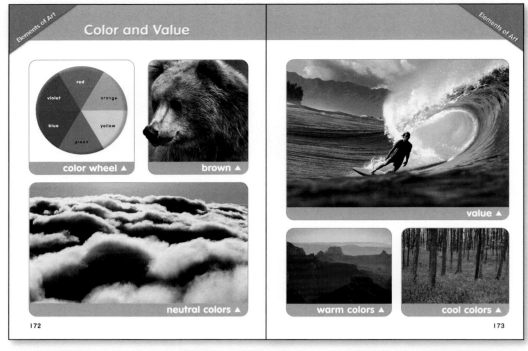

Elements of Art

Color and Value

red
orange
yellow
green
blue
violet

color wheel ▲

brown ▲

neutral colors ▲

value ▲

warm colors ▲

cool colors ▲

172

173

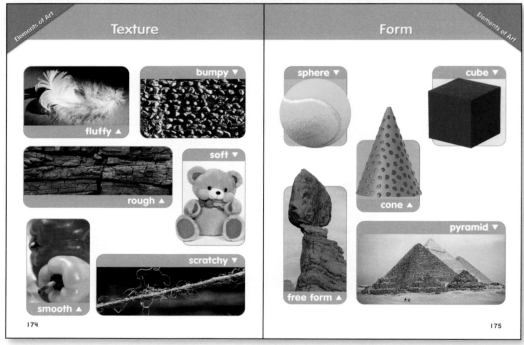

Elements of Art

Texture

bumpy ▼

fluffy ▲

soft ▼

rough ▲

smooth ▲

scratchy ▼

174

Elements of Art

Form

sphere ▼

cube ▼

cone ▲

free form ▲

pyramid ▼

175

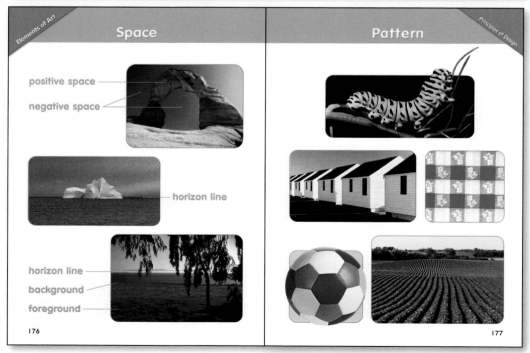

Elements of Art

Space

positive space

negative space

horizon line

horizon line

background

foreground

176

Principles of Design

Pattern

177

Rhythm and Movement
Principles of Design

178

Balance
Principles of Design

179

Emphasis
Principles of Design

180

Variety and Unity
Principles of Design

variety ▼

variety ▲

unity ▲

181

Gallery of Artists

Ansel Adams
(1902–1984) page 110

Buckeye Blake
(1946–) page 91

Sofonisba Anguissola
(1532–1625) pages 42–43

Pieter Brueghel
the Elder
(1525?–1569)
pages 102–103

Thomas Hart Benton
(1889–1975) pages 62–63

182

Deborah Butterfield
(1949–) page 88

Edna Crawford
(1968–) pages 56–57

Eric Carle
(1929–) page 44

Nancy Curry
(1961–) page 74

Mary Cassatt
(1844–1926) pages 130–131

183

Gallery of Artists

Edgar Degas
(1834–1917) page 114

Albrecht Dürer
(1471–1528) page 78

Abastenia St. Leger Eberle
(1878–1942) page 28

Flor Garduño
(1957–) page 111

Paul Gauguin
(1848–1903) page 104

Glenna Goodacre
(1939–) pages 82–83

Jonathan Green
(1955–) page 46

Ann Hanson
(1959–) page 78

Ichiryusai Hiroshige
(1797–1858) page 106

Katsushika Hokusai
(1760–1849) page 108

184

185

Gallery of Artists

Winslow Homer
(1836–1910) page 58

Luis Jaso
(1926–1983) page 38

Jasper Johns
(1930–) page 67

William H. Johnson
(1901–1970) page 132

Frida Kahlo
(1907–1954) pages 116–117

Phillip King
(1934–) page 86

Jacob Lawrence
(1917–2000) pages 76–77

Doris Lee
(1905–1983) page 33

Gerhard Marcks
(1889–1981) page 88

Henri Matisse
(1869–1954) pages 34, 106

186

187

Gallery of Artists

Gerald McDermott
(1941–) pages 136–137

Claude Monet
(1840–1926) pages 49, 98

Grandma Moses
(1860–1961) pages 22–23

Miriam Tewaguna Nampeyo
(1956–) page 86

Georgia O'Keeffe
(1887–1986) pages 50–51

I. M. Pei
(1917–) page 95

Pablo Picasso
(1881–1973) pages 26, 36–37

Brian Pinkney
(1961–) page 24

Rembrandt van Rijn
(1606–1669) page 115

Diego Rivera
(1886–1957) pages 28, 48

188

189

R10 *ART EVERYWHERE*

Norman Rockwell
(1894–1978) page 124

Wayne Thiebaud
(1920–) page 32

Henri Rousseau
(1844–1910) pages 27, 72

Suzanne Valadon
(1865–1938) page 52

Amos Supuni
(1970–) page 84

Vincent van Gogh
(1853–1890) page 54

Frank Lloyd Wright
(1867–1959) pages 96–97

Jacob van Hulsdonck
(1582–1647) page 132

Stefano Vitale
(1958–) page 64

190

191

Glossary

abstract   balance

A

abstract [ab′strakt]
Artwork with lines, shapes, and colors used in a way that does not look real. (page 36)

architect [är′kə•tekt]
A person who plans and designs buildings, bridges, or cities. (page 94)

architecture [är′kə•tek•chər]
The art and science of planning buildings. (page 94)

B

background [bak′ground]
The part of an artwork that seems farthest away. (page 98)

balance [bal′əns]
An arrangement of parts of an artwork that makes the parts seem equal. (page 112)

color wheel   emphasis

C

color wheel [kul′er (h)wēl]
A chart that shows primary and secondary colors in rainbow order. (page 47)

contrast [kon′trast]
A big difference between two parts of an artwork, like the difference between a light and a dark color. (page 114)

cool colors [kōōl kul′erz]
Colors such as blue, green, and violet that give a feeling of coolness and calmness. (page 48)

D

design [di•zīn′]
A plan for the way lines, shapes, and colors are placed in an artwork. (page 118)

E

emphasis [em′fə•sis]
The use of size, shape, or color to make part of an artwork stand out. (page 106)

192

193

foreground   graphic art

F

foreground [fôr′ground]
The part of an artwork that seems closest. (page 98)

form [fôrm]
An object that is not flat. It has height, width, and depth. (page 86)

free-form shapes
[frē′fôrm shāps]
Curved or uneven shapes that are not geometric. (page 34)

G

geometric shapes
[jē•ə•met′rik shāps]
Shapes used in math that have simple lines and curves, such as squares, triangles, and circles. (page 32)

graphic art [graf′ik ärt]
Designs used on products, such as signs and TV ads. (page 138)

horizon line   mosaic

H

horizon line [hə•rī′zən līn]
The place where the land or water meets the sky. (page 58)

L

landscape [land′skāp]
An outdoor scene showing things like fields, trees, gardens, roads, and mountains. (page 98)

lines [līnz]
Marks that go from one point to another and that can be thin, thick, straight, curved, or zigzag. (page 26)

M

mood [mōōd]
The way an artwork makes you feel, such as happy or sad. (page 54)

mosaic [mō•zā′ik]
An artwork made by fitting together small pieces of glass, tile, stone, or paper. (page 126)

194

195

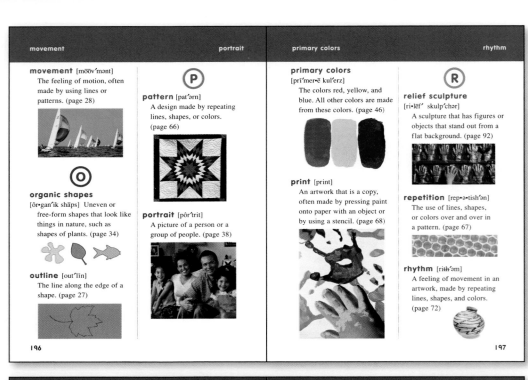

movement [mōōv′mənt]
The feeling of motion, often made by using lines or patterns. (page 28)

O

organic shapes
[ôr•gan′ik shāps] Uneven or free-form shapes that look like things in nature, such as shapes of plants. (page 34)

outline [out′līn]
The line along the edge of a shape. (page 27)

P

pattern [pat′ərn]
A design made by repeating lines, shapes, or colors. (page 66)

portrait [pôr′trit]
A picture of a person or a group of people. (page 38)

196

primary colors
[prī′mer•ē kul′erz]
The colors red, yellow, and blue. All other colors are made from these colors. (page 46)

print [print]
An artwork that is a copy, often made by pressing paint onto paper with an object or by using a stencil. (page 68)

R

relief sculpture
[ri•lēf′ skulp′chər]
A sculpture that has figures or objects that stand out from a flat background. (page 92)

repetition [rep•ə•tish′ən]
The use of lines, shapes, or colors over and over in a pattern. (page 67)

rhythm [rith′əm]
A feeling of movement in an artwork, made by repeating lines, shapes, and colors. (page 72)

197

S

sculpture [skulp′chər]
An artwork, often made from stone, wood, metal, or clay, that has height, width, and depth. (page 88)

seascape [sē′skāp]
A picture that has a water setting, such as the ocean or the sea. (page 58)

secondary colors
[sek′ən•der•ē kul′erz]
The colors orange, green, and violet, each made by mixing two primary colors. (page 46)

self-portrait [self′•pôr′trit]
An artist's picture of himself or herself. (page 38)

shade [shād]
A darker color made by adding black to a color. (page 52)

198

space [spās]
The empty areas within, between, above, below, or around objects or parts of an artwork. (page 88)

still life [stil līf]
An artwork that shows objects arranged in an interesting way. (page 132)

story cloth [stôr′ē klôth]
An artwork on cloth or other textiles that tells a story. (page 134)

subject [sub′jikt]
What an artwork is about. (page 108)

symbol [sim′bəl]
A person or object that has a special meaning and stands for something else. (page 128)

199

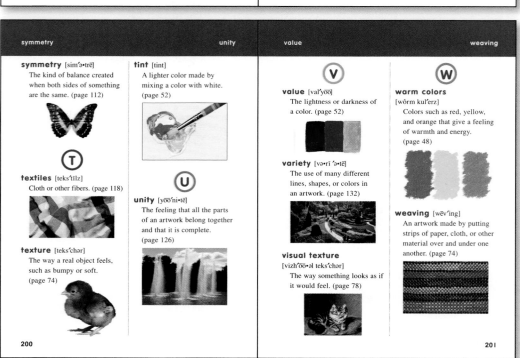

symmetry [sim′ə•trē]
The kind of balance created when both sides of something are the same. (page 112)

T

textiles [teks′tilz]
Cloth or other fibers. (page 118)

texture [teks′chər]
The way a real object feels, such as bumpy or soft. (page 74)

tint [tint]
A lighter color made by mixing a color with white. (page 52)

U

unity [yōō′ni•tē]
The feeling that all the parts of an artwork belong together and that it is complete. (page 126)

200

V

value [val′yōō]
The lightness or darkness of a color. (page 52)

variety [və•rī ′ə•tē]
The use of many different lines, shapes, or colors in an artwork. (page 132)

visual texture
[vizh′ōō•əl teks′chər]
The way something looks as if it would feel. (page 78)

W

warm colors
[wôrm kul′erz]
Colors such as red, yellow, and orange that give a feeling of warmth and energy. (page 48)

weaving [wēv′ing]
An artwork made by putting strips of paper, cloth, or other material over and under one another. (page 74)

201

Index of Artists and Artworks

Index

Acknowledgments

Index

Acknowledgments

For permission to reprint copyrighted material, grateful acknowledgment is made to the following sources:

Flint Public Library, 1026 East Kearsley, Flint, MI 48502–1994: "Two Little Friends" (Retitled: "Friends") from *Ring a Ring o' Roses: Finger Plays for Pre-School Children,* 11th Edition. Text copyright © 1996 by Flint Public Library.

Tim Gallagher: From "Harvest Breeze" by Tim Gallagher in *Sunflower Road Journal.* Text copyright © 1990–2002 by Tim Gallagher.

Harcourt, Inc.: Cover illustration from *Coyote: A Trickster Tale from the American Southwest* by Gerald McDermott. Copyright © 1994 by Gerald McDermott.

HarperCollins Publishers: Cover illustration from *Dinosaur Bob and His Adventures with the Family Lazardo* by William Joyce. Copyright © 1988, 1996 by William Joyce. "Stardust Crooner" illustration from *The World of William Joyce Scrapbook* by William Joyce. Illustration copyright © 1997 by William Joyce.

Felice Holman: "At the Top of My Voice" from *At the Top of My Voice and Other Poems* by Felice Holman. Text copyright © 1970 by Felice Holman. Published by Charles Scribner's Sons.

Photo Credits

Page Placement Key: (t)-top (c)-center (b)-bottom (l)-left (r)-right

All photos property of Harcourt except the following:

Frontmatter

6 (tr) Roger Wood / Corbis; 7 (bc) Miriam Tewogians / Harcourt; (tr) Blackstar / Harcourt; 8 (tl) Araldo de Lucia / Corbis; 12 Harper Collins Publishers; 14 (t) David Butow / Corbis Saba; 15 (t) Geoffrey Clements / Corbis; (b) LM Otero / AP / Wide World; 16 Francis G. Mayer / Corbis; 19 (t) Royalty-Free / Corbis (cl) Alamy Images; 20 (bl) Alamy Images; (tr) Steve Terrill / Corbis; 21 Royalty-Free / Corbis; (c) Alamy Images; (b) Koji Kitagawa / Superstock.

Unit 1

22 Grandma Moses, Autumn / Collections of the Bennington Museum, Bennington, VT / Copyright © 1985 Grandma Moses Properties Co., New York; 23 (b) Bettmann / Corbis; 24 Reprinted with the permission of Simon & Schuster Books for Young Readers, an imprint of Simon & Schuster Children's Publishing Division from *Max Found Two Sticks* by Brian Pinkney. Copyright © 1994 Brian Pinkney; 26 © 2006 The Estate of Pablo Picasso / Artist Rights Society (ARS), New York / Art Resource, NY; 27 (t) The Metropolitan Museum of Art, Gift of Marshall Field, 1929, (29. 15); 28 (t) Scholkopf / Art Resource, NY; 29 (b) Gift of Mrs. W.E. Chilton II / National Museum of Women in the Arts; 30 (tl) John and Lisa Merrill / Corbis; (bl) Owaki-Kulla / Corbis; 31 (tl) The Purcell Team / Corbis; (br) Andrew J.G. Bell; Eye Ubiquitous / Corbis; 32 Wayne Thiebaud, *Desserts* / The UBS Art Collection / Licensed by VAGA, New York; 33 (t) Gift of Wallace and Wilhelmina Holladay / National Museum of Women in the Arts; 34 © 2006 Succession H. Matisse, Paris / Artist Rights Society (ARS), New York; The Bridgeman Art Library; 36 © 2006 The Estate of Pablo Picasso / Artist Rights Society (ARS), New York / Digital Image © The Museum

of Modern Art / Licensed by SCALA / Art Resource, NY; 37 (t) © 2006 The Estate of Pablo Picasso / Artist Rights Society (ARS), New York / Philadelphia Museum of Art / Corbis; (b) © 2006 The Estate of Pablo Picasso / Artist Rights Society (ARS), New York / Giraudon / Art Resource, NY; 38 (t) Antonia Monte / Parkview Elementary, Miami, FL; (b) Lee Jaso; V- (b) Grandma Moses, Autumn / Collections of the Bennington Museum, Bennington, VT / Copyright © 1985 Grandma Moses Properties Co., New York.

Unit 2

42 Ali Meyer / Corbis; 43 Scala / Art Resource, NY; 44 Eric Carle Studio; 46 Balloons For A Dime, 1946, Acrylic on Paper, 15" x 22" - Jonathan Green; 48 Diego Rivera Museum, Guanajuato, Mexico; 49 (t) Museo d'Orsay, Paris / Bridgeman Art Library, London / Superstock; 50 © 2006 The Georgia O'Keeffe Foundation / Artist Rights Society (ARS), New York / Columbus Museum of Art, Ohio; 51 (t) National Portrait Gallery, Smithsonian Institution / Art Resource, NY; 52 © 2006 The Georgia O'Keeffe Foundation / Artist Rights Society (ARS), New York; The Nelson-Atkins Museum of Art, Kansas City, Missouri (Gift of Mrs. Louis Sosland); 53 © Gustavo / Constellation www.constellationart.org; 54 Private Collection / Bridgeman Art Library; 54 The Metropolitan Museum of Art, Gift of George N. and Helen M. Richard, 1964, (64.165.2) Photograph copyright 1996; The Metropolitan Museum of Art; 57 Edna Crawford; 58 Francis G. Mayer / Corbis; 60 (br) Francis G. Mayer / Corbis; V- (b) Balloons For A Dime, 1946, Acrylic on Paper, 15" x 22"- Jonathan Green.

Unit 3

62 Lyle Peterzell / National Gallery of Art, Washington / Gift of the Artist / Licensed by VAGA, New York; 63 (b) Bettmann / Corbis; 64 Used by permission of HarperCollins Publishers; 66 The Newark Museum / Art Resource, NY; 67 (t) Whitney Museum of American Art, New York, USA / Bridgeman Art Library / Licensed by VAGA, New York, NY; 68 (b) Heather Burton / Shortland Elementary; 70–71 (b) Erich Lessing / Art Resource, NY; 70 (t) Roger Wood / Corbis; 71 (t) Erich Lessing / Art Resource, NY; 72 (t) Norton Simon Collection, Pasadena, CA / Bridgeman Art Library; 72 (r) Jan Chen / Art Resource, NY; 74 Nancy Curry; 76 (b) Chris Eden / Eden Arts; (b) The Butler Institute of American Art / The Jacob and Gwendolyn Lawrence Foundation; 77 Hirshhorn Museum and Sculpture garden, Smithsonian Institution, gift of Joseph H. Hirshhorn, 1966 / The Jacob and Gwendolyn Lawrence Foundation; 78 (t) On loan from Wallace and Wilhelmina Holladay / National Museum of Women in the Arts; 78 (c) Erich Lessing / Art Resource, NY; 81 (b) On loan from Wallace and Wilhelmina Holladay / National Museum of Women in the Arts.

Unit 4

82 Glenna Goodacre; 83 (b) Kelly-Mooney Photography / Corbis; 84 (t) Werner Forman Archive, Private Collection / Art Resource, NY; 85 Blackstar / Harcourt; 86 (t) Miriam Tewogians / Harcourt; 90 Lewis Museums and Galleries (City Art Gallery), U.K. / Bridgeman Art Library; 88 (t) Dave Bartruff / Corbis; (c) Deborah Butterfield / San Diego Museum of Art (Museum Purchase); 90 San Antonio Museum of Art, Nelson A. Rockefeller Mexican

207

Acknowledgments

Folk Art Collection; 91 (t) (r) National Cowboy & Western Heritage Museum; 92 (detail) Reunion des Musees Nationaux / Art Resource, NY; 94 Superstock; 95 (t) Dallas and John Heaton / Corbis; 96 Richard A. Cooke / Corbis; 97 (t) Angelo Hornak / Corbis; 97 (c) Underwood & Underwood / Corbis; 98 (t) Sotheby's, London / AKG, Berlin / SuperStock; 98 (b) Kacy / Ridgemont Elementary; 101 Dave Bartruff / Corbis.

Unit 5

102 Erich Lessing / Art Resource, NY; 103 (b) Historical Picture Archive / Corbis; 104 Collection of Mr. and Mrs. Paul Mellon / National Gallery of Art, Washington; 106 (t) © 2006 Succession H. Matisse, Paris / Artist Rights Society (ARS), New York / Pushkin Museum of Fine Arts, Moscow / SuperStock; (c) Ichiryusai Hiroshige / The Minneapolis Institute of Arts, Bequest of Richard P. Gale; 108 (t) The Metropolitan Museum of Art, H.O. Havemeyer Collection, Bequest of Mrs. H.O. Havemeyer, 1929 (jp1917) Photograph © 1991 The Metropolitan Museum of Art; 108 (b) Teri Rash / Hilltop Elementary, Lynwood, WA; 110 (t) Roger Ressmeyer / Corbis; (c) Araldo de Luca / Corbis; (c) Giraudon / Art Resource, NY; 114 Reunion des Musees Nationaux / Art Resource, NY; 115 (t) Rijksmuseum, Amsterdam / SuperStock; 116 Banco de Mexico Trust / CNAC / MNAM; Diol Reunion des Musees Nationaux / Art Resource, NY; 112 (t) Araldo de Luca / Corbis; 117 (b) Photography Credit : Ben Blackwell / San Francisco Museum of Modern Art; 118 (t) Danny Lehman / Corbis; (c) The Newark Museum / Art Resource, NY; 121 The Metropolitan Museum of Art, H.O. Havemeyer Collection, Bequest of Richard P. Gale.

Unit 6

122 Museum for Volkerkunde, Wien oder MVK, Wien; 124 © 1966 The Rockwell Family Entities; 126 (t) Gilles Mermet / Art Resource, NY; (b) Karolu Mattison / St. John Central Middle School; 128 (bl) The British Museum; 129 (br) The British Museum; 130 The Detroit Institute of Arts 1978, gift of Edward Chandler Walker, accession number 08.8; 131 (t) The Metropolitan Museum of Art, Bequest of Edith H. Proskauer, 1975 (1975.319.1) photograph © 1998 The Metropolitan Museum of Art; (b) Armand Hammer Foundation, Los Angeles / Superstock; 132 (t) Smithsonian American Art Museum, Washington, DC / Art Resource, NY; 134 (c) Christie's Images / Superstock; 136 (t) Todd Bigelow / Black Star / Harcourt; 137 Gerald McDermott / Harcourt Trade; 138 (t) (c) (br) US Postal Service; 138 (br) US Postal Service; 141 Armand Hammer Foundation, Los Angeles / Superstock.

Elements of Art

170 (tr) Getty Images; (br) Chase Swift / Corbis; 174 (br) Royalty-Free / Corbis.

Gallery of Artists

Adams: AP / Wide World Photos; Anguissola: Scala / Art Resource, NY; Benton: Bettmann / Corbis; Brueghel: Historical Picture Archive / Corbis; Butterfield: Buck Butterfield, Inc.; Carle: Motoko Inoue / Eric Carle Studio; Cassatt: The Metropolitan Museum of Art, Bequest of Edith H. Proskauer 1975 (1975.319.1); Crawford: Harcourt / Edna Crawford; Curry: Nancy Curry; Degas: Giraudon / Art Resource, NY; Durer: Mary Evans Picture Library; Eberle: Kendall Young Library in Webster City, Iowa / Kendall Young Library; Garduno: Flor Garduno; Gauguin: AKG Images; Goodacre: Kelly-Mooney Photography / Corbis; Green: The History Makers; Hanson: Joson

Henstman / Ann Hanson; Hiroshige: Peter Harholdt / Corbis; Hokusai: The Granger Collection; Homer: Bettmann / Corbis; Jasc: Arturo Jasc Y Asociados; Johns: Christopher Felver / Corbis; Johnson: Smithsonian American Art Museum, Washington, DC / The Art Resource, NY; Kahlo: Bettmann / Corbis; King: Phil Sayer / Royal Academy of Arts; Lawrence: Chris Eden / Eden Arts; Lee: National Museum of Women in the Arts; Marcks: AKG Images; Matisse: © 2006 Succession H. Matisse, Paris / Artist Rights Society (ARS), New York / AKG Images; McDermott: Gerald McDermott / Harcourt; Monet: Reunion des Musees Nationaux / Art Resource, NY; Moses: Bettmann / Corbis; Nampeyo: University of New Mexico Press; O'Keeffe: National Portrait Gallery, Smithsonian Institution / Art Resource, NY; Pei: Pei Huber / Stock Photo; Picasso: © 2006 The Estate of Pablo Picasso / Artist Rights Society (ARS), New York / Philadelphia Museum of Art / Corbis; Pinkney: Hyperion Books for Children; Rijn: Scala / Art Resource, NY; Rivera: Bettmann / Corbis; Rockwell: Underwood & Underwood / Corbis; Rousseau: Erich Lessing / Art Resource, NY; Saguak: Deborah Tote-Collins of SAIBU, Inc. / Sobu Inc.; Thiebaud: Christopher Felver / Corbis; Veladon: 2006 Artist Rights Society (ARS), New York / ADAGP, Paris; Christie's Images / SuperStock; Van Gogh: Reunion des Musees Nationaux / Art Resource, NY; Vitale: Stefano Vitale; Wright: Underwood & Underwood / Corbis.

Glossary

162 (bl) Rachel Epstein / PhotoEdit; 163 (tr) Lindsay Hebberd / Corbis; 194 (bl) Private Collection / Marilee Whitehouse-Holm / Superstock; 195 (tl) (cr) Alamy Images; (br) Index Stock Imagery, Inc.; 196 (b) Alamy Images; (tr) Roman Soumar / Corbis; 197 (tr) Alamy Images; (cr) Ralph A. Clevenger / Corbis; (br) George H. H. Huey / Corbis; 198 (tl) (tr) Alamy Images; 199 (bl) Michelle Garrett / Corbis; (cr) Tretyakov Gallery, Moscow / AKG Berlin / SuperStock; 200 (b) (tr) Alamy images; (cl) Getty Images; 201 (cr) Douglas Peebles / Corbis; (bl) Bonhams, London / Bridgeman Art Library, London / SuperStock; (br) Photodisc Green / Getty Images.

208

Media & Techniques

Creating art is an exhilarating process of self-expression.

Children who are experienced in basic art techniques have the confidence to take risks and try new approaches, with surprisingly original pieces of artwork often resulting. Here are some brief descriptions of media and techniques suitable for students in elementary school.

• TYPES OF PAPER

BUTCHER PAPER
Available in wide rolls and several colors, this hard-surfaced paper is useful for murals and other large art projects.

CONSTRUCTION PAPER
Available in different colors, this paper is useful for crayon and tempera projects. It is easy to cut or tear, and can be used in collages and paper sculptures.

DRAWING AND PAINTING PAPER
This slightly rough paper is useful for drawing and watercolor painting projects, especially at the elementary level.

NEWSPRINT
This thin, inexpensive paper is good for sketching, printmaking, and making papier-mâché.

TISSUE PAPER
Available in bright colors, tissue paper is especially useful for making collages and for projects that require transparent color.

OTHER KINDS OF PAPER
Wallpaper and gift-wrapping paper can be cut into shapes and used in collages. Photographs in old magazines can be cut out and arranged into photomontages.

• ART BOARDS

POSTER BOARD
This lightweight, flexible art board comes in a variety of colors. It has a smooth, hard surface and is easily cut with dull scissors. It can be used for tempera painting projects, collages, and for mounting paper artworks.

CARDBOARD
Used boxes are a good source of cardboard. Pieces of cardboard can be used to back a framed artwork or to build three-dimensional forms. They can also be used as bases for sculptures. Teachers should use sharp scissors to cut boxes ahead of time.

FOAMCORE BOARD
This lightweight board is made by laminating a layer of foam between two pieces of poster board. Foam boards come in various thicknesses and are easy to cut. They are useful for mounting artwork and building three-dimensional forms.

MATBOARD
Matboard is a stiff, heavy, professional-quality board used for framing photographs and paper artworks. Matboards are cut with a razor-edge mat knife.

Safety Tips

Closely supervise students when they are using hard or pointed instruments.

• GLUE, STARCH, AND PASTE

WHITE GLUE

This nontoxic, creamy liquid comes in plastic squeeze bottles and in larger containers. It is recommended for use with cardboard, wood, cloth, plastic foam, and pottery. White glue causes wrinkling when used with paper, especially when too much is used.

POWDERED ART PASTE OR STARCH

Mixed to a thin, watery consistency, this material is recommended for use in making tissue-paper collages.

SCHOOL PASTE (LIBRARY PASTE)

Although this substance is nontoxic, young children like its smell and may be tempted to eat it. It should be used by the teacher for pasting pieces of paper onto other pieces of paper or onto cardboard. School paste and glue sticks are not recommended for more elaborate projects because they may not hold the materials together.

USING GLUE OR PASTE

1. Spread out sheets of newspaper.
2. Place the artwork to be glued facedown. Spread the glue or paste evenly from the center, using a finger or a piece of cardboard. Be sure the edges and corners of the paper are covered.
3. Lift the paper and carefully lay it in the desired position on the surface to which it will be affixed. Place a sheet of clean paper over the artwork and smooth it with the palm of the hand.

Starch and powdered art paste should be mixed by the teacher without students present.

• DRAWING TOOLS AND TECHNIQUES

PENCILS

Many different effects can be created with an art pencil, depending on how it is held and how much pressure is applied. Art pencil leads vary from 6B, which makes the darkest, softest mark, to 9H, which makes the lightest, hardest mark.

Students can also achieve a variety of effects with regular number 2 or $2\frac{1}{2}$ pencils. Shading or making light and dark values can be made by using the flat side of the lead.

Colored pencils are most effectively used by first making light strokes and then building up the color to develop darker areas.

CRAYONS

When applied with heavy pressure, crayons produce rich, vivid colors. Always save crayon stubs. Allow students to unwrap them so they can experiment with using the side of the crayon rather than the tip.

Crayon etching is a technique in which layers of light-colored crayon are built up on shiny, nonabsorbent paper. The colors are covered with black crayon or black tempera paint that has been mixed with a small amount of liquid soap. Students must press hard with all the crayons to apply enough wax to the paper. With a toothpick, fingernail, or other pointed tool, students etch, or scratch away, the black layer to expose the colors or the white paper underneath (**Figure 1**).

Figure 1. Crayon etching

OIL PASTELS

Softer than wax crayons, oil pastels produce bright, glowing color effects. Pressing an oil pastel hard on the paper creates rich, vibrant color; less pressure produces a softer color. Oil pastels smudge more easily than crayons. As with crayons, drawing can be done with the points or with the unwrapped sides, and students may wish to break their oil pastels in half.

Colors can be mixed by adding one over another or by placing dots of different colors side by side and blending them by rubbing.

COLORED MARKERS

Nonpermanent felt- or plastic-tipped markers are safe and easy to use, and they are available in a wide range of colors and sizes. They are useful for outdoor sketching, for making contour drawings, and for other art assignments. Dried-out markers can be renewed by running warm water on the tip.

· PAINTING TOOLS AND TECHNIQUES

TEMPERA

Tempera paint works best when it has the consistency of thick cream. It is available in powder or, more commonly, liquid form. Tempera is opaque—the paper beneath cannot be seen through paint of normal consistency.

Tempera powder is available in cans or boxes, and it should be mixed in small amounts. Mix water and powder to the desired consistency. Tempera may be mixed with wheat paste to make a very thick paint for impasto painting. Dried-out tempera paint should not be used again.

Safety Tips

Powdered tempera can irritate eyes and nasal passages during mixing. If you use powdered tempera, wear a mask and mix it ahead of time.

Liquid tempera is available in jars or plastic containers and is ready to use. Shake the container well before using. Keep a lid on the paint when it is not being used, and keep paint cleaned out of the cap to prevent sticking.

Some manufacturers supply helpful pouring spouts. If you use them, put a galvanized nail in the spout openings when not in use to keep them from stopping up.

WATERCOLORS

Watercolors should be softened ahead of time by placing a drop of water on each color cake. Paintings can be done with a dry or wet brush for different effects. Students may use the top of the open box to mix colors. Small, soft-bristle brushes are used with watercolors to achieve the transparent, fluid quality of the medium.

Interesting effects with watercolors include
* making a watercolor wash by painting a line and then smudging the line with a wet brush.
* blotting watercolors with crumpled paper.
* sprinkling salt on a wet watercolor picture.
* painting on wet paper.

BRUSHES

Choose well-made brushes with metal ferrules (the ring around the paintbrush shaft near the bristles). Ferrules should be tightly bonded to the handles so the bristles will not come off onto students' paintings.

Dozens of sizes and varieties of brushes are available, from nylon-bristle brushes to fairly expensive sable brushes. Students should have access to a wide variety of brushes—round and flat, thick and thin, square-ended and oval-tipped. After each art session, brushes should be cleaned in a warm solution of mild detergent and water. Students can experiment with other painting tools, such as toothbrushes, eye-makeup brushes, sponges, and cotton swabs.

PAINT CONTAINERS

Mixing trays or paint palettes can be made from many free or inexpensive materials, such as pie pans, muffin tins, plastic food trays, and paper plates. Egg cartons make good mixing trays because they can be closed, labeled with the student's name, and stored for later use.

When storing tempera paint in a mixing tray for later use, add a little water to keep the paint from drying out overnight. You can use a spray bottle to wet the paints before storing.

Always provide students with containers of water for cleaning their brushes while painting. Use plastic margarine containers or other small plastic tubs. Demonstrate for students how to rinse the brush in water before dipping it into a new color. Students can dry the brush as needed by stroking it across a folded paper towel.

Make your own portable paint holder by cutting holes in the lid of a shoe box. Place babyfood jars filled with paint into the openings.

COLOR-MIXING TECHNIQUES

When mixing **tints**, start with white and gradually add small amounts of a color to make the desired tint. When mixing **shades**, gradually add small amounts of black to a color.

Mix the **primary colors** (red, yellow, and blue) to create the **secondary colors** (green, orange, and violet).

- To make green, add small amounts of blue to yellow.
- To make orange, add small amounts of red to yellow.
- To make violet, add small amounts of blue to red.

To make **neutral colors**, such as brown, combine **complementary color pairs** (red plus green, yellow plus violet, blue plus orange).

• PRINTMAKING TOOLS AND TECHNIQUES

Prints can be made from a wide variety of materials, including plastic foam meat trays with indented designs, dried glue lines on cardboard, and flat shapes or objects glued to cardboard.

The following technique may be used for printmaking:

1. Pour water-based printing ink on a plastic tray or a cookie sheet.
2. Roll a brayer or roller over the ink.
3. Roll the coated brayer over the printing surface until it is evenly covered. Roll first in one direction and then at right angles.
4. Place a piece of paper on top of the inked surface. Rub the back of the paper with the fingertips or the back of a spoon, being careful not to move it.
5. Pull the paper away from the surface. This is called "pulling the print." The print is ready to dry.

Even water-based ink stains clothing. Have students wear smocks or old shirts when they are making prints.

PRINTMAKING PAPER

Recommended paper for printing includes newsprint, construction paper, and tissue paper. Avoid using paper with a hard, slick finish because it absorbs ink and paint poorly.

To use paint instead of ink for a relief print, mix several drops of glycerine (available in drugstores) with one tablespoon of thick tempera paint. If brayers are not available, have students apply the ink or the paint with a foam brush.

CLEANUP

Drop a folded piece of newspaper into the pan filled with printmaking ink. Roll the brayer on the newspaper. This removes most of the ink from both the pan and the brayer. Lift the newspaper, refold it with the ink inside, and throw it away. Repeat until most of the ink is out of the pan, and then rinse the pan and the brayer at the sink.

• ASSEMBLAGE

An assemblage is an artwork made by joining three-dimensional objects. It can be either free-standing or mounted on a panel, and it is usually made from "found" materials—scraps, junk, and objects from nature. Students can help you collect and sort objects such as

- carpet, fabric, foil, leather, paper, and wallpaper scraps.
- boxes in all sizes, film cans, spools, corks, jar lids.
- packing materials such as foam peanuts and cardboard.
- wire, rope, twine, string, yarn, ribbon.

• SCULPTING TOOLS AND TECHNIQUES

Sculpture is three-dimensional art. It is usually made by carving, modeling, casting, or assembling. Sculptures can be created by adding to a block of material (**additive**) or taking away from a block of material (**subtractive**).

Materials recommended for additive sculpture include clay, papier-mâché, wood, and other materials that can be joined together.

Materials appropriate for subtractive sculpture in school include child-safe clay, wax, soft salt blocks, and artificial sandstone. Synthetic modeling materials are also available.

In the primary grades, salt dough may be substituted for clay in some art activities. Combine 2 cups of flour with 1 cup of salt. Add 1 cup of water and mix thoroughly. Press the mixture into a ball and then knead for several minutes on a board.

Foil offers interesting possibilities for sculpture and embossing. Heavy aluminum foil works best. In addition to making three-dimensional forms with foil, students can smooth it over textured objects to make relief sculptures or jewelry.

Wire, including pipe cleaners, telephone wire, and floral wire, is easily shaped and reshaped. Teachers should cut wire into pieces ahead of time. When using long wires, tape the ends to prevent injury. Students should wear safety goggles and sit a safe distance from each other.

Media & Techniques

PAPER SCULPTURE

Stiff paper or poster board, cut in a variety of shapes and sizes, yields colorful and inventive three-dimensional forms. For best results, students should always use glue, not paste, when assembling a paper sculpture. They can use a paper clip or tape to hold parts together while the glue is drying.

CLAY

Clay comes from the ground and usually has a gray or reddish hue. It is mixed with other materials so that it is flexible, yet able to hold a shape.

Oil-based clay is mixed with oil, usually linseed, and cannot be fired or glazed. It softens when it is molded with warm hands. When the clay becomes old and loses oil, it becomes difficult to mold and will eventually break apart. Oil-based clay is available in a variety of colors.

Water-based or wet clay comes in a variety of textures and can be fired to become permanent. It should be stored in a plastic sack to keep it moist until it is used. If the clay begins to dry out, dampen it with a fine spray of water. If it has not been fired, dried water-based clay can be recycled by soaking it in water.

Before firing, or baking clay in a kiln, there are two important considerations:

- Read and carefully follow the instructions for operating the kiln.
- Be certain that the clay has been kneaded before being molded to prevent air pockets that can explode during firing.

PREPARING CLAY

If clay is reused or made from a powder mix, knead thoroughly to remove air pockets.

- Take a chunk of soft clay and form it into a ball. Then use a wire cutting tool to cut the ball in half. From a standing position, throw the clay onto a tabletop to flatten it.
- Press down on the clay with the palms of both hands against a hard surface. Fold the clay, and press hard again. Keep folding and pressing in this manner until the air pockets have been removed.

Figure 2. Pinch method

METHODS FOR MOLDING CLAY

Clay can be molded and formed using the pinch, slab, and coil methods.

- To make a pot using the **pinch method (Figure 2)**, mold a chunk of clay into a ball. Holding the ball in one hand, press the thumb in and carefully squeeze the clay between thumb and forefinger. Begin at the bottom, and gradually work upward and out. Continually turn the ball of clay while pinching it.
- To make a **slab**, use a rolling pin to flatten a chunk of clay between a quarter of an inch and half an inch thick. Shapes cut from the slab **(Figure 3)** can be draped over bowls or crumpled newspapers and left to dry. Clay shapes can also be joined together to form containers or sculptures.

Figure 3. Slab method

Textures can be added by pressing found objects, such as combs, coins, buttons, bottle caps, and other interesting objects, into the clay. Designs can also be etched with tools such as pencil points, paper clips, and toothpicks.

To create a **coil**, use the whole hand to roll a chunk of clay against a hard surface until it forms a rope of even thickness **(Figure 4)**. Ropes can be attached to each other and coiled into a shape, or they can be added to a slab base and smoothed out.

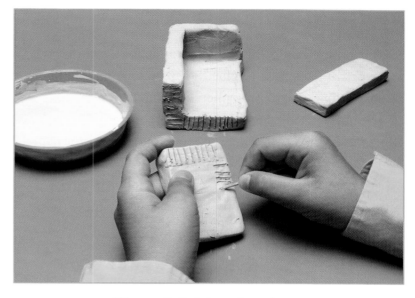

Figure 5. Joining clay pieces

JOINING CLAY TOGETHER

Oil-based clay pieces can be pressed together and blended with the fingertips.

Water-based clay pieces should be joined by **scoring**, or scratching the surface, of the adjoining pieces with the tip of a toothpick. Adding **slip**, or water-thinned clay, will make the two pieces adhere **(Figure 5)**.

Figure 4. Coil method

Plastic spray bottles provide an easy way to keep clay pieces moist.

Clean up dry clay with a wet cloth or a wet mop to keep silica dust from dispersing into the air.

PAPIER-MÂCHÉ

This art material is made by mixing paper pulp or strips with art paste or glue. It can be molded into three-dimensional forms or applied to a foundation form, or **armature**, then painted when dry.

Good forms that can be used as foundations for papier-mâché include inflated balloons, plastic bottles, paper sacks stuffed with newspapers, and wire armatures shaped into skeletal forms.

PREPARING PULP

Shred pieces of soft paper, such as newsprint, paper towels, or facial tissue, into small bits or thin strips. Soak them for several hours in water, then drain them, squeeze out the extra water, and mix the pulp with prepared paste until it reaches the consistency of soft clay. Let the mixture stand for an hour before beginning to work with it.

PREPARING STRIPS

Tear newsprint into long strips about one-half inch wide. Dip the strips into art paste or a white-glue mixture, and put down a layer of wet strips over the foundation form. Allow the piece to dry after every two layers of application. Continue putting strips on the form until there are five or six layers. This thickness is strong enough to support most papier-mâché projects.

Do not use pages from a printed newspaper to make papier-mâché. The printing inks may contain toxic pigments.

MAKING PAPER

Help children tear up scrap paper and put it in a blender with water to make pulp. Pour it into a basin. Children can add things from nature like seeds, flower petals, or leaves. Dip a section of screen into the pulp and raise it up, covering it with a thin, even layer. Place a towel over the pulp, push on it to drain out the water, and flip it over carefully so that the layer of pulp is lying on the towel. Place another towel over the pulp and iron until it is dry. Spray on starch to make the paper easier to write on.

FABRIC ARTS

BATIK

The traditional batik method of dyeing fabric is a **wax-resist** technique. First, patterns are drawn on the fabric with wax. When the fabric is dyed, waxed areas resist the dye. When the wax is removed, the pattern emerges. To make an acrylic batik, draw patterns on the fabric with acrylic white paint, rather than wax. Then dye the fabric or brush it with a water-based paint. After it has dried, scratch the white paint off to reveal the pattern (**Figure 6**).

Figure 6. Simple batik

• WEAVING

A weaving is an artwork created on a **loom** by lacing together or interlocking strands of thread, yarn, or other materials. Simple square looms can be made by stretching thick rubber bands across stiff cardboard. Circular weavings can be made on looms formed from wire hangers bent into a circle. Students can weave a variety of materials through the loom, including ribbon, yarn, strands of beads, twine, and fabric strips **(Figure 7)**.

Figure 7. Weaving

• DISPLAYING ARTWORK

Frames usually improve the appearance of artwork, and they make attractive displays.

MOUNTING

The simplest kind of frame is a **mount**, or a solid sheet of paper or cardboard attached to the back of an artwork. It should be at least an inch larger than the work on all sides.

MATTING

A **mat** is a piece of paper or cardboard with a cut-out center. A picture is taped in place behind it, with the mat forming a border. Professional-style mats made from matboard should be cut only by the teacher.

To make a mat, use a piece of cardboard that extends two or three inches beyond the picture on all sides. On the back of the board, mark the position where the art is to be placed. Then measure one-fourth inch in from the outer edge of the artwork. This will make the picture overlap the cutout window on all sides.

FRAMING

Students can turn cardboard mats into finished frames. Have them paint and decorate a mat, attach their artwork to the back of it, and then attach a solid piece of cardboard to the back of the mat.

Teachers should work carefully when using a mat knife. Keep the blade pointed away from you, and retract the blade or return the knife to its container when not in use.

Art instruction can be particularly useful in helping to meet a wide spectrum of individual needs in the classroom. Knowing some of the characteristics of the developmental stages in art can help teachers make better decisions concerning individual needs.

▲ **Preschematic Stage**

▲ **Late Schematic Stage**

STAGES OF ARTISTIC DEVELOPMENT

Students' interests and skills in art develop at different rates, just as they do in other disciplines. The following information describes five basic stages of artistic development. Of course, at any age, individual students may show characteristics of various stages.

Scribbling (2–4 YEARS)

- Children begin drawing disorganized scribbles, progress to controlled scribbling, and then advance to named scribbling.
- Children work with art materials for the joy of manipulating them.

Preschematic (4–6 YEARS)

- Drawings are often direct, simple, and spontaneous, showing what children believe is most important about the subject.
- There is usually little concern about technical skill or physical appearance, and color is selected for emotional reasons.
- There is little understanding of space, and objects may be placed haphazardly throughout pictures. The self often appears in the center.

Schematic (7–9 YEARS)

- An understanding of space is demonstrated in most drawings, and objects have a relationship to what is up and down.
- In drawings, a horizon becomes apparent, and items are spatially related.
- Exaggeration between figures, such as humans taller than a house, is used to express strong feelings about subjects.

Beginning of Realism (9–11 YEARS)

- Children begin using perspective.
- Overlapping objects and three-dimensional effects are achieved, along with shading and use of subtle color combinations.
- Drawings may appear less spontaneous than in previous stages because of the students' attempts at achieving realism.

Increasing Realism (11–13 YEARS)

- Students may value the finished product over the process.
- Students strive to show things realistically and in three dimensions.
- Perspective and proportion are used.

ESL

Art instruction provides an exceptional opportunity for English-language learners to build both language ability and self-esteem because of the abundance of visual images, hands-on experiences, and peer interaction involved.

Strategies for Success

To help English-language learners:

Use physical movement and gestures, realia, and visuals to make language comprehensible and to encourage oral language development. You may want to use Harcourt's *Picture Card Collection* and *Picture Card Bank CD-ROM* to reinforce concepts visually.

Introduce concepts and words using rhymes and poetry. At Grades 1–3, you will find rhymes and poems in the unit openers.

Explain concepts, using the Grades 1–2 *Big Books* and Grades 1–5 *Art Prints*.

Encourage students to speak, but never force them to do so. All responses should be voluntary.

Display the *Posters of Elements, Principles, and Safety* in both English and Spanish. *Artist's Workshop Activities: English and Spanish* are also available.

EXTRA SUPPORT

Students may need extra support due to insufficient background experiences or home support or because of learning disabilities that affect the way they receive and process information. Some of the problems these students may have include difficulty in organizing work, expressing ideas through speech and language, following directions, or maintaining attention.

Strategies for Success

To help students who need extra support:

Involve students in setting goals and in determining rubrics.

Modify art instruction to meet students' learning styles.

Maintain a consistent art-program schedule.

Simplify complex directions or use fewer words to explain them.

Give students a desk copy of board work or directions.

Model directions for art activities.

Provide concrete examples of concepts and vocabulary to aid retention.

Review regularly what students have previously done or learned.

Allow student choice, and build on student interests.

Look for

CHALLENGE NOTES

KEEP IN MIND

Gifted children may

■ become bored with routine tasks.

■ be overly critical of others or perfectionistic.

■ dominate or withdraw in cooperative learning situations.

■ resist changing from activities they find interesting.

GIFTED AND TALENTED

Gifted and talented students are those who consistently perform at a high level in art.

Characteristics

When gifted and talented students produce art, they typically:

• show willingness to experiment and try new materials and techniques.
• appear keenly interested in the art of other artists.
• produce art frequently.
• show originality.
• display ease in using materials and tools.

Strategies for Success

Use these strategies with gifted and talented students:

Provide more challenging art assignments and projects. See the Challenge Activities in the *Teacher Resource Book*.

Enable students to participate in long-term projects in which they explore techniques or styles in depth.

Encourage and provide opportunities for individual exploration.

Challenge students with cross-disciplinary experiences in which they combine aspects of two disciplines, such as making a "sound collage."

Plan for additional outlets and audiences for students' work—in the community as well as at school.

Arrange for additional art opportunities, such as noon "drop-in" classes or after-school classes.

SPECIAL NEEDS

Special-needs students may have mobility, visual, or hearing impairments; be multiply disabled; or have behavioral or developmental disabilities. Art experiences can provide these students with unique opportunities to express their ideas and feelings and to improve their self-esteem and independence.

Strategies for Success

Here are a few of the many strategies you can use to help these students achieve success. Not all strategies work with all students or situations. Check individualized educational plans for each student's personal goals as well as the objectives of your curriculum.

Mobility Impairments

Consider whether a different medium might be easier to use, such as oil pastels instead of tempera paints.

Use assistive technology, or use or make adaptive devices. For example, for a student who has trouble gripping a crayon, place the crayon inside a foam curler.

Tape paper to the table to hold it in place while students draw.

Visual Impairments

Demonstrate for the child, allowing the student to touch your hands as you model.

Provide tactile materials in lieu of primarily visual ones, such as yarn for forming lines, clay for sculpting, and finger paints for painting.

Tape a shallow box lid or frame in the student's workspace, where the student's tools can be kept and easily located.

Hearing Impairments

Provide additional visual models.

Repeat demonstrations of skills, such as mixing colors.

Use signing, if known.

Behavioral Disabilities

Praise students for all tasks well done.

Provide opportunities for working with three-dimensional materials.

Make these students your helpers.

Developmental Disabilities

Explain each task separately, allowing it to be done before starting another.

Allow frequent opportunities for free drawing.

Repeat each direction, demonstrating it several times.

Look for

SPECIAL NEEDS NOTES

KEEP IN MIND

You may want to share the work of some artists with disabilities:

■ **Chuck Close (mobility)**

■ **Dale Chihuly (vision)**

■ **Francisco Goya (hearing)**

■ **Auguste Renoir (mobility)**

■ **Frida Kahlo (mobility)**

For more information and resources:

• http://www.vsarts.org

• http://finearts.esc20.net/fa_forall.htm

• http://www.vsatx.org

Assessment involves the selection, collection, and interpretation of information about student performance. The goal of assessment is to help children show what they know and what they can do. Effective assessment in an art program should include both creating and responding experiences that engage a variety of knowledge and skills in studio production, art criticism, art history, and aesthetics. Learning may be demonstrated in products, paper-pencil format, and discussions or conferences.

Art Everywhere includes a variety of tools that teachers may use to construct a complete picture of a child's accomplishments.

TOOLS AND STRATEGIES

Student Edition Review and Reflect Pages

Use to determine whether the child

- Responds to questions of art and design using appropriate vocabulary through discussion, writing, and visual analysis

- Applies knowledge in art criticism, art history, and aesthetics

Two pages at the end of each instructional unit in the *Student Edition* provide exercises and activities for children to review and reflect upon the unit content. These activities encourage children to demonstrate their knowledge of visual art vocabulary, to apply reading and thinking skills to art, to write in response to art, and to describe, analyze, interpret, compare, and evaluate works of art.

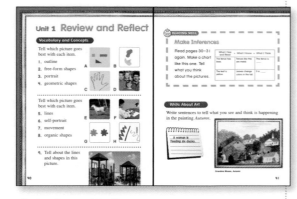

▲ Review and Reflect

Studio Production Activities

Use to determine whether the child

- Demonstrates and applies technical skills and control of media and tools in studio production

- Constructs and communicates meaning by using different media, techniques, and processes to communicate ideas and experiences and solve problems

The Artist's Workshop, a production activity in each lesson in the *Student Edition*, provides an opportunity for children to demonstrate technical skills and control of media and tools and to apply elements and principles taught in the lesson. The Artist's Workshop Rubrics on pages R30–R31 may be used to help children assess their own work and to discuss personal art-works with peers and the teacher. The completed forms may serve to guide a student-teacher conference or a student-student discussion.

▲ Artist's Workshop

Unit Tests

Use to determine whether the child

- Uses appropriate vocabulary to respond to questions of art and design through discussion, writing, and visual analysis

The *Teacher Resource Book* includes a set of multiple-choice and short-answer questions, in blackline master format, which may be duplicated and used to assess children's knowledge of visual art vocabulary and concepts orally or in writing.

Portfolio

> Use to determine whether the child
>
> - Recognizes personal strengths and weaknesses and discusses own work
>
> - Constructs and communicates meaning by using different media, techniques, and processes

A portfolio, a purposeful collection of a child's work, provides a continuous record of a child's growth and learning. It is an effective strategy to be used to compare a child's current work to earlier work.

Organized chronologically, a portfolio benefits both the child and the teacher. Children reflect on their own growth and development as they self-assess and select materials to include in their portfolio. For the teacher, a portfolio provides a forum for a student-teacher discussion or conference. See page R32 for the Portfolio Recording Form.

Art Prints and Discussion Cards

> Use to determine whether the child
>
> - Responds to works of art and design, using appropriate vocabulary, through discussion and visual analysis
>
> - Identifies specific works of art as belonging to particular cultures, times, and places
>
> - Recognizes connecting patterns, shared concepts, and connections between and among works of art

The Discussion Cards, found on pages R34–R42, may be used to help children focus their thoughts as they view the program *Art Prints*. Each card provides a framework for children to respond to works of art and design using technical vocabulary appropriately

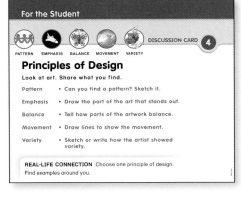

▲ Student Discussion Card

and to demonstrate an understanding of the nature and meaning of artworks.

Observations

> Use to determine whether the child
>
> - Demonstrates and applies technical skills and control of media, tools, and processes
>
> - Applies art knowledge in art criticism, art history, and aesthetics

A checklist or inventory is one of the easiest tools for recording children's progress. Observe children at various times and in various circumstances, and record observations. The Progress Recording Form, found on page R33, is a checklist based on instructional objectives that may be used for monitoring children's acquisition of art skills and knowledge.

Self- and Peer Assessment

> Use to determine whether the child
>
> - Describes, analyzes, interprets, and judges or evaluates design or artwork done by self, peers, or other artists
>
> - Recognizes personal strengths and weaknesses and discusses own work
>
> - Responds to works of art and design, using technical vocabulary that describes visual experiences and supports assertions

Self-assessment helps children learn to reflect on their own artwork and on their strengths and weaknesses as artists. The Artist's Workshop Rubric for Self/Teacher Assessment, on page R30, provides a format for both the child and the teacher to assess student artwork and habits.

▲ Peer Assessment Rubric

Peer assessment provides children with a forum to share their ideas as artists and as viewers of art in a positive and constructive setting. In evaluating each other's work, children can use art-specific vocabulary and knowledge, exercise their art-response skills, and reflect on their own learning and development. Use the Artist's Workshop Rubric for Peer Assessment on page R31 to guide children's responses.

Artist's Workshop Rubric
Self/Teacher Assessment

Artist _____ Artwork _____

Teacher _____ Date _____

Rate your own work.

My work is creative.	☺	☺	☺	☺
I used what I learned.	☺	☺	☺	☺
I used the materials well.	☺	☺	☺	☺
I followed directions.	☺	☺	☺	☺
I cleaned up and put things away.	☺	☺	☺	☺

Knowledge and Skills   Teacher Rating

Creativity Work shows creativity. Work is imaginative and original.	1	2	3	4
Design Work shows application of art principles and elements.	1	2	3	4
Technique Shows skillful use of tools, techniques, and media.	1	2	3	4
Following Directions Stays on task. Completes activity as directed.	1	2	3	4
Work Habits Applies self to activity. Shows safe and proper use of tools.	1	2	3	4
Scoring: 4 — Excellent; 3 — Above Average; 2 — Satisfactory; 1 — Unsatisfactory				

Harcourt

Artist's Workshop Rubric
Peer Assessment

Artist _____ Artwork _____

Reviewer _____ Date _____

Circle the word or words to complete each sentence.

The artist used _____.

good ideas   imagination

I like how the artist used _____.

lines   colors   shapes

patterns   balance   materials

The artwork shows _____.

a main idea   good details   hard work

Something that makes this artwork special is _____

_____

_____

Harcourt

Portfolio Recording Form

Name _____

Artwork   Date Done

_____

_____

_____

_____

I chose these artworks because _____

_____ .

My favorite artwork in my portfolio is _____

because

_____ I used different tools and materials.

_____ it shows how I can use my imagination.

_____ I enjoyed working on it.

_____ it shows my feelings and ideas.

The artwork that was hardest for me is _____

because _____ .

One thing that makes me a good artist is _____

_____ .

Harcourt

Progress Recording Form

Name _____ Teacher _____

Knowledge and Skills

Date

Perception						
Identifies variations in objects and subjects from the environment, using the senses.						
Identifies art elements such as color, texture, form, line, and space and art principles such as emphasis, pattern, and rhythm.						
Creative Expression/Performance						
Expresses ideas and feelings in artworks, using a variety of colors, forms, and lines.						
Creates effective compositions, using design elements and principles.						
Identifies and practices skills necessary for producing drawings, paintings, prints, constructions, and modeled forms, using a variety of art materials.						
Historical/Cultural Heritage						
Identifies stories and constructions in a variety of artworks.						
Compares ways individuals and families are depicted in different artworks.						
Identifies different kinds of jobs in art.						
Response/Evaluation						
Defines reasons for preferences in personal artworks.						
Identifies ideas in original artworks, portfolios, and exhibitions by peers and artists.						

Key: R = Rarely or never exhibits behavior
         S = Sometimes exhibits behavior
         C = Consistently exhibits behavior

Comments

Harcourt

Looking at Art

1. **Help children scan and describe the *subject* and *details* of each artwork.**

   QUESTION: *What do you see?*
   STUDENT RESPONSE: *I see a landscape. I see trees, grass, and sky.*

2. **Use prompts to encourage children to talk about the artwork's *elements, principles, materials,* and *meaning*. Use one or two prompts like these from each category.**

ELEMENTS
- What kinds of lines are used? **LINE**
- What colors do you see? Where do you see lighter colors? Darker colors? **COLOR**

PRINCIPLES
- What is the first thing you see when you look at the artwork? **EMPHASIS**
- Tell which shapes are repeated. Where do they lead your eyes? **RHYTHM**

MATERIALS
- What materials make up this artwork? **MEDIA**
- How was this artwork put together? **TECHNIQUE**

MEANING
- How does the artist want you to feel? **IDEAS AND FEELINGS**
- What is the purpose of this art? **PURPOSE**

3. **Present *historical information* about the art.**

Harcourt

Art Criticism

DESCRIPTION
1. **Have children look at and describe the artworks, using *facts* about what they see.**
   - What kind of artwork is this? (portrait, landscape, still life, sculpture)
   - What *elements* do you see in the artwork? (lines, shapes, colors, and so on)

ANALYSIS
2. **Have children identify the *characteristics* of the artwork—or how the artist used design principles.**
   - How does this artwork show *balance*? *pattern*?
   - How does the artist want you to *feel*?

INTERPRETATION
3. **Guide children in determining the artwork's *purpose* and *meaning*.**
   - What is the *purpose* of the artwork? (for example, show nature, show feelings, tell a story, or persuade)
   - What does this artwork say or *mean* to you?

EVALUATION
4. **Encourage children to make evaluations that use *criteria* or *reasons* for attributing value.**
   - How is this artwork *important*? Give *reasons*.
   - Do you like this artwork? Give *reasons*.

Harcourt

For the Teacher

DISCUSSION CARD ③

 LINE    SHAPE    COLOR    FORM    TEXTURE

Elements of Art

Look at art. Share what you find.

Line   • Draw lines that you see.

Shape   • Draw the free-form shapes. Circle organic shapes. Draw geometric shapes.

Color   • Show the colors used most.

Form   • Draw the two biggest forms that you see.

Texture • Sketch or write about the textures.

REAL-LIFE CONNECTION Choose one element of art. Find examples around you.

Harcourt

PATTERN   EMPHASIS   BALANCE   MOVEMENT   VARIETY

DISCUSSION CARD

4

Principles of Design

Look at art. Share what you find.

Pattern
- Can you find a pattern? Sketch it.

Emphasis
- Draw the part of the art that stands out.

Balance
- Tell how parts of the artwork balance.

Movement
- Draw lines to show the movement.

Variety
- Sketch or write how the artist showed variety.

REAL-LIFE CONNECTION Choose one principle of design. Find examples around you.

Harcourt

PORTRAIT

SELF-
PORTRAIT

GROUP
PORTRAIT

FAMILY
PORTRAIT

Portraits

Look at a portrait. Answer the questions.

1. What kind of portrait is this? How do you know?

2. What can you tell about the people?

3. How do you think the people are feeling?

4. What do the clothes tell you about the people?

5. What materials were used to make this portrait?

REAL-LIFE CONNECTION Where do you see portraits at school?
Tell about them.

Harcourt

DISCUSSION CARD

6

LANDSCAPE

SEASCAPE

CITYSCAPE

Landscapes

Look at art. Answer the questions.

1. Is the artwork a landscape, a seascape, or a cityscape? How can you tell?

2. Find the horizon line. What is nearest you?

3. What is the weather like? What time of year is it?

4. How did the artist show the difference between things that are near and far away?

5. Would you like to visit this place? Why?

REAL-LIFE CONNECTION If you could draw a landscape of your neighborhood, what would you show?

CHARACTERS   SETTING   BEGINNING   MIDDLE   END

Stories in Art

Look at art. Share what you find.

1. Who or what is shown in the art?

2. What is the setting of the artwork?

3. What is happening in the artwork?
   What do you think will happen next?

4. How do the colors help tell the story?

5. How do you think the artist wants you to feel?

REAL-LIFE CONNECTION Find a favorite picture book.
Tell how the art helps tell the story.

Harcourt

DISCUSSION CARD

Abstract Art

SHAPES

FEELINGS

COLOR

Look at an abstract artwork. Answer the questions.

1. What does the artwork show?

2. What shapes, lines, and colors do you see?

3. Does the title help you understand the artwork? Why?

4. What do you think the artist wants you to feel?

5. Would you like to put the artwork in your room? Why?

REAL-LIFE CONNECTION Look at an object in your classroom. Sketch it in an abstract way.

DISCUSSION CARD **9**

DESCRIBE   ANALYZE   INTERPRET   EVALUATE

Art Criticism

Look at art. Discuss these questions.

1. Describe
   - What do you see in the artwork? Is this artwork a portrait, landscape, still life, or something else?

2. Analyze
   - What colors, lines, and shapes do you see? How does the art show balance?

3. Interpret
   - What does this artwork mean to you?

4. Evaluate
   - Do you like this artwork? Give reasons.

REAL-LIFE CONNECTION Look through your portfolio. Choose one artwork. Answer the questions about your own artwork.

Harcourt

DISCUSSION CARD

10

PARK

GARDEN

MURAL

PLAYGROUND

Community Art

Look at art, and discuss these questions.

1. Where is this art? What is the subject?

2. What elements of art do you see?

3. Tell about the form and space used.

4. How does the art make you feel? Why?

5. How was this art made? Why do you think it was made?

REAL-LIFE CONNECTION Think of a park you have visited. What could you add to it to make it more beautiful?

Materials

	UNIT					
PAPER	1	2	3	4	5	6
butcher paper			●			
cardboard			●	●	●	
construction paper	●	●	●	●	●	●
tissue paper	●		●			
white drawing paper	●	●		●		●
PAINTING, DRAWING, PRINTMAKING						
crayons	●	●	●		●	
fabric paints						●
markers	●	●	●		●	●
oil pastels		●	●		●	●
paintbrushes	●	●	●	●	●	●
pencils	●		●		●	●
tempera paints	●	●	●	●	●	●
watercolor paints		●	●	●	●	●
CLAY						
carving tools (paper clips, toothpicks, plastic knives, and other objects for carving and making patterns.)				●		
clay				●		

continued

Materials

OTHER MATERIALS

OTHER MATERIALS	UNIT					
	1	2	3	4	5	6
aluminum foil				●		●
boxes (examples: small milk cartons, shoeboxes)				●		
brads		●				
clothespins			●			
craft sticks		●		●		
foam plates						●
found objects—includes recyclables, objects from nature, craft supplies			●	●	●	●
glue	●	●	●	●	●	●
glue sticks	●	●				
hole punch					●	
paper bags (large)					●	
paper plates	●					●
paper tubes				●		
pillowcases, plain (optional)						●
rolling pin				●		
rulers			●			
scissors	●	●	●	●	●	●
sponges			●			
stapler			●			
still-life items (examples: stuffed animals, fruit, flowers)						●
straws		●				
tape			●	●		
wallpaper		●				
yarn			●	●	●	●

FREE AND INEXPENSIVE MATERIALS

GENERAL CLASSROOM MATERIALS	WHERE TO FIND THEM
artificial flowers, leaves	fabric stores, department stores, craft stores
building materials (dowels, scrap lumber, wood shavings, bricks, screws, nuts, bolts)	contractors, builders, lumberyards
carpet scraps, foam	carpet manufacturers and retailers
fabric scraps, ribbon, yarn	fabric stores, craft stores
hangers	discount department stores, consignment shops, thrift stores
leaves, woodchips	local lawn services
magazines, catalogs, and newspapers	libraries, bookstores
packing supplies (Styrofoam™ noodles, cardboard scraps, bubble wrap, etc.)	storage and moving suppliers
shoe boxes	shoe stores, discount department stores
straws, napkins	fast food or restaurant chains
Styrofoam™	packing supply stores, hardware stores, retail stores
tile (damaged, samples, seconds)	hardware/paint stores, plumbers, tile manufacturers
wallpaper samples	home improvement stores, discount stores
watercolor paints, regular paints	art supply stores, school resources
wire	television repair shops, florists, hardware stores, plumbers, telephone/power companies
wood scraps	home improvement stores, lumberyards

TECHNOLOGY RESOURCES

Visit *The Learning Site*
www.harcourtschool.com

Link Bank for Teachers
- Links to museum sites
- Links to sites that offer free and inexpensive materials
- Links to key educational organizations

Alternative Planners

TEACHING BY MEDIA

The following chart shows the pages you can use if you wish to teach with the same media across different grades.*

MEDIA	PAGES GRADE 1	GRADE 2	GRADE 3	GRADE 4	GRADE 5
Clay	73, 89	87, 93	39, 127	105	71, 135
Colored Pencils/ Crayons/Markers	27, 35, 39, 75, 93, 109, 129	27, 29, 39, 59, 79, 109, 113, 135, 139	27, 29, 49, 67, 89, 95, 99, 107, 139	31, 91, 125, 131, 155, 161, 165	31, 35, 65, 91, 105, 121, 141, 171, 195
Computers	– –	57	– –	201	201
Drawing Pencils/ Charcoal	93	39, 115, 133	29, 67, 89, 95, 99, 107	75	– –
Fiber/Textiles	87, 129	75, 135	55, 73, 75, 119	121	185
Found Objects	79, 87, 95, 127	67, 75, 79, 95, 109, 119	135	191	111
Oil Pastels	49	55, 73, 109, 113, 115, 139	69, 109	81, 95, 151	151, 155
Paper/Foil/Tissue Paper	33, 59, 69, 93, 109, 127, 129, 135, 139	27, 29, 33, 35, 47, 67, 69, 75, 79, 107, 113, 127	33, 119, 133	51, 65, 125, 131, 195	121
Photographic Imagery	133	113	133	51, 161, 195	45
Tempera Paints	29, 47, 53, 55, 67, 107, 113, 115, 127	39, 47, 49, 53, 69, 99, 107, 119, 129, 133	35, 47, 53, 79, 93, 113, 115, 129, 135	35, 41, 45, 61, 71, 125, 135, 141, 171, 181, 185, 191	41, 131
Watercolor Paints	99, 119, 135	59, 99, 107, 139	59, 87	71	51, 61, 81, 95, 101, 125, 161, 165

* See also **Challenge Activities**, *Teacher Resource Book*.

TEACHING BY ELEMENTS AND PRINCIPLES

The following chart shows the pages you can use if you wish to teach the same elements and principles across different grades.

ELEMENTS & PRINCIPLES	PAGES				
	GRADE 1	GRADE 2	GRADE 3	GRADE 4	GRADE 5
Balance	106–107, 108–109, 110–111, 120	112–113, 114–115, 116–117, 118–119	106–107, 108–109, 112–113, 120–121	122–125, 128–131, 132–135, 138–141, 159, 162–165	148–151, 152–155, 158–161, 162–165
Color	42–43, 46–47, 48–49, 52–53, 54–55, 58–59, 60	46–47, 48–49, 50–51, 52–53, 54–55, 58–59	30–31, 46–47, 48–49, 50–51, 52–53, 60–61, 72–73, 94–95, 98–99, 106–107, 114–115	38–41, 42–45, 48–51, 58–61, 68–71, 152–155, 159, 183, 193–194, 198–199	38–41, 42–45, 48–51, 98–101, 148–151, 158–161, 162–165, 168–171, 178–181, 183–185, 188–191, 193, 200
Emphasis	102–103, 112–113, 114–115, 118–119, 120	106–107, 108–109, 110–111	94–95, 98–99, 100–101	78–81, 182–185	88–91, 158–161, 163–164, 169, 194
Form	82–83, 86–87, 88–89, 92–93, 94–95, 96–97, 100	86–87, 88–89, 90–91, 92–93, 94–95, 96–97	38–39, 40–41, 98–99, 134–135	102–105, 108–111	72–75, 78–81, 132–135
Line	26–27, 28–29, 30–31, 32–33, 36–37, 40	26–27, 28–29, 58–59	26–27, 28–29, 30–31, 40–41, 72–73, 92–93, 94–95, 106–107	28–31, 62, 149, 153–154, 183, 193–194, 198	28–31, 32–35, 58–59, 102–105, 130, 162
Movement	28–29, 68–69	28–29, 72–73	68–69, 78–79, 80–81	158–161, 168–171	93–94, 163, 192–195
Pattern	58–59, 62–63, 66–67, 68–69, 70–71, 76–77, 80	66–67, 68–69, 70–71, 72–73, 74–75, 78–79	72–73, 74–75, 77, 79, 80–81	118–121, 128–131	58–61, 68–71
Proportion	– –	98–99, 108–109	66–67, 80–81	88–91, 92–95	92–95, 103, 119, 124, 125
Rhythm	62–63, 66–67, 68–69, 76–77, 80	72–73	128–129, 132–133, 140–141	98–101	178–185, 189–191, 192–195
Shape	32–33, 34–35, 36–37, 38–39, 40, 86–87	32–33, 34–35, 36–37, 38–39, 86–87	30–31, 32–33, 34–35, 36–37, 40–41, 72–73, 74–75, 92–93, 94–95, 112–113, 126–127	32–35, 48–51, 79, 92–95, 99, 183, 198–199	28–31, 32–34, 58, 62–65, 148–151, 152–155
Space	94–95, 96–97, 98–99, 100	88–89, 92–93, 94–95, 96–97, 98–99	86–87, 88–89, 91, 92–93, 97, 100–101	102–105, 148–151, 152, 155	68–71, 89–91, 92–95, 98–101, 103, 164
Texture	62–63, 72–73, 74–75, 78–79, 80	74–75, 78–79	54–55, 58–59, 60–61, 94–95, 118–119	62–65, 72–75, 160, 198, 200	129–131, 135, 198
Unity	122–123, 132–133, 136–137, 138–139, 140	126–127, 128–129, 130–131, 132–133, 134–135, 138–139	114–115, 118–119, 120–121	158–161, 162–165, 168–171, 178–181, 188–190, 192	152–155
Value	42–43, 52–53, 54–55, 60	52–53, 58–59	52–53, 60–61, 115	58–61, 62–65, 68–71, 72–75, 78, 183, 200	38–41, 48–49, 129, 159, 168–171, 199
Variety	122–123, 126–127, 128–129, 130–131, 136–137, 140	132–133, 134–135, 138–139	126–127, 129, 132–133, 134–135, 138–139, 140–141	178–181, 182–185, 188–191, 192–195, 198–201	178–181, 182–185, 189–191

These pages provide additional information about the artists and art history terms in this grade level.

Adams, Ansel (1902–1984) American photographer known for his dramatic, black-and-white images of American landscapes, especially western mountains. Adams's first camera, a Kodak Brownie, was a gift from his parents to use on a summer trip to Yosemite National Park. He became a master of photographic technique, publishing numerous photography collections and how-to manuals. Adams worked to gain public acceptance of photography as a fine art. He helped build the first-ever museum collection of photographs, at New York's Museum of Modern Art. Adams was also a dedicated environmentalist and used his work to push for the preservation of scenic areas. *Images by this artist: Student Edition p. 110.*

Anguissola, Sofonisba

[ahn•GWEES•soh•lah, soh•foh•NIS•bah] (1532–1625) Italian painter renowned for introducing new techniques in portraiture. Born in Cremona, Italy, she was the oldest of seven children. Of her five sisters, three of them—Elena, Anna Maria, and Lucia—also became painters. In mid-sixteenth-century Italy, during the height of the Renaissance, Anguissola's father, Amilcare, was a minor member of the Cremonese nobility. Although the activities of young women who lived at this time were very limited—most women were not taught to read—Amilcare and his wife, Bianca, made sure their daughters got as much education as their son. Anguissola began studying with Bernardino Campi, a painter and teacher, when she was about eleven years old. She soon began painting a new type of portrait, posing sitters in informal domestic settings, and her work was praised by Michelangelo and the Italian aristocracy. In 1559, King Philip II of Spain invited Anguissola to Madrid. In Madrid, she worked for many years as a court painter, producing portraits of the royal family and teaching art to Queen Isabel. *Images by this artist: Student Edition pp. 42–43.*

Aztec art Type of art produced by American Indian people who ruled an empire in what is now Mexico during the 1400s and 1500s. The Aztecs had an advanced society for their time. Their craftspeople used feathers to decorate headdresses that were worn only by nobles, often during rituals. Featherwork was considered one of the most prestigious crafts in Aztec art.

Benton, Thomas Hart (1889–1975) Painter and muralist who was part of the American Regionalist movement of the 1930s. Benton, who was born in Neosho, Missouri, studied for a year at the Art Institute of Chicago and then in Paris and New York. His early works were abstracts, but by 1920, he had rejected modernism and begun painting straightforward, recognizable scenes based on American history, daily life, folktales, and song lyrics. He used strong colors and dark, dramatic outlines, depicting people and objects with distorted, almost cartoon-like features. Benton received commissions to paint numerous murals for public buildings, including the New School for Social Research in New York City, the Missouri State Capitol in Jefferson City, and the Truman Presidential Museum & Library in Independence, Missouri. He settled in Kansas City, Missouri, in the mid-1930s and is said to have died with a paintbrush in his hand. *Images by this artist: Student Edition pp. 62–63.*

DID YOU KNOW?

At five feet three inches tall, Thomas Hart Benton was so small that he is said to have bought his clothes from boys' shops his entire life.

Blake, Buckeye (1946–) American painter and sculptor best known for his realistic style of paintings and sculptures of the Old West. Blake was born in Fullerton, California. As a child, he won many school art contests, even though he had no formal art training. At the age of seventeen, Blake went to Hollywood, where he painted scenery for movie studios. In 1978, he and his wife moved to Augusta, Montana, where he built an art studio in which he produces leather furniture, bronze sculptures, and painted ceramics. *Images by this artist: Student Edition p. 91.*

Brueghel the Elder, Pieter [BROY•guhl] (1525?–1569) Dutch painter renowned for his landscape paintings and his witty scenes of peasant life. Brueghel was born in Breda, the Netherlands. He learned to work in tempera—a method of watercolor painting—and traveled to France and Rome, where he studied with local artists. He rejected the influences of classical art. Instead, he drew figures in realistic situations and placed them in contemporary settings. *The Netherlandish Proverbs* is the first of Brueghel's paintings to show his distinctive style. Brueghel had an interest in portraying movement in his paintings. In *The Tower of Babel,* the tower appears to be rotating. Today, fewer than fifty of Brueghel's paintings exist. Although Brueghel enjoyed success during his lifetime, critics did not like his realistic human figures and contemporary subjects. In breaking away from the classical style, Brueghel paved the way for contemporary artists. *Images by this artist: Student Edition pp. 102–103.*

Butterfield, Deborah (1949–) American sculptor known for her modern sculptures of horses. Born in San Diego, California, on the day of the seventy-fifth running of the Kentucky Derby, Butterfield has loved horses since she was a child. At first, she wanted to become a veterinarian. However, two art professors at the University of California encouraged her to study art. Butterfield received a master of fine arts degree from the University of California at Davis, where she studied modern ceramics and sculpture. The ceramic horses of China's Tang dynasty influenced her to use natural materials such as mud, straw, and charred sticks. She also used found objects such as barbed wire, metal pipes, wood fencing, and crushed steel. Butterfield continues to raise and train horses on her ranch in Montana. *Images by this artist: Student Edition p. 88.*

Carle, Eric (1929–) Award-winning author and illustrator of numerous highly acclaimed children's books. Eric Carle was born in Syracuse, New York, and his passion for art began in kindergarten. He remembers how excited he was to create colorful paintings with big paintbrushes on large sheets of paper. At the age of six, he moved with his parents to Stuttgart, Germany, his father's original home. Carle enrolled in the Fine Arts Academy and designed posters for the American information center in Stuttgart. Confident and prepared, he returned to the United States with his portfolio. A few years later, after serving in the United States Army, Carle worked as a designer and art director. Eventually he quit that job and became a freelance artist. Carle's illustration of his first children's book led to his true course as a writer and illustrator. His first two books, *1, 2, 3 to the Zoo* and *The Very Hungry Caterpillar,* contain bold, colorful collage illustrations of various animals. His love of nature comes from fond childhood memories of time spent with his father. The two used to take long walks through the countryside, where they would lift rocks and pull back tree bark to see what lived beneath. The simple text and brilliantly colorful illustrations in Carle's many award-winning books reveal his youthful artistic passions. *Images by this artist: Student Edition p. 44.*

Cassatt, Mary [kuh•SAT] (1844–1926) American-born painter and printmaker known for her intimate depictions of women and children. Cassatt was born in Allegheny City, now part of Pittsburgh, Pennsylvania. She had a privileged upbringing and spent much of her childhood in Paris, where she decided to become an artist. Her parents eventually supported her decision and paid for her to attend the Pennsylvania Academy of Fine Arts in Philadelphia. Afterward, Cassatt traveled, studied, and painted in Europe, ultimately settling in Paris. In the late 1870s, she became friends with Edgar Degas, who invited her to exhibit with a cutting-edge group of painters, the Impressionists. Cassatt incorporated Impressionist techniques into her work, using bright colors and rapid, visible brushstrokes to paint light-filled, casually arranged snapshots of modern life, especially scenes of mothers and their children. In her fifties, Cassatt's eyesight began to fail, and by 1914, she had stopped painting. By the time she died, she was almost completely blind. *Images by this artist: Student Edition pp. 130–131; Art Print 17. See also* **Impressionism.**

DID YOU KNOW?

Mary Cassatt painted mothers and children but chose not to marry or have children of her own. After her death, her country home outside Paris became a home for abandoned children.

Cordero, Helen (1915–1994) Native American potter best known as the inventor of the "Storyteller" figure. Cordero, a native of the Cochiti Pueblo near Santa Fe, New Mexico, first began working with clay in the 1950s but had difficulty with the craft until she switched from bowls and jars to figurines, first of birds and animals and then of people. Her first Storyteller, created in 1964, was modeled after her grandfather. Like countless other Storytellers that followed, the figure is open-mouthed, seated, and surrounded by children. Cordero was credited with reviving the Pueblo figure-making tradition as well as with contributing to the economic success of her own people and of other Pueblos. *Images by this artist: Art Print 10.*

Crawford, Edna (1968–) Hispanic American artist who was born and raised in New York. Crawford is a freelance computer animator but has also painted and worked in collage and graphic arts in her free time. She likes to make her art playful and fun so that it is "child-friendly." Crawford uses a sketchbook to write down ideas and draw rough sketches. However, once she has a solid idea, she tries out different versions of images directly on her computer. *Images by this artist: Student Edition pp. 56–57.*

Cubism Movement in twentieth-century painting and sculpture developed jointly by Pablo Picasso and Georges Braque from around 1907 to 1914. Cubists reacted against the Impressionists' use of color and their style of painting from a single viewpoint. Cubists paint a subject as it appears to them rather than paint an imitation. The Cubist style is divided into two categories—analytical and synthetic. In analytical Cubism, painters use monochromatic colors and fragmented geometric shapes to place subjects in different presentations in a composition. Synthetic Cubists use color and the technique of collage to give texture and illusion to the painting. Other artists who have worked in the Cubist style include Robert Delaunay and Juan Gris.

Cuna people, Panama Group of Indian people whose women hand-sew and wear molas. Molas are brightly colored blouses that consist of at least two layers of cloth and are considered a distinct achievement in folk art. The first mola was made more than a hundred years ago, and the earliest designs featured abstract, geometric patterns. Depending on the level of detail, one mola can take up to six months to complete. The unique designs and bright colors keep molas in high demand, bringing in profits for the women who make them.

Curry, Nancy Stamp artist who lives in Cincinnati, Ohio. Curry is known for using the design elements of texture and depth in her work. She teaches art and paint techniques along with stamping and book arts. *Images by this artist: Student Edition p. 74.*

Da Vinci, Leonardo *See* Leonardo da Vinci.

Degas, Edgar [duh•GAH] (1834–1917) French painter, sculptor, and draftsman known as the painter of dancers. Degas came from a wealthy Parisian family. He originally studied law, but at the age of twenty, he convinced his father to support his interest in art. In 1861, he met Edouard Manet, who introduced him to the Impressionists. Like the Impressionists, Degas painted scenes that seemed spontaneous and unplanned. Unlike these artists, however, he painted only indoors and did not work directly from nature; his work also reflected his intense training and his mastery of drawing the human form. He may be best known for his scenes of female ballet dancers, often in class or rehearsal, depicted from an unusual or off-center point of view. When Degas's eyesight began to fail in the 1880s, he turned to creating bold, simple pastels, primarily of women, as well as wax sculptures of dancers and horses. *The Little 14-Year-Old Dancer,* perhaps Degas's most recognized sculpture, was the only one exhibited during his lifetime. *Images by this artist: Student Edition p. 114.*

Dürer, Albrecht [DYUR•er, AHL•brekt] (1471–1528) German painter, draftsman, printmaker, scholar, and writer, considered one of the greatest German artists. Dürer was born in Nuremberg. Showing great artistic talent as a boy, he was apprenticed to a painter and later traveled to learn from other artists. He visited Venice, and his work combined characteristics of Italian paintings with the more conservative German tradition. He is best known for his religious images. Dürer later devoted more of his time to art theory, including the mathematics of perspective and proportion in the human body. He was honored as a German national hero in the mid-1800s, and year-long celebrations were held in 1928, to commemorate the 400th anniversary of his death, and in 1971, to mark the 500th anniversary of his birth. *Images by this artist: Student Edition p. 78.*

Eberle, Abastenia St. Leger (1878–1942) American sculptor who was born in Webster City, Iowa. In 1899, Eberle began her studies at the Art Students League in New York City. She created a multitude of portrait sculptures. Much of her work stemmed from her observations of street life. *Images by this artist: Student Edition p. 28.*

Egyptian art Art of ancient Egypt from about 3000–300 B.C. The purpose of Egyptian art was to glorify kings and honor the deceased by burying them with personal belongings. Evidence of this idea was discovered in the early 1920s when King Tut's tomb was opened, revealing personal treasures that included jewelry, weapons, and a mask made of gold and decorated with gems. Egyptian art is renowned for the sculptures and wall paintings that adorned the tombs within the pyramids. The wall paintings depicted the pursuits of the king and his family. Egyptians used a unique system of writing called hieroglyphs, in which symbols represented letters. These symbols were often carved in stone and were an important feature of Egyptian art.

Fauvism Early twentieth-century artistic movement originating in France. Fauvism flourished in Paris from 1905 to 1907. It is considered the first avant-garde European art movement. Like the Impressionists, Fauvists painted scenes directly from nature, but they rejected the way Impressionists used color. Fauvist painters use pure, brilliant, luminous colors straight from the tube and then aggressively apply them to the canvas in broad, flat areas. They also use rough brushstrokes, thick outlines, and contrasting hues, and they often leave areas of the canvas exposed. Painters practice Fauvism to create a feeling of space and light and to express personal feelings through the vigorous application of color. The Fauvist style can be found in the work of Henri Matisse.

Folk art Natural art style that aims to convey simplicity in art while expressing the beliefs and interests that a group of people have in common. For example, the Hmong people, an Asian culture nearly 4,000 years old, create needlework story cloths as a way of documenting Hmong history. Folk art has been created in numerous countries for hundreds of years, but American folk art gained popularity from 1780 to 1860. It represents everyday life and includes pottery, carving, needlework, weaving, quilting, and other decorative art forms. Folk artists are often self-taught. This art style can be found in the works of Grandma Moses and Horace Pippin.

French, Daniel Chester (1850–1931) American sculptor. French was born in Exeter, New Hampshire, and is known for his large-scale sculptures. Some of his more famous sculptures include a marble bust of Ralph Waldo Emerson and the statue of Abraham Lincoln in the Lincoln Memorial in Washington, D.C. French was influenced by Louisa May Alcott

and the Transcendentalist movement. In 1940, he was one of five artists featured in a series of postage stamps honoring distinguished Americans. *Images by this artist: Art Print 11.*

Garduño, Flor [gahr•DOO•nyoh] Mexican photographer born in Mexico City. Garduño studied art at the San Carlos School of Fine Arts. Garduño worked as an assistant to Manuel Alvarez Bravo, a highly skilled Mexican photographer, before becoming a professional photographer herself. She has taken pictures of people all over the world. *Images by this artist: Student Edition p. 111.*

Gauguin, Paul [goh•GAN] (1848–1903) French painter whose innovative style had a profound influence on the development of modern art. Gauguin was born in Paris. By young adulthood, he had lived in Lima, Peru; spent six years sailing the world in a merchant marine service; and lost both his parents. Between 1871 and 1883, Gauguin lived a typical middle-class life in Paris. He worked as a stockbroker, married, had five children, and developed an interest in collecting art and painting. In 1891, Gauguin left France on a government grant to paint the people and customs of Tahiti. Except for a two-year period when health problems forced him back to France, Gauguin spent the rest of his time living and working in Tahiti and the nearby Marquesas Islands. Three years after his death, a Paris exhibition of nearly 300 of his paintings brought his work to the attention of a new generation of artists. His bold use of color and rejection of Realism inspired both the Fauvist and Expressionist movements. *Images by this artist: Student Edition p. 104.*

DID YOU KNOW?

In 1888, Paul Gauguin spent two months in Arles, France, where he worked with Vincent van Gogh. The two appreciated each other's art but quarreled bitterly about almost everything else. A particularly heated argument between them is said to have sent van Gogh into a mental breakdown, during which he cut off one of his earlobes.

Gogh, Vincent van *See* Van Gogh, Vincent.

Goodacre, Glenna (1939–) American sculptor renowned for her creation of the *Vietnam Women's Memorial,* honoring the women who served in the Vietnam War. Goodacre was born in Texas. Early in her career, she was known for her bronze sculptures and portraits of children in action. Goodacre created the obverse, or head-side, design of the Sacagawea gold dollar that debuted in 2000. *Images by this artist: Student Edition pp. 82–83.*

Graphic arts Term that applies to pictures and designs that can be reproduced by printing processes, allowing a multitude of people to view the same work of art. Graphic arts are used commercially in advertising that appears in magazines, newspapers, posters, pamphlets, and brochures. They are used in the fine arts as well, through the techniques of block printing, etching, engraving, lithography, and silkscreen printing. Today, graphic art forms can be created and manipulated on a computer.

Greek art Type of art and architecture that originated in ancient Greece. With its new ideas and depiction of ideal beauty, Greek art influenced Roman art, particularly in the areas of painting and sculpting. The use of form, line, and decoration was important to the Greeks, as were structure and composition. Sculptures and pottery were two of the major art forms. The sculptures were created out of marble and were then painted. Greek artists often portrayed their subjects in profile, and their art took on a geometric, symmetrical look.

Green, Jonathan (1955–) African American painter and printmaker best known for painting scenes of the everyday lives of the Gullah people of South Carolina. Green was born in Gardens Corner, South Carolina. He attended the Art Institute of Chicago and earned a bachelor's degree in fine arts and is the first known artist of Gullah heritage to receive formal training at a professional art school. Green's artistic style is described as Narrative Realism. He prefers to paint in oils. Green's figures are featureless, and he uses a combination of pattern, abstraction, and bright colors to compose his paintings. *Images by this artist: Student Edition p. 46; Art Print 14.*

Guaymí Indians [wy•MEE] Also known as the Ngobe-Bugle Indians, they are predominantly from Panama. They specialize in making *chaquiras,* which are multicolored, beaded necklaces. The first of these necklaces were dull in color and were made of pebbles, bone fragments, seeds, and shells. The *chaquiras* were originally worn by Guaymí men during festivals and cultural ceremonies. Today, they are mass-produced and sold in tourist markets.

Hanson, Ann (1959–) American artist born in Montgomery County, Maryland. Hanson's inspiration comes from nature and, more specifically, animals. She is amazed by their skin and feather patterns and uses her art as a way of expressing her admiration of these creatures. In an interview in the *Montgomery County Journal,* she said, "My work is mostly to entertain people, to cause people to smile, to reflect on some of the happy things in life. . . . Animals are what I'm well known for. Everything is dancing . . . dancing or springing or [moving]." *Images by this artist: Student Edition p. 78.*

Hiroshige, Ando (other first names also include Ichiryusai or Ichiryusu or Utagawa) [hee•roh•shee•gay] (1797–1858) Japanese painter and printmaker, renowned for his full-color landscape prints. Hiroshige was born in Edo, Japan (present-day Tokyo). As a child, Hiroshige liked to sketch. The prints of the great artist Katsushika Hokusai inspired him to become an artist. From 1830 to 1844, he traveled throughout Japan, creating a series of landscape prints. His most successful print series, titled *Fifty-three Stages on the Tokaido,* was made from sketches about life along the Tokaido highway connecting the ancient Japanese cities of Edo and Kyoto. Hiroshige's technique of using sweeping brushstrokes to suggest vast landscapes influenced the Impressionist movement. *Images by this artist: Student Edition p. 106.*

Hokusai, Katsushika [hoh•kus•eye, kaht•soo•shee•kah] (1760–1849) Japanese painter and printmaker, renowned for his landscape prints. Hokusai was born in Edo, Japan (present-day Tokyo). He used a wide range of artistic techniques, ranging from Ming-period Chinese painting to Western-style painting. His art forms included ink paintings, woodblock prints, book illustrations, silkscreens, and landscape paintings. Hokusai drew upon the legends, traditions, and everyday lives of the Japanese to create his images. He produced more than 30,000 drawings. In his constant pursuit of new forms of artistic expression, Hokusai moved ninety-three times. He also changed his name more than fifty times. The last name he used was Gakyo Rojin, which means "old man mad about drawing." *Images by this artist: Student Edition p. 108.*

Homer, Winslow (1836–1910) American painter, illustrator, and lithographer, known as the era's leading representative of Realism. Homer was born in Boston and grew up in Cambridge, Massachusetts. In 1855, he became a lithographer's apprentice; he then moved on to work as a free-lance magazine illustrator. In 1859, the magazine *Harper's Weekly* hired Homer and eventually made him an artist-correspondent covering the Civil War. After the war, Homer focused on oil painting. His early oils were inspired by his wartime illustrations and were somber in color. During the 1860s and 1870s, Homer began painting in watercolor, choosing rural or idyllic scenes of farm life as his subjects. He eventually moved to the Maine coast, and the sea became the leading subject of his paintings. Homer's paintings are characterized by their directness, realism, objectivity, and splendid color. He said about his art, "When I have selected the thing carefully, I paint it exactly as it appears." *Images by this artist: Student Edition p. 58; Art Print 6.*

DID YOU KNOW?

Winslow Homer was twenty-four when he received his first important assignment with *Harper's Weekly*. He sketched Abraham Lincoln's first inauguration.

Impressionism Late nineteenth-century artistic movement originating in France. Impressionism flourished in France from 1860 to 1900. The Impressionists were a group of artists with different styles who exhibited their work together. They reacted against traditional painting techniques and the Romantics' belief that paintings should portray emotion. Impressionists attempt to capture the visual impression made by a scene, usually a land-scape or city scene painted outdoors. Their primary goal is to show the effect of natural light and color on a subject and quickly transmit it to the canvas. Painters use unmixed bright, soft colors applied with swift, loose brushstrokes to intensify luminosity and brilliance. The Impressionist style can be found in the works of Claude Monet, Pierre-Auguste Renoir, Edgar Degas, and Mary Cassatt.

Jaso, Luis [HAH•soh, loo•EES] (1926–1983) Mexican-born painter and architect who lived in Germany for some time. Jaso traveled to Spain, Italy, and the cities of San Francisco and New York on journeys that were inspired by his appre-ciation of art. His parents encouraged his interest in art and architecture, and he surrounded himself with creative friends—authors, actors, musicians, and other artists. Jaso was a student at the Universidad Nacional Autónoma de México and won prizes, awards, and recognition for his art and architecture. *Images by this artist: Student Edition p. 38.*

Johns, Jasper (1930–) American painter, sculptor, and printmaker. Johns was born in Augusta, Georgia, and grew up in South Carolina. In the early 1950s, he worked in a bookstore and as a commercial artist in New York City, designing store window displays with friend and artist Robert Rauschenberg. In 1954, Johns created the first of his now-famous flag paintings. In 1958, his first solo exhibition made him one of the world's best-known—and best-paid—living artists. Along with Rauschenberg, Johns is credited with laying the groundwork for Pop Art. Since the late 1990s, he has lived and worked in Connecticut. *Images by this artist: Student Edition p. 67. See also* **Pop Art.**

Johnson, William H. (1901–1970) American painter best known for his vivid, primi-tive scenes of African American life, culture, and history. Johnson was born in Florence, South Carolina. He showed artistic talent at an early age. At seventeen, he followed an uncle to New York City. Johnson worked at odd jobs and saved enough money to enroll in art school. His work impressed supporters, who paid for a three-year stint in Paris. There, he exhibited Expressionist-style paintings. He returned to the United States in 1930, where his work won prestigious awards. Johnson's style evolved to include bold, vibrantly contrasting colors; heavy, black outlines; and fig-ures with exaggerated, even cartoonish features. *Images by this artist: Student Edition p. 132.*

Kahlo, Frida [KAH•loh, FREE•dah] (1907–1954) Mexican painter noted for her self-portraits and primitive artistic style. Kahlo was born in Coyoacan, Mexico. She never planned to become an artist, wanting instead to go to medical school. However, devastating injuries in a traffic accident left her permanently disabled. During her slow recovery, Kahlo taught herself to paint. She painted mostly self-portraits and still lifes. In 1929, Kahlo married Diego Rivera, Mexico's most famous artist. Rivera encouraged Kahlo to focus on her Mexican heritage as the subject of her paintings. In her second self-portrait, Kahlo took Rivera's advice and portrayed herself in traditional Mexican folk dress. In 1943, Kahlo was appointed professor of painting at the Education Ministry's School of Fine Arts. Throughout her life, she refused to let her physical problems interfere with her art. *Images by this artist: Student Edition pp. 116–117; Art Print 15.*

DID YOU KNOW?

As a result of her accident, Frida Kahlo endured thirty-two operations. She could not paint for more than an hour at a time. At one exhibit of her paintings, Kahlo was too ill to leave her bed, so she had it moved into the gallery in order to become a part of the exhibit.

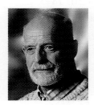

King, Phillip (1934–) British sculptor and member of the New Generation—a group of British sculptors who achieved recognition in the mid-1960s. King started creating sculptures between 1954 and 1957 while studying modern languages at Christ's College, Cambridge. King's sculptures, particularly his series of cones, illustrate his desire to create simple, translucent forms. *Images by this artist: Student Edition p. 86.*

Kuba people, Democratic Republic of the Congo

Multiethnic group that used art objects to demonstrate its power, wealth, and social status. The Kuba kingdom was at its peak from 1835 to 1885, as there was a high demand for the exportation of its hand-woven embroidered raffia cloths. The Kuba people wore masks and costumes decorated with beads, copper, feathers, and shells to honor the royal dynasty and their matrilineal, or maternal, ancestors. Their ceremonial clothing often depicted abstract geometric patterns and designs in a somewhat conservative fashion.

Lawrence, Jacob (1917–2000) African American painter renowned for his realistic narrative scenes of African American life and history. Lawrence was born in Atlantic City, New Jersey, but when he was thirteen, his family moved to Harlem. He attended classes at the Harlem Art Workshop and the American Artists School, developing an artistic style influenced by Cubism and Expressionism. He drew simple geometric figures and painted them in brilliant colors, using the water-based media of gouache and tempera. Lawrence researched

and painted many series of works about famous Africans and African Americans, the best known of which is titled *Migration of the Negro*. Lawrence became the first African American painter to have his work placed in the permanent collection of the Museum of Modern Art. In 1970, the National Association for the Advancement of Colored People awarded him the Spingarn Medal, and in 1990, he received the United States National Medal of Arts. *Images by this artist: Student Edition pp. 76–77; Art Print 9.*

Lee, Doris (1905–1983) American painter known for painting realistic American scenes. Lee was born in Aledo, Illinois, into a family of artists. She studied with many artists, including Andre Lhote, Ernest Lawson, and Arnold Blanch, whom she later married. In 1931, Lee moved to the Woodstock Artists Colony in Woodstock, New York. Lee's paintings are described as lively, humorous, and colorful, combining the styles of Realism and modernism. Lee's style is illustrated in her painting *Thanksgiving,* which won the Logan Medal from the Art Institute of Chicago in 1935. *Images by this artist: Student Edition p. 33.*

Leonardo da Vinci [lay•oh•NAR•doh dah VIN•chee] (1452–1519) Italian painter, sculptor, scientist, engineer, architect, and musician known as the original "Renaissance man." Leonardo was one of the most influential artists of all time. He produced two of the world's best-known and most-admired paintings—the *Mona Lisa* (now in the Louvre in Paris) and *The Last Supper* (a fresco in the Santa Maria della Grazie, in Milan, Italy). Leonardo pioneered painting techniques now called *sfumato* (a softening of outlines that creates the suggestion of movement in a still painting) and *chiaroscuro* (the use of dramatic light and shadow to create a sense of volume). He was one of the first artists to sketch what he intended to paint before he painted it. Because of Leonardo, people stopped thinking of artists as poor laborers and started viewing them as potentially genius-level creative thinkers. Leonardo spent much of his working life on his notebooks—huge volumes in which he sketched his observations of plants and animals; his plans for buildings, sculptures, bridges, and canals; and even his designs for an airplane, helicopter, and underwater diving suit. Leonardo was born in Vinci, near Florence (*da Vinci* means "from Vinci"), and lived mostly in Florence and Milan. He spent his last years in Amboise, France, under the patronage of Francis I, king of France. *Images by this artist: Art Print 3.*

Marcks, Gerhard (1889–1981) German-born sculptor, teacher, printmaker, and painter who is best known for producing sculptures in the Expressionist style. Marcks was born in Berlin and in 1919 became one of the first teachers appointed to the faculty of the Bauhaus School. He later traveled to Greece to study classical sculpture. While in Greece, Marcks developed a form of abstraction based on the human body. After World War II, Marcks was appointed professor of sculpture at an art school in Hamburg. He also created monuments to those who had died during the war. *Images by this artist: Student Edition p. 88.*

Matisse, Henri [mah•TEES, ahn•REE] (1869–1954) French painter, sculptor, and graphic artist. Matisse is widely considered the greatest French painter of the twentieth century and one of the major figures of contemporary art. Matisse did not become interested in art until he was in his twenties when, against his father's wishes, he left law school to become an artist. He studied in Paris, where the work of Paul Cézanne, Claude Monet, Paul Gauguin, and other revolutionary artists influenced him. Matisse emphasized color and line over the realistic depiction of people and objects. A 1913 New York show that introduced Matisse and other contemporary European artists to the United States enhanced his reputation, and he was soon one of the world's best-known—and best-paid—living artists. Until about 1920, Matisse divided his time between a studio in Paris, another in Nice on the French Riviera, and his family home in the Paris suburbs. By the 1940s, Matisse's eyesight was failing, and arthritis limited the use of his hands. During this time, he experimented with what he called "drawing with scissors," producing compositions of cut paper that today are among his most recognizable works. *Images by this artist: Student Edition pp. 34, 106; Art Print 7. See also* **Fauvism.**

McDermott, Gerald (1941–) American author, filmmaker, illustrator, graphic designer, and storyteller who is renowned for his films and children's books based on folktales from other countries. Born in Detroit, McDermott attended weekend art classes at the Detroit Institute of Art. During college, he began making animated films about folklore. McDermott chose the Japanese folktale *The Stonecutter* to develop his unique method. After designing a storyboard for the film, he drew 6,000 frames, each synchronized to the notes of a musical score. McDermott went on to make *Anansi the Spider,* *The Magic Tree,* and *Arrow to the Sun.* He then turned these three films into children's books. *Arrow to the Sun* won the prestigious Caldecott Medal. *Images by this artist: Student Edition pp. 136–137.*

Miró, Joan [mee•ROH, hoh•AHN] (1893–1983) Spanish painter, sculptor, printmaker, etcher, and lithographer best known as one of the leaders of Surrealism. Miró was born in Barcelona and worked as an accountant for two years before deciding to become a full-time artist. In 1919, Miró visited Paris, where he studied the paintings of Pablo Picasso and the Fauvists. He also associated with the Surrealists and joined their movement. Miró's artistic technique combined elements of folk art, the bright colors of Fauvism, and the expressive lines and odd geometric forms of Cubism. Miró's Surrealist painting *Harlequin's Carnival* features humorous insect-like creatures dancing and making music. He said, "I begin painting and as I paint the picture begins to assert itself, or suggest itself, under my brush." Miró wanted his artwork to be available to the public. In 1947, he painted a large mural for the Terrace Hilton Hotel in Cincinnati. He also painted a mural for Harvard University. Miró later took up stained-glass design. *Images by this artist: Art Print 2.*

Monet, Claude [moh•NAY] (1840–1926) French painter renowned as the leader of the Impressionist movement. Born in Paris, Monet spent his childhood in Le Havre, France. In 1862, he moved back to Paris to study art. There, he met several other artists, including Pierre-Auguste Renoir. In 1874, Monet and his friends held an independent exhibition of their paintings, including Monet's landscape titled *Impression: Sunrise.* That apparently inspired one art critic to call the entire exhibition Impressionist, which gave the movement its name. The Impressionists attempted to capture a visual impression of a scene, especially the effect natural light has on the setting. Monet painted the same view many times to capture the light at different times of the day, as can be seen in his *Rouen Cathedral* series. Monet once said, "I want the unobtainable. Other artists paint a bridge, a house, a boat, and that's the end. They are finished. I want to paint the air which surrounds the bridge, the house, the boat, the beauty of the air in which the objects are located, and that is nothing short of impossible." Despite failing eyesight, Monet continued to paint until his death. *Images by this artist: Student Edition pp. 49, 98. See also* **Impressionism.**

Moses, Grandma (Anna Mary Robertson) (1860–1961) American painter

best known for her folk art paintings. Grandma Moses was born Anna Mary Robertson in Greenwich, New York. Robertson had no formal art training. As a child, she drew and painted on unused newsprint. She used berry juice to brighten her pictures. She married Thomas Salmon Moses in 1887, and the couple became farmers. Moses loved to work in needlepoint, and she won prizes for her embroidery. In 1927, she began to paint full time. Her first art exhibition was held in a drugstore in Hoosick Falls, New York, where an art collector discovered her work. In 1940, an exhibition in Manhattan titled *What a Farm Wife Painted* launched her career. Five years later, Hallmark bought the rights to reproduce her paintings on Christmas cards, making her an instant celebrity. Moses published her autobiography, *My Life's History,* in 1952. At the age of one hundred, she illustrated *'Twas the Night Before Christmas* by Clement Moore. *Images by this artist: Student Edition pp. 22–23.*

Nampeyo, Miriam Tewaguna

[nahm•PAY•oh, tay•wah•GOO•nuh] (1956–) Native American of the Southwest and member of the Hopi reservation. Nampeyo is gaining popularity as a potter. She is the daughter of Elva Tewaguna Nampeyo, the granddaughter of the well-known Fannie Polacca Nampeyo, and the great-granddaughter of Nampeyo of Hano—also potters. Nampeyo's pottery is characterized by its abstract designs and earthy tones. *Images by this artist: Student Edition p. 86.*

O'Keeffe, Georgia (1887–1986) American

painter renowned for her abstract paintings and still-life compositions. Born in Sun Prairie, Wisconsin, O'Keeffe became interested in art after she saw a pen-and-ink drawing of a Grecian maiden in one of her mother's books. O'Keeffe studied art at many prestigious schools, including the Art Institute of Chicago and Columbia University. She worked as a teacher and commercial artist but after 1918 began to paint full time. O'Keeffe's life changed when she married photographer Alfred Stieglitz in 1924. She learned about photography and began to use certain elements of the photographic process in her work. O'Keeffe moved to New Mexico and was inspired by the state's beautiful landscapes. In New Mexico, she painted abstracts and still lifes of flowers, animal bones, mountains, and other natural forms. Near the end of her life, O'Keeffe lost her sight, but she did not give up her art. She pursued pottery instead. *Images by this artist: Student Edition pp. 50–51; Art Print 5.*

DID YOU KNOW?

Georgia O'Keeffe mixed paints on a glass tray on which she also kept a separate brush for each color. In order to keep track of every color, O'Keeffe put a sample of each on a white card. This enabled her to easily reproduce the color to use in another painting.

Pei, I. M. [PAY] (1917–) Chinese-born

American architect best known for his use of simple geometric forms to create contemporary, functional buildings. In 1935, Pei went to the United States to study architectural engineering at the Massachusetts Institute of Technology. He also earned a graduate degree from Harvard University. He started his own architectural firm in 1955. As he developed his own personal style, Pei's designs often included prism shapes, soaring airy spaces, and skylights in vaulted ceilings. Some of his most famous designs are the John Hancock Tower in Boston and the glass pyramid that was built in the courtyard of the Louvre Museum in Paris. In 1979, Pei received a Gold Medal from the American Institute of Architects, the organization's highest award, for his design of the JFK Memorial Library. *Images by this artist: Student Edition p. 95.*

Picasso, Pablo [pih•KAHS•soh] (1881–1973)

Spanish painter, sculptor, printmaker, ceramicist, and illustrator renowned for pioneering the artistic style of Cubism. Picasso was born in Malaga, Spain. His father, an art teacher, recognized Picasso's early talent and gave him art lessons. At fifteen, Picasso qualified to enter the Academy of Fine Arts in Barcelona. After one year, he left school and went to Paris. There, he painted the poor and social outcasts of the city using blue tones to express their sadness. In 1904, Picasso changed his style and began to paint happy circus performers in rose and pink tones. After studying Paul Gauguin's paintings of non-Western cultures and the artistic style of ancient Iberian sculpture, Picasso became inspired to experiment with the element of distortion. In 1907, he collaborated with fellow artist Georges Braque to produce a new artistic style called Cubism. Picasso was also the first artist to create sculptures out of various materials, rather than by carving or modeling. *Images by this artist: Student Edition pp. 26, 36–37; Art Print 1. See also* **Cubism.**

Pinkney, Brian (1961–) American artist renowned for his illustrations using a technique called scratchboard. Born in Boston, Massachusetts, Pinkney grew up surrounded by art. His mother writes children's books, and his father is a children's book illustrator. Pinkney knew that he wanted to become an illustrator. Pinkney attended the Philadelphia College of Art, and later, the School of Visual Arts in New York. There, he learned to work with scratchboard, a technique that involves scratching black ink off a white board. He received a Caldecott Honor award for illustrating *Duke Ellington: The Piano Prince and His Orchestra. Images by this artist: Student Edition p. 24.*

Pop Art Movement in painting, sculpture, and printmaking that began in Britain in the 1950s and shifted to the United States in 1960. Pop Art focused on images from popular culture, including advertising, comic strips, and brand-name packaged goods. Inspired by Dada, which broke new ground in both subject matter and technique, Pop Art is sometimes called Neo-Dada. Major Pop artists include Roy Lichtenstein, Jasper Johns, Claes Oldenburg, and Andy Warhol.

Post-Impressionism General term for trends in modern art that developed as a reaction against Impressionism and Neo-Impressionism. The three major Post-Impressionist artists were Paul Cézanne, Vincent van Gogh, and Paul Gauguin, but Henri Matisse and Pablo Picasso were also involved for part of their careers. All produced early work that was Impressionist in style but later developed styles that used flat areas of bright color and emphasized solid structures and simplified forms. Most Post-Impressionist work was created between 1886 and 1905.

Rembrandt van Rijn [REM•brant fuhn RYN] (1606–1669) Dutch painter, etcher, and draftsman, considered one of the greatest Western artists. Rembrandt was born in Leiden, the Netherlands. At age fourteen, he entered the University of Leiden, but he soon left to study with a local artist. Rembrandt also studied for six months with painter Pieter Lastman, who taught him to use exaggerated gestures in his subjects' poses, vivid lighting effects and colors, and a glossy finish on the canvas. Rembrandt painted portraits, landscapes, historical and biblical scenes, and scenes of everyday life. Rembrandt's group portrait titled *Anatomy Lesson of Professor Tulp* established him as a premier portrait painter. He invented a new kind of painting called a *tronie,* or portrait head, which is a combination of a portrait and a historical painting. *The Night*

Watch is one of the best examples of this style. *Images by this artist: Student Edition p. 115.*

Renaissance Movement that began in Italy and gradually spread into northern Europe. In the visual arts, the Renaissance of the fourteenth and fifteenth centuries marked a gradual transition from medieval to modern ways of thinking and viewing the world. Specific changes included a renewed interest in the characteristics of Greek and Roman art and architecture; the expansion of patronage and subject matter outside the realm of the church; the application of scientific and mathematical principles to the representation of realistic human forms and spatial perspective; and an overall rise in the status of artists and their work. Among the dozens of major Renaissance artists are Sandro Botticelli, Leonardo da Vinci, and Michelangelo.

Rivera, Diego [ree•VAY•rah, DYAY•goh] (1886–1957) Mexican painter known for his murals and as the co-founder of the Mexican School of Painting. Rivera was born in Guanajuato, Mexico. As a young boy, he wanted to paint all the time. To accommodate his son, Rivera's father covered the walls of a room in their house with paper so that Diego could paint on them. At the age of ten, Rivera received a scholarship to study art in Mexico City. Later, he went to France and also toured Italy to study the fresco techniques of the Renaissance artists. He wanted to paint murals on the walls of public buildings to make art accessible to all people. For his murals, Rivera used fresco, a technique where paint is placed on wet plaster, and also encaustic painting, a method that uses heat to fuse wax colors onto a surface. Rivera's best-known mural is at the National Palace in Mexico City. It depicts the history of Mexico from ancient to modern times. In 1929, Rivera married Frida Kahlo, an accomplished Mexican painter. *Images by this artist: Student Edition pp. 28, 48; Art Print 4.*

Rockwell, Norman (1894–1978) American illustrator and painter renowned for his realistic illustrations of everyday small-town life in the United States. Rockwell was born in New York City and studied at the Art Students League, the Chase School of Art, the National Academy of Design, and in Paris. Rockwell's big break came when he sold five color illustrations to the *Saturday Evening Post* magazine in 1916. Rockwell's illustrations told the story of American family values, usually with a humorous twist. His most acclaimed *Saturday Evening Post* cover, *Saying Grace,* was done for a Thanksgiving issue. Rockwell's magazine illustrations brought him much success and were very popular with the public. In 1977, President Gerald Ford awarded Rockwell the Presidential Medal of Freedom. *Images by this artist: Student Edition p. 124.*

DID YOU KNOW?

Although Norman Rockwell is best known for his *Saturday Evening Post* illustrations, he also worked for other magazines, including *Look.* For his *Look* magazine illustrations, Rockwell chose contemporary subjects such as politics and the American space program.

Roman art Type of art intended for decoration and display, rather than the expression of ideas and beliefs. The Romans were renowned for their statues, paintings, and mosaics. Mosaics are made up of small painted stones arranged to create an image. Roman mosaics depicted scenes of everyday living. The two basic mosaic styles are *opus sectile,* which refers to mosaics made of geometric stones arranged in a certain way to produce a desired shape, and *opus tessellatum,* which are square mosaics that were often used as patterns on floors.

Rousseau, Henri [roo•SOH, ahn•REE] (1844–1910) French painter renowned for his modern primitive-style paintings. Born in Laval, France, Rousseau came from a working-class family. His family could not afford art lessons, but he taught himself to paint. He did not begin painting full time until he retired at the age of forty-nine. At first, critics ridiculed his work, but he believed in himself and continued painting. Rousseau developed an unusual painting technique. He painted from the top to the bottom of the canvas. He also painted the different colors one by one. For example, he would paint first the reds, then the blues, and then the other colors. Rousseau liked to paint jungle landscapes and wild animals. His best-known jungle landscape is entitled *Tiger in a Tropical Storm.* He got his inspiration from walks through Paris gardens and from looking at photographs of wild animals in books. *Images by this artist: Student Edition pp. 27, 72; Art Print 18.*

Supuni, Amos (1970–) African sculptor who was born in Malawi in south-central Africa. Supuni grew up in neighboring Zimbabwe, where his parents moved when he was only a few months old. He was nearly twenty years old when he learned to carve in stone at a community center for unemployed youth. Supuni remained with the center, which became known as Silvera House, until 1996, when he was selected to join Zimbabwe's Chapungu artists' residency program, whose traveling exhibitions have brought worldwide attention to his work. *Images by this artist: Student Edition p. 84.*

Symbols in art Pictures or signs that represent something to a group of people who share knowledge, beliefs, or values. American culture has many symbols, including the eagle, the American flag, Uncle Sam, and the Statue of Liberty. Images of these symbols appear frequently in famous paintings and photographs, as well as on medals, coins, and buildings.

Thiebaud, Wayne [TEE•boh] (1920–) American painter and commercial artist best known for his still lifes of sweet foods. Thiebaud was born in Mesa, Arizona, and has spent much of his life in California. In the early 1950s, Thiebaud earned a master's degree in art and began working as a college art professor. By the early 1960s, he had begun the paintings for which he is best known—small still lifes of commonplace objects, especially cakes, pies, and other desserts, against an empty, white background. Thiebaud was linked to Pop Art in part because of his everyday subject matter and emphasis on basic shapes, but he has always considered himself a traditional painter, applying paint in what has been described as a thick, juicy style. In the late 1960s, Thiebaud began painting landscapes, especially city scenes viewed at a distance from overhead angles. *Images by this artist: Student Edition p. 32.*

Valadon, Suzanne (1865–1938) French painter whose works are known for their rich colors, dark, heavy outlines, and crowded backgrounds. Valadon was born near Limoges, France. She spent a lonely childhood in Paris, and before she was a teenager, she was working as a waitress and a circus acrobat. By about 1880 she began to work as an artist's model, posing for such artists as Henri de Toulouse-Lautrec and Pierre-Auguste Renoir. Valadon had drawn since childhood, but she learned painting techniques by watching the artists who painted her. In 1883, Valadon gave birth to Maurice Utrillo, who also became a well-known painter. Valadon and her work became internationally known in the 1920s and 1930s. *Images by this artist: Student Edition p. 52.*

Van Gogh, Vincent [van GOH]
(1853–1890) Dutch painter born in the small
village of Groot-Zundert, Holland, renowned
as one of the greatest Post-Impressionist artists.
In 1869, van Gogh became an apprentice in his
uncle's art business and later pursued his interest
in religious studies. He became a missionary and went to live in
the coal-mining district of southern Belgium. There, he decided
to become an artist, and he began to draw pictures chronicling
the miners' harsh living conditions. After studying drawing in
Brussels and watercolor with Anton Mauve, van Gogh began to
paint in oils. He moved to a desolate area of the Netherlands,
where he painted the remote landscape and local peasants. In
1885, he produced his first masterpiece based on the daily life
of peasants, titled *The Potato Eaters.* The works of Rubens, the
Japanese printmakers Hiroshige and Katsushika Hokusai, and the
French Impressionists influenced his work. In 1888, he went to
paint in southern France; his works created there reflect the sunlight, landscapes, and vivid colors of the countryside. In France,
he began to exhibit erratic behavior. Paul Gauguin joined him,
they argued, and after cutting off his own earlobe, van Gogh was
hospitalized for mental illness. He spent the last nineteen months
of his life fighting this illness. *Images by this artist: Student
Edition p. 54; Art Print 13. See also* **Post-Impressionism.**

Van Hulsdonck, Jacob (1582–1647) Flemish painter
who specialized in still lifes, mostly of flowers and fruit. Van
Hulsdonck began studying painting as a youth in Middleburg,
Germany. At the age of twenty-seven, he joined the painters'
guild in his native Antwerp. Viewers were captivated by the lus-
cious colors and varied textures that filled van Hulsdonck's paintings. *Images by this artist: Student Edition p. 132.*

Vitale, Stefano [vee•TAHL•ee, stay•FAHN•oh]
(1958–) Italian-born children's book illustrator.
Vitale's drawings have graced the pages of several
children's books. His artwork has also appeared
in magazines, including *Time, Newsweek,* and
Reader's Digest. He has an original style, similar
to primitive painting or folk art, using wood-grain texture and
vibrant colors in many of his illustrations. *Images by this artist:
Student Edition p. 64.*

Wood, Grant (1891–1942) American painter best known
for his painting *American Gothic.* Wood was born in Anamosa,
Iowa. As a young man, he supported himself as a metalworker
and handyman while he studied and practiced painting. He produced Impressionist-inspired landscapes and architectural scenes
until the late 1920s, when he began to paint distinctly Midwestern themes in a hard-edged, almost cartoonish American
Regionalist style. Wood painted Iowa landscapes and gently
satirical portraits of local people, often farmers, in everyday
situations and dress. *American Gothic,* which Wood painted in
1930, depicts a gaunt Iowa farmer and his equally stern-looking
daughter in front of their farmhouse. The piece made Grant Wood
famous and has since become an American icon and one of the
most-recognized paintings in the world. Through the 1930s,
Wood also worked on numerous New Deal Public Works Art
Projects, founded an experimental art colony at Stone City,
Iowa, and taught at Iowa State University. *Images by this artist:
Art Print 8.*

Wright, Frank Lloyd (1867–1959) Most
influential American architect of the twentieth
century. Born in Richland Center, Wisconsin,
Wright entered the University of Wisconsin at
fifteen as an engineering student. However, he
stayed for only a few months before moving to Chicago. There,
he worked as a draftsman for architect Joseph Lyman Silsbee
and later for Louis Sullivan, before establishing his own practice.
He became known as the developer of the Prairie School architectural style, characterized by low-pitched roofs designed to
blend into the surrounding landscape. Wright's work remained
controversial in the United States, but he had a strong influence
on the development of architecture in Europe and Asia. In 1916,
he designed the Imperial Hotel in Tokyo, Japan, in such a way
that it would float on a sea of mud. As a result of Wright's
design, the hotel sustained little damage in the catastrophic
earthquake of 1923. Wright described his architectural style
as "organic architecture," which, he said, "proceeds, persists,
creates, according to the nature of man and his circumstances
as they both change." *Images by this artist: Student Edition
pp. 96–97; Art Print 12.*

DID YOU KNOW?

Wright designed the Guggenheim Museum in New York
City. His design for the structure, a spiral ramp that
rises from the bottom to the top of the building, was
an innovative idea at the time.

Scope & Sequence

PERCEPTION: DEVELOP AND ORGANIZE IDEAS FROM THE ENVIRONMENT	GRADE 1	2	3	4	5
Use Sensory Knowledge and Life Experiences to Identify Ideas					
About self	•	•	•	•	•
About family, school, community	•	•	•	•	•
About visual symbols, life events		•	•	•	•
Elements of Art					
Line					
Identify and discuss line as an element of art	•	•	•	•	•
Examine and explore line in art	•	•	•	•	•
curved, straight, diagonal	•	•	•	•	•
vertical, horizontal		•	•	•	•
outline; contour; expressive			•	•	•
crosshatch; sketched			•	•	•
actual; implied				•	
continuous					•
Shape					
Identify and discuss shape as an element of art	•	•	•	•	•
Recognize shape as two-dimensional	•	•	•	•	•
Examine and explore shape in art	•	•	•	•	•
geometric; organic/free-form; repeated; symbols/pictures	•	•	•	•	•
symbols/letters; positive, negative					•
Color					
Identify and discuss color as an element of art	•	•	•	•	•
Examine and explore color in art	•	•	•	•	•
primary, secondary, neutral	•	•	•	•	•
warm, cool	•	•	•	•	•
intermediate, complementary		•	•	•	•
monochromatic, dominant				•	•
analogous; hue; saturation; intensity					•
Space					
Identify and discuss space as an element of art	•	•	•	•	•
Examine and explore space in art	•	•	•	•	•
three-dimensional; horizon line	•	•	•	•	•
foreground, background		•	•	•	•
overlapping; illusion of depth		•	•	•	•
placement; proportion		•	•	•	•
atmospheric perspective; linear perspective; vanishing point				•	•
middle ground, positive, negative				•	•
points of view					•
Value					
Identify and discuss value as an element of art	•	•	•	•	•
Examine and explore value in art	•	•	•	•	•
dark, light	•	•	•	•	•
brightness		•	•	•	•
shadows; gray scale; color gradations	•	•	•	•	•
shades, tints	•	•	•	•	•
contrast		•	•	•	•

	1	2	3	4	5
Texture					
Identify and discuss texture as an element of art	•	•	•	•	•
Recognize texture as simulated (drawn or painted on a surface) and real (tactile); distinguish between visual and tactile textures	•	•	•	•	•
Examine and explore texture in art	•	•	•	•	•
visual, tactile; repeated lines	•	•	•	•	•
values				•	•
Form					
Identify and discuss form as an element of art	•	•	•	•	•
Recognize form as three-dimensional	•	•	•	•	•
Examine and explore form in art	•	•	•	•	•
geometric, organic	•	•	•	•	•

Principles of Design

	1	2	3	4	5
Pattern/Repetition					
Identify and discuss pattern as a principle of design	•	•	•	•	•
Recognize repetition of art elements to create pattern	•	•	•	•	•
Examine and explore pattern in art	•	•	•	•	•
Proportion					
Identify and discuss proportion as a principle of design			•	•	•
Emphasis					
Identify and discuss emphasis as a principle of design	•	•	•	•	•
Identify emphasis by indicating what parts of an artwork are most important	•	•	•	•	•
Examine and explore emphasis in art	•	•	•	•	•
center of interest; color; contrast	•	•	•	•	•
visual weight		•	•	•	•
Balance					
Identify and discuss balance as a principle of design	•	•	•	•	•
Understand balance as a composition that achieves equilibrium in the eyes of the viewer		•	•	•	•
Examine and explore balance in art	•	•	•	•	•
symmetrical	•	•	•	•	•
radial; asymmetrical; midline		•	•	•	•
vertical axis; visual weight				•	•
horizontal axis; exact symmetry, near symmetry					•
Rhythm					
Identify and discuss rhythm as a principle of design	•	•	•	•	•
Understand that rhythm is achieved by repeating elements in artwork	•	•	•	•	•
Examine and explore rhythm in art (repetition; movement)	•	•	•	•	•
Movement					
Identify and discuss movement as a principle of design		•	•	•	•
Examine and explore movement on two-dimensional surfaces		•	•	•	•
Unity					
Identify and discuss unity as a principle of design	•	•	•	•	•
Examine and explore unity in art	•	•	•	•	•
Variety					
Identify and discuss variety as a principle of design	•	•	•	•	•
Examine and explore variety in art (variety in line, color, texture, shape)	•	•	•	•	•

Scope & Sequence

	GRADE 1	2	3	4	5
CREATIVE EXPRESSION/PERFORMANCE: EXPRESS IDEAS THROUGH ORIGINAL ARTWORKS					
Safety in Art Processes					
Display an awareness of and respect for art tools and materials	•	•	•	•	•
Demonstrate the proper care for and use of tools, materials, and art area	•	•	•	•	•
Follow art safety rules and procedures	•	•	•	•	•
Develop and Apply Art Knowledge and Skills					
Apply elements (line, shape, color, form, texture, value, space) in original artworks	•	•	•	•	•
Apply design principles (pattern, rhythm, movement, unity, variety, balance, proportion, emphasis) in original artworks	•	•	•	•	•
Creative Expression					
Create artworks based on personal observations and experiences	•	•	•	•	•
Integrate a variety of ideas about self, life experiences, family, and community in original artworks	•	•	•	•	•
Combine information from personal observations, experiences, and imagination to express ideas about self, family, and community in original artworks	•	•	•	•	•
Organization and Composition					
Compare relationships between design and everyday life	•	•	•	•	•
Use design skills to develop effective compositions in original artworks		•	•	•	•
Production					
Follow directions and solve problems	•	•	•	•	•
Produce artworks using a variety of art media appropriately	•	•	•	•	•
Produce drawings, paintings, prints, constructions, clay/ceramics, textiles/fiberart	•	•	•	•	•
Produce art that reflects knowledge of a variety of cultures		•	•	•	•
HISTORICAL/CULTURAL HERITAGE: UNDERSTAND ART HISTORY AND CULTURE					
Understanding the Visual Arts in Relation to History and Cultures					
Historical Background					
Understand that art reflects values, beliefs, traditions, expressions, or experiences in a historical context	•	•	•	•	•
Recognize or describe art as a visual record of humankind	•	•	•	•	•
Recognize that media, tools, materials, and processes available to artists have changed through history	•	•	•	•	•
Relate art to different kinds of jobs in everyday life	•	•	•	•	•
Identify main ideas expressed in art	•	•	•	•	•
Recognize a variety of artworks as being from various historical eras		•	•	•	•
Investigate major themes in historical/contemporary eras				•	•
Identify the roles of art in American society				•	•
Cultural Influences					
Understand that art reflects values, beliefs, traditions, expressions, or experiences in a cultural context	•	•	•	•	•
Compare and contrast art from various cultures	•	•	•	•	•
Recognize a variety of artworks as being from various cultures	•	•	•	•	•
Determine ways in which artworks reflect or express cultural themes	•	•	•	•	•
Acknowledge and appreciate the artistic contributions of various ethnic groups in our culture	•	•	•	•	•
Compare ways individuals and families are depicted in art	•	•	•	•	•
Identify stories and constructions in art		•	•	•	•
Identify the characteristics of art from other cultures, and value the images, symbols, and themes distinguishing a specific culture		•	•	•	•
Artists and Artistic Styles					
Identify and discuss the artworks of a particular artist	•	•	•	•	•

	GRADE				
	1	2	3	4	5
Value the diverse contributions of artists	•	•	•	•	•
Recognize various artistic styles	•	•	•	•	•
Recognize artists' roles in history and society (to inform, define, interpret, enlighten, entertain; to raise questions and cause reflection; to provide a visual record of humankind; to communicate values, beliefs, feelings; to reveal social and political customs)	•	•	•	•	•
Learn that art is universal, made by people in all cultures throughout history	•	•	•	•	•
Recognize that artists are influenced by artists of the past		•	•	•	•

Understanding the Visual Arts in Relation to the Environment and Everyday Lives

Art in the Environment

	1	2	3	4	5
Develop an awareness of art in natural and human-made environments	•	•	•	•	•
Respond to art elements and design principles (formal structure) found in natural and human-made environments	•	•	•	•	•
Identify art that reflects, celebrates, or communicates sensitivity to natural and human-made environments	•	•	•	•	•

Art in the Community

	1	2	3	4	5
Recognize art as an important part of daily life	•	•	•	•	•
Recognize that art can contribute to the quality of daily life	•	•	•	•	•
Develop awareness of the historical relationship between art and daily life	•	•	•	•	•
Recognize the function of visual arts in the family, the neighborhood, and the community		•	•	•	•
Recognize the importance of art careers		•	•	•	•

RESPONSE/EVALUATION: MAKE INFORMED JUDGMENTS ABOUT ARTWORKS

Apply Simple Criteria to Make Informed Judgments About Art

	1	2	3	4	5
Analyze art elements in art	•	•	•	•	•
Analyze design principles in art	•	•	•	•	•
Analyze media, processes, techniques in art	•	•	•	•	•
Form conclusions about artworks	•	•	•	•	•
Analyze and interpret moods, meanings, symbolism, themes, stories, constructions in art		•	•	•	•

Evaluate Personal Artworks

	1	2	3	4	5
Identify general intent in art	•	•	•	•	•
Identify expressive qualities in art	•	•	•	•	•
Form conclusions about art	•	•	•	•	•
Interpret meaning in art	•	•	•	•	•

Evaluate Artworks by Peers and Others

	1	2	3	4	5
View and respond to original art and reproductions	•	•	•	•	•
Use art vocabulary in discussions about artworks	•	•	•	•	•
Recognize characteristics that make artworks similar and different	•	•	•	•	•
Distinguish characteristics of style in art	•	•	•	•	•
Respond to evidence of skill and craftsmanship found in art	•	•	•	•	•
Respect the differences in others' responses to and perceptions of art	•	•	•	•	•
Identify ideas/moods in original artworks, portfolios, and exhibitions by peers and others	•	•	•	•	•
Recognize that the aim of criticism is to clarify the meaning of and to share discoveries about art			•	•	•

CONNECTIONS BETWEEN AND AMONG THE ARTS AND OTHER CONTENT AREAS

	1	2	3	4	5
Discover and identify connections between the visual arts and other disciplines	•	•	•	•	•
Construct meaning and express ideas, feelings, experiences, and responses through connections to the other subjects	•	•	•	•	•
Analyze and interpret similarities and differences between characteristics of the visual arts and other disciplines		•	•	•	•

Index

Cross-Curricular
Themes and Topics

READING	Examples of Artworks and Artist's Workshop Activities from *Art Everywhere*, Grade 2	
Animals and Plants	Zebras, p. 31	*Rabbit Devouring a Bunch of Grapes*, p. 126
	The Waterlily Pond, p. 49	*Still Life of Fruit and Flowers in a Basket*, p. 132
	Exotic Landscape, p. 72	Artist's Workshop: Foil Sculpture, p. 89
	Dancing Lizard Couple, p. 78	Art Print 1: *Dove with Flowers*
	Birds, p. 84	Art Print 4: *Girl with Sunflowers*
	The Bremen Town Musicians, p. 88	Art Print 5: *Poppy*
	Macaw on a Pine Branch, p. 106	Art Print 18: *Flowers in a Vase*
Biographies	Pablo Picasso, pp. 36–37	Frank Lloyd Wright, pp. 96–97
	Georgia O'Keeffe, pp. 50–51	Frida Kahlo, pp. 116–117
	Edna Crawford, pp. 56–57	Mary Cassatt, pp. 130–131
	Jacob Lawrence, pp. 76–77	Gerald McDermott, pp. 136–137
Celebrations	Illustration from *Max Found Two Sticks*, p. 24	*Balloons for a Dime*, p. 46
	La Piñata, p. 28	*Olympic Wannabes*, pp. 82–83
Communities/ Neighborhoods	*Autumn*, pp. 22–23	*The Street*, p. 76
	Illustration from *Max Found Two Sticks*, p. 24	*The Hay Harvest*, pp. 102–103
	Illustration from *Draw Me a Star*, p. 44	*The Great Wave off Kanagawa*, p. 108
	Balloons for a Dime, p. 46	Hmong story cloth of village life, p. 134
	La Era, p. 48	Artist's Workshop: "Around the Town" Painting, p. 107
	Gloucester Harbor, p. 58	Art Print 8: *Fall Plowing*
	Trail Riders, pp. 62–63	Art Print 16: *Cosecha (Harvest)*
Cooperation	*The Chess Game*, pp. 42–43	*The Hay Harvest*, pp. 102–103
	Illustration from *Draw Me a Star*, p. 44	*Breton Girls Dancing, Pont-Aven*, p. 104
	Dancing Lizard Couple, p. 78	*Heroes*, p. 139
	The Bremen Town Musicians, p. 88	Art Print 16: *Cosecha (Harvest)*
Creativity	Illustration from *Max Found Two Sticks*, p. 24	*The Bremen Town Musicians*, p. 88
	Untitled, p. 28	Frank Lloyd Wright and architectural model, p. 97
	The Horse, the Rider, and the Clown, p. 34	*Breton Girls Dancing, Pont-Aven*, p. 104
	Three Musicians, p. 36	*Two Dancers in Blue Costumes*, p. 114
	Self Portraits, p. 37, p. 116, p. 131	*The Music Man*, p. 124
	Vaudeville, p. 77	Artist's Workshop: Dance for Joy Drawing, p. 29
	Olympic Wannabes, pp. 82–83	Art Print 10: *Grandfather Storyteller*
Cultures and Traditions	Illustration from *Max Found Two Sticks*, p. 24	*The Great Wave off Kanagawa*, p. 108
	La Piñata, p. 28	Ancient Greek hydria; Turkish plate, p. 112
	My Family Before I Was Born, p. 38	*Frida and Diego Rivera*, p. 117
	Guaymí necklaces, p. 68	Child's blouse with geometric mola, p. 118
	Egyptian art, pp. 70–71, p. 84	Hmong story cloth of village life, p. 134
	Hopi olla, p. 86	Illustration from *Coyote*, p. 137
	Cowboys and cowgirls, p. 91	Art Print 10: *Grandfather Storyteller*

Explorations/Travel	*Gloucester Harbor*, p. 58	*Neuschwanstein Castle*, p. 94
	Trail Riders, pp. 62–63	*The Great Wave off Kanagawa*, p. 108
	Exotic Landscape, p. 72	*Dog Stamp*, p. 138
	Pyramids of Giza, pp. 70–71	Art Print 6: *Breezing Up (A Fair Wind)*
Families and Friendship	*Hand with Flowers*, p. 26	*The Street*, p. 76
	La Piñata, p. 28	*Olympic Wannabes*, pp. 82–83
	My Family Before I Was Born, p. 38	*Scenes from the life of a child*, p. 92
	The Chess Game, pp. 42–43	*Breton Girls Dancing, Pont-Aven*, p. 104
	Illustration from *Draw Me a Star*, p. 44	*Women Admiring a Child*, p. 130
	Balloons for a Dime, p. 46	Artist's Workshop: Favorite-People Portrait, p. 39
	First Steps, after Millet, p. 54	Art Print 17: *Nurse and Child*
Growth and Change	*Autumn*, pp. 22–23	*Scenes from the life of a child*, p. 92
	First Steps, after Millet, p. 54	*The Hay Harvest*, pp. 102–103
	Autumn Leaves, Lake George, N.Y., p. 50	*Women Admiring a Child*, p. 130
	The Street, p. 76	Art Print 17: *Nurse and Child*
Seasons	*Autumn*, pp. 22–23	*Summertime*, p. 131
	Illustration from *When the Wind Stops*, p. 64	Artist's Workshop: Fall Bouquet Painting, p. 53
Self-Discovery	Student art, p. 38	Photographers, pp. 110–111
	First Steps, after Millet, p. 54	*Heroes*, p. 139
	Fanny Sperry Steele, p. 91	Artist's Workshop: Story-Cloth Collage, p. 135
	Scenes from the life of a child, p. 92	Art Print 6: *Breezing Up (A Fair Wind)*

SOCIAL STUDIES	**Examples of Artworks and Artist's Workshop Activities from** *Art Everywhere*, **Grade 2**	
HISTORY • understanding communities and neighborhoods	Illustration from *Max Found Two Sticks*, p. 24	*Trail Riders*, pp. 62–63
	La Piñata, p. 28	*The Street*, p. 76
	My Family Before I Was Born, p. 38	*Breton Girls Dancing, Pont-Aven*, p. 104
	The Chess Game, pp. 42–43	*Women Admiring a Child*, p. 130
	Illustration from *Draw Me a Star*, p. 44	Hmong story cloth of village life, p. 134
	Balloons for a Dime, p. 46	*Greetings from Texas*, p. 138
	La Era, p. 48	*Heroes*, p. 139
	Gloucester Harbor, p. 58	Art Print 16: *Cosecha (Harvest)*
• understanding ancient times, periods, and chronology	*My Family Before I Was Born*, p. 38	Ancient Greek hydria, p. 112
	The Chess Game, pp. 42–43	Aztec feather headdress, pp. 122–123
	Egyptian art, pp. 70–71	Hmong story cloth of village life, p. 134
	Vaudeville, p. 77	Artist's Workshop: Amazing School Model, p. 95
	Fanny Sperry Steele, p. 91	Art Print 3: *Mona Lisa*
	Scenes from the life of a child, p. 92	Art Print 11: *Statue of Abraham Lincoln*
GEOGRAPHY • understanding maps	*Autumn*, pp. 22–23, pp. 144–147	*Olympic Wannabes*, pp. 82–83, pp. 144–147
	The Chess Game, pp. 42–43, pp. 144–147	*The Hay Harvest*, pp. 102–103, pp. 144–147
	Trail Riders, pp. 62–63, pp. 144–147	Aztec feather headdress, pp. 122–123, pp. 144–147

• **understanding landforms, bodies of water, and regions**	*La Era*, p. 48 *Gloucester Harbor*, p. 58 *Trail Riders*, pp. 62–63 *Exotic Landscape*, p. 72 *The Hay Harvest*, pp. 102–103	*The Great Wave off Kanagawa*, p. 108 *Moon Over Half Dome*, p. 110 Art Print 6: *Breezing Up (A Fair Wind)* Art Print 8: *Fall Plowing* Art Print 16: *Cosecha (Harvest)*
• **understanding natural resources and hazards**	*La Era*, p. 48 *Trail Riders*, pp. 62–63 *Exotic Landscape*, p. 72	*Aluminum Horse #5*, p. 88 *The Great Wave off Kanagawa*, p. 108 Art Print 8: *Fall Plowing*
• **understanding interaction between people and the environment**	*Autumn*, pp. 22–23 *La Era*, p. 48 *Gloucester Harbor*, p. 58 *Trail Riders*, pp. 62–63 *Neuschwanstein Castle*, Germany, p. 94	Exterior of *Fallingwater*, p. 96 *The Hay Harvest*, pp. 102–103 *The Great Wave off Kanagawa*, p. 108 Hmong story cloth of village life, p. 134 Art Print 16: *Cosecha (Harvest)*
ECONOMICS • **understanding goods and services**	Food products, pp. 32–33 Star of Bethlehem quilt, p. 66 Guaymí necklace, p. 68	Hopi olla, p. 86 Child's blouse with geometric mola, p. 118 Art Print 16: *Cosecha (Harvest)*
• **understanding work and jobs**	Edna Crawford, Animator, pp. 56–57 Frank Lloyd Wright and his architectural model, p. 97 Ansel Adams photographing the Big Sur coast, p. 110	Flor Garduño photographing a volcano, p. 111 Gerald McDermott, Book Illustrator, pp. 136–137 *Heroes*, p. 139
GOVERNMENT AND CITIZENSHIP • **understanding citizenship/symbols**	Texas bluebonnets, p. 30 *Three Flags*, p. 67 *Olympic Wannabes*, pp. 82–83 Money from Around the World, pp. 128–129	Stamps from Around the World, pp. 138–139 Artist's Workshop: Money Design, p. 129 Art Print 11: *Statue of Abraham Lincoln* Art Print 16: *Cosecha (Harvest)*
• **understanding leadership**	Gold mask of Tutankhamen, p. 70 Aztec feather headdress, pp. 122–123 One-dollar bill, U.S., front, p. 128	Twenty peso bill, Mexico, p. 128 Artist's Workshop: Famous-Person Portrait, p. 115 Art Print 11: *Statue of Abraham Lincoln*
CULTURE • **understanding diversity in work and interests**	*La Era*, p. 48 Cowboys and cowgirls, p. 91 *The Hay Harvest*, pp. 102–103	*Basket of Light*, p. 111 Olympic Soccer—Ghana, Africa, p. 138 *Heroes*, p. 139
• **understanding exploration**	*Trail Riders*, pp. 62–63 *Exotic Landscape*, p. 72	Photographers, pp. 110–111 *Dog Stamp*, p. 138
SCIENCE	**Examples of Artworks and Artist's Workshop Activities from** *Art Everywhere*, **Grade 2**	
LIFE SCIENCE Animals, Plants, and Habitats	*Autumn*, pp. 22–23 *The Banks of the Bièvre near Bicêtre*, p. 27 Texas bluebonnets, p. 30 Zebras, p. 31	*The Waterlily Pond*, p. 49 *Trail Riders*, pp. 62–63 *Exotic Landscape*, p. 72 *In the Meadow*, p. 98

This correlation shows where the Texas Essential Knowledge and Skills are developed in the *Teacher Edition* for grade 2.

ART

(2.1)   **Perception.** The student develops and organizes ideas from the environment.

The student is expected to:	Teacher Edition pages
(A) identify variations in objects from the environment, using the senses;	30, 31, 36, 40, 46, 58, 62, 64, 66, 68, 70, 71, 74, 79, 84, 85, 86, 92, 94, 96, 97, 98, 101, 102, 117, 118, 132, 138
identify variations in subjects from the environment, using the senses; and	30, 54, 62, 64, 71, 88, 96, 97, 102, 108, 116, 117, 127, 132
(B) identify art elements such as color, texture, form, line, and space.	23, 26, 27, 28, 30, 31, 32, 33, 34, 35, 36, 37, 38, 39, 40, 41, 46, 47, 48, 50, 51, 52, 58, 61, 62, 63, 64, 66, 71, 74, 75, 78, 79, 81, 84, 86, 87, 88, 89, 90, 92, 95, 97, 98, 99, 101, 106, 107, 111, 112, 117, 130, 132, 133, 137, 139, 140
identify art principles such as emphasis, pattern, and rhythm.	63, 66, 67, 68, 69, 70, 71, 72, 73, 74, 76, 78, 81, 84, 87, 90, 106, 107, 108, 109, 111, 112, 113, 114, 117, 118, 119, 120, 121, 126, 127, 128, 129, 132, 133, 137, 139, 140

(2.2)   **Creative expression/performance.** The student expresses ideas through original artworks, using a variety of media with appropriate skill.

The student is expected to:	Teacher Edition pages
(A) express ideas in artworks, using a variety of colors;	39, 43, 47, 49, 53, 55, 69, 77, 115, 120, 129, 131
express ideas in artworks, using a variety of forms;	69, 87, 91, 93, 95
express ideas in artworks, using a variety of lines;	27, 29, 31, 69, 97, 129
express feelings in artworks, using a variety of colors;	39, 43, 47, 49, 53, 55, 69, 77, 115, 120, 129, 131
express feelings in artworks, using a variety of forms;	69, 87, 91, 93, 95
express feelings in artworks, using a variety of lines;	27, 29, 31, 69, 97, 129
(B) create effective compositions, using design elements;	27, 29, 33, 35, 39, 47, 49, 51, 53, 55, 59, 67, 69, 75, 79, 87, 91, 93, 95, 97, 99, 129, 131, 135
create effective compositions, using design principles; and	29, 67, 73, 75, 87, 91, 109, 113, 115, 119, 127, 129, 133, 135
(C) identify skills necessary for producing drawings, using a variety of art materials.	27, 29, 31, 73, 115

identify skills necessary for producing paintings, using a variety of art materials.	39, 49, 51, 53, 99
identify skills necessary for producing prints, using a variety of art materials.	63, 69, 113, 129
identify skills necessary for producing constructions, using a variety of art materials.	47, 67, 75, 89, 91, 95, 109, 119, 135
identify skills necessary for producing modeled forms, using a variety of art materials.	83, 87, 89, 93
practice skills necessary for producing drawings, using a variety of art materials.	26, 27, 29, 31, 57, 58, 59, 63, 73, 83, 103, 111, 115, 133, 137, 139
practice skills necessary for producing paintings, using a variety of art materials.	39, 47, 49, 51, 53, 58, 59, 99, 103, 107, 117, 133, 137
practice skills necessary for producing prints, using a variety of art materials.	63, 69, 113, 129
practice skills necessary for producing constructions, using a variety of art materials.	47, 55, 71, 75, 89, 91, 95, 109, 119, 127, 135
practice skills necessary for producing modeled forms, using a variety of art materials.	83, 87, 89, 93

(2.3) **Historical/cultural heritage.** The student demonstrates an understanding of art history and culture as records of human achievement.

The student is expected to:	**Teacher Edition pages**
(A) identify stories in a variety of artworks;	22, 24, 26, 34, 37, 38, 41, 42, 44, 45, 46, 52, 54, 56, 58, 61, 73, 76, 77, 81, 86, 88, 90, 102, 104, 109, 116, 118, 124, 125, 134, 135, 138
identify constructions in a variety of artworks;	36, 37, 68, 70, 71, 76, 77, 86, 94, 108, 109, 116, 117, 128, 131, 136, 137
(B) compare ways individuals are depicted in different artworks;	36, 39, 76, 82, 92, 116, 128, 130
compare ways families are depicted in different artworks; and	38, 42, 44, 54, 58, 76, 92, 116, 130
(C) identify different kinds of jobs in art.	56, 57, 60, 80, 100, 110, 136

(2.4) **Response/evaluation.** The student makes informed judgments about personal artworks and the artworks of others.

The student is expected to:	**Teacher Edition pages**
(A) define reasons for preferences in personal artworks; and	29, 33, 41, 53, 61, 67, 68, 75, 79, 81, 95, 101, 119, 121, 127, 141
(B) identify ideas in original artworks by peers.	27, 29, 31, 33, 35, 49, 55, 57, 59, 69, 71, 89, 91, 93, 99, 109, 111, 113, 115, 119, 121, 127, 133, 137
identify ideas in portfolios by peers.	31, 57, 71, 91, 111, 121, 137
identify ideas in exhibitions by peers.	31, 57, 71, 91, 109, 111, 137

identify ideas in original artworks by artists.	28, 36, 37, 40, 48, 50, 51, 52, 54, 55, 56, 59, 61, 74, 76, 77, 81, 86, 91, 94, 96, 97, 98, 101, 102, 105, 106, 108, 112, 114, 116, 117, 118, 120, 121, 125, 130, 131, 135, 141
identify ideas in portfolios by artists.	37, 51, 77, 97, 117, 131
identify ideas in exhibitions by artists.	37, 51, 77, 97, 117, 131

READING

(2.1) **Listening/speaking/purposes.** The student listens attentively and engages actively in a variety of oral language experiences.

The student is expected to:	Teacher Edition pages
(C) participate in rhymes, songs, conversations, and discussions (K-3);	22, 36–37, 42, 50–51, 62, 76–77, 82, 96–97, 102, 116–117, 122, 130–131
(D) listen critically to interpret and evaluate (K-3);	22–23, 42–43, 62–63, 82–83, 122–123

(2.2) **Listening/speaking/culture.** The student listens and speaks to gain knowledge of his/her own culture, the culture of others, and the common elements of cultures.

The student is expected to:	Teacher Edition pages
(B) compare language and oral traditions (family stories) that reflect customs, regions, and cultures (K-3).	22, 38, 39, 42, 54, 55, 76, 77, 110, 116–117, 134, 135, 137

(2.3) **Listening/speaking/audiences/oral grammar.** The student speaks appropriately to different audiences for different purposes and occasions.

The student is expected to:	Teacher Edition pages
(D) present dramatic interpretations of experiences, stories, poems, or plays (K-3);	29, 35, 55

(2.4) **Listening/speaking/communication.** The student communicates clearly by putting thoughts and feelings into spoken words.

The student is expected to:	Teacher Edition pages
(B) clarify and support spoken messages using appropriate props such as objects, pictures, or charts (K-3);	25, 41, 47, 55, 59, 61, 65, 81, 85, 95, 101, 105, 107, 113, 119, 121, 125, 129, 133, 135, 139, 141

(2.6) **Reading/fluency.** The student reads with fluency and understanding in texts at appropriate difficulty levels.

The student is expected to:	Teacher Edition pages
(A) read regularly in independent-level materials (texts in which no more than approximately 1 in 20 words is difficult for the reader) (2);	22d, 32, 34, 38, 42d, 46, 48, 52, 54, 58, 62d, 66, 68, 72, 74, 78, 82d, 92, 98, 102d, 108, 112, 114, 118, 122d, 126, 132, 134, 138
(B) read regularly in instructional-level materials that are challenging but manageable (texts in which no more than approximately 1 in 10 words is difficult for the reader; a "typical" second grader reads approximately 70 wpm) (2);	24–41, 44–61, 64–81, 84–101, 104–121, 124–141

(2.8) **Reading/vocabulary development.** The student develops an extensive vocabulary.

The student is expected to:	Teacher Edition pages
(A) discuss meanings of words and develop vocabulary through meaningful/concrete experiences (K-2);	23, 40, 43, 60, 63, 80, 83, 100, 103, 120, 123
(D) use resources and references such as beginners' dictionaries, bilingual dictionaries, glossaries, available technology, and context to build word meanings and to confirm pronunciation of words (2-3).	23, 43, 63, 83, 103, 123, R11–R12

(2.9) **Reading/comprehension.** The student uses a variety of strategies to comprehend selections read aloud and selections read independently.

The student is expected to:	Teacher Edition pages
(A) use prior knowledge to anticipate meaning and make sense of texts;	24, 44, 64, 84, 104, 124
(E) draw and discuss visual images based on text descriptions (1-3);	27, 29, 33, 35, 39, 47, 49, 53, 55, 59, 67, 69, 73, 75, 79, 87, 89, 93, 95, 99, 107, 109, 113, 115, 119, 127, 129, 133, 135, 139
(F) make and explain inferences from texts such as determining important ideas, causes and effects, making predictions, and drawing conclusions (1-3);	24–25, 26, 28, 32, 34, 38, 41, 44–45, 46, 48, 52, 54, 58, 61, 64–65, 66, 68, 72, 74, 78, 81, 104–105, 106, 108, 112, 114, 118, 121, 124–125, 126, 128, 132, 134, 138, 141
(I) represent text information in different ways including story maps, graphs, and charts (2-3).	25, 41, 45, 47, 53, 61, 65, 73, 75, 79, 81, 85, 87, 89, 93, 101, 105, 121, 125, 141

(2.10) **Reading/literary response.** The student responds to various texts.

The student is expected to:	Teacher Edition pages
(A) respond to stories and poems in ways that reflect understanding and interpretation in discussion (speculating, questioning) in writing, and through movement, music, art, and drama (2-3);	22, 41, 42, 44–45, 54–55, 56–57, 61, 62, 82, 92–93, 102, 122, 134–135
(B) demonstrate understanding of informational text in various ways such as through writing, illustrating, developing demonstrations, and using available technology (2-3);	22d, 22–41, 42d, 42–61, 62d, 62–81, 82d, 82–101, 102d, 102–121, 122d, 122–141

(2.11) **Reading/text structures/literary concepts.** The student analyzes the characteristics of various types of texts.

The student is expected to:	Teacher Edition pages
(D) recognize the distinguishing features of familiar genres including stories, poems, and informational texts (1-3);	xx–xxi, 22, 42, 62, 82, 102, 122
(H) analyze characters including their traits, relationships, and changes;	44–45, 46, 52, 54, 58, 61
(I) identify the importance of the setting to a story's meaning (1-3); and	44–45, 46, 48, 52, 54, 58, 61
(J) recognize the story problem(s) or plot (1-3).	44–45, 46, 52, 54, 58, 61

Texas Essential Knowledge and Skills

(2.12) **Reading inquiry/research.** The student generates questions and conducts research using information from various sources.

The student is expected to:	Teacher Edition pages
(B) use alphabetical order to locate information (1-3);	23, 37, 43, 57, 63, 77, 83, 97, 103, 117, 123, 131
(C) recognize and use parts of a book to locate information, including table of contents, chapter titles, guide words, and indices (1-3);	xx–xxi, 22, 42, 62, 82, 102, 122
(D) use multiple sources including print, such as an encyclopedia, technology, and experts to locate information that addresses questions (2-3);	22d, 22, 23, 30, 36, 37, 42d, 42, 43, 50, 51, 57, 62d, 62, 63, 70, 76, 77, 82d, 82, 83, 90, 91, 96, 97, 102d, 102, 103, 110, 116 117, 122d, 123, 131, 137
(E) interpret and use graphic sources of information such as maps, charts, graphs, and diagrams (2-3);	22, 25, 41, 42, 45, 47, 61, 62, 65, 73, 79, 81, 82, 85, 87, 89, 101, 102, 105, 119, 121, 122, 125, 135, 139, 141, R3
(G) demonstrate learning through productions and displays such as murals, written and oral reports, and dramatizations (2-3);	27, 29, 33, 35, 39, 47, 49, 53, 55, 59, 67, 69, 73, 75, 79, 87, 89, 93, 95, 99, 103, 107, 109, 113, 115, 119, 123, 127, 129, 133, 135, 139, 141

(2.13) **Reading/culture.** The student reads to increase knowledge of his/her own culture, the culture of others, and the common elements of culture.

The student is expected to:	Teacher Edition pages
(A) connect life experiences with the life experiences, language, customs, and culture of others (K-3);	22, 24–25, 28, 36–37, 38–39, 42, 46, 54, 55, 58, 62, 68, 70–71, 76–77, 82, 86, 90–91, 92–93, 94–95, 96–97, 102, 108, 110–111, 112, 114–115, 116–117, 118–119, 122, 128, 130–131, 132, 134–135, 136–137, 138–139

(2.14) **Writing/purposes.** The student writes for a variety of audiences and purposes, and in various forms.

The student is expected to:	Teacher Edition pages
(A) write to record ideas and reflections (K-3);	26–29, 32–35, 38–39, 41, 46–49, 52–55, 58–59, 61, 66–69, 72–75, 78–79, 81, 86–89, 92–95, 98–99, 101, 106–109, 112–115, 118–119, 121, 126–129, 132–135, 138–139, 141

(2.15) **Writing/penmanship/capitalization/punctuation.** The student composes original texts using the conventions of written language such as capitalization and handwriting to communicate clearly.

The student is expected to:	Teacher Edition pages
(C) use basic capitalization and punctuation correctly, including capitalizing names and first letters in sentences, using periods, question marks, and exclamation points (1-2);	29, 33, 39, 49, 59, 69, 75, 95, 107, 109, 115, 133

(2.17) **Writing/grammar/usage.** The student composes meaningful texts applying knowledge of grammar and usage.

The student is expected to:	Teacher Edition pages
(B) compose complete sentences in written texts and use the appropriate end punctuation (1-2);	41, 49, 69, 75, 81, 89, 95, 101, 107, 109, 115, 121, 129, 133, 135, 139, 141

(2.18) **Writing/writing processes.** The student selects and uses writing processes for self-initiated and assigned writing.

The student is expected to:	Teacher Edition pages
(C) revise selected drafts for varied purposes including to achieve a sense of audience, precise word choices, and vivid images (1-3);	61, 73, 101, 109, 119, 127, 129, 133, 135

(D)	edit for appropriate grammar, spelling, punctuation, and features of polished writings (2-3);	29, 33, 39, 47, 49, 59, 67, 69, 75, 87, 95, 101, 107, 109, 115, 129, 133, 139

(2.20) **Writing/inquiry/research.** The student uses writing as a tool for learning and research.

The student is expected to:	**Teacher Edition pages**
(B) record his/her own knowledge of a topic in various ways such as by drawing pictures, making lists, and showing connections among ideas;	23, 27, 31, 43, 47, 53, 55, 61, 63, 73, 75, 79, 83, 87, 89, 93, 97, 103, 123, 133, 141

MATHEMATICS

(2.6) **Patterns, relationships, and algebraic thinking.** The student uses patterns to describe relationships and make predictions.

The student is expected to:	**Teacher Edition pages**
(A) generate a list of paired numbers based on a real-life situation such as number of tricycles related to number of wheels;	67
(C) identify, describe, and extend patterns to make predictions and solve problems.	66–67, 68–69, 70, 72–73, 74–75, 76–77, 78, 80, 81, 90, 126, 127, 136–137

(2.7) **Geometry and spatial reasoning.** The student uses attributes to identify, compare, and contrast shapes and solids.

The student is expected to:	**Teacher Edition pages**
(A) identify attributes of any shape or solid;	23, 30, 32, 33, 34, 35, 36–37, 40, 67, 86, 87, 90, 94, 95, 97, 101
(B) use attributes to describe how two shapes or two solids are alike or different; and	30, 32, 33, 35, 36, 38, 39, 40, 86, 87, 94, 95, 112, 113
(C) cut geometric shapes apart and identify the new shapes made.	33

(2.11) **Probability and statistics.** The student organizes data to make it useful for interpreting information.

The student is expected to:	**Teacher Edition pages**
(A) construct picture graphs and bar-type graphs;	47

(2.12) **Underlying processes and mathematical tools.** The student applies Grade 2 mathematics to solve problems connected to everyday experiences and activities in and outside of school.

The student is expected to:	**Teacher Edition pages**
(A) identify the mathematics in everyday situations;	23, 26–27, 28–29, 30–31, 32–33, 36–37, 40, 66–67, 68–69, 70–71, 86–87, 94–95, 96–97, 112–113, 118–119, 129
(B) use a problem-solving model that incorporates understanding the problem, making a plan, carrying out the plan, and evaluating the solution for reasonableness;	27, 29, 33, 35, 39, 47, 49, 53, 55, 59, 67, 69, 73, 75, 79, 87, 89, 93, 95, 99, 107, 109, 113, 115, 119, 127, 129, 133, 135, 139
(D) use tools such as real objects, manipulatives, and technology to solve problems.	57, 75, 79, 87, 89, 91, 93, 95, 99, 109, 119, 129

Texas Essential Knowledge and Skills

SCIENCE

(2.2) **Scientific processes.** The student develops abilities necessary to do scientific inquiry in the field and the classroom.

The student is expected to:	Teacher Edition pages
(B) plan and conduct simple descriptive investigations;	27, 49, 51, 64, 74, 99, 109, 113, 133
(D) gather information using simple equipment and tools to extend the senses;	49, 51, 59, 74, 99, 107, 109, 113, 133
(E) construct reasonable explanations and draw conclusions using information and prior knowledge;	30, 31, 49, 50–51, 59, 69, 75, 89, 99, 107

(2.4) **Scientific processes.** The student uses age-appropriate tools and models to verify that organisms and objects and parts of organisms and objects can be observed, described, and measured.

The student is expected to:	Teacher Edition pages
(A) collect information using tools including rulers, meter sticks, measuring cups, clocks, hand lenses, computers, thermometers, and balances;	57, 112, 113, 114, 133

(2.5) **Science concepts.** The student knows that organisms, objects, and events have properties and patterns.

The student is expected to:	Teacher Edition pages
(A) classify and sequence organisms, objects, and events based on properties and patterns;	30, 31, 34, 40, 51, 66, 67, 68, 69, 70, 71, 78, 79, 81, 89, 127, 133

(2.6) **Science concepts.** The student knows that systems have parts and are composed of organisms and objects.

The student is expected to:	Teacher Edition pages
(C) observe and record the functions of plant parts; and	27, 51, 52, 79, 133
(D) observe and record the functions of animal parts.	31, 52, 56–57, 69, 79, 89, 107

(2.7) **Science concepts.** The student knows that many types of change occur.

The student is expected to:	Teacher Edition pages
(A) observe, measure, record, analyze, predict, and illustrate changes in size, mass, temperature, color, position, quantity, sound, and movement;	27, 28, 29, 47, 49, 51, 57, 58, 75, 89, 99, 107, 108–109, 111, 133
(D) observe, measure, and record changes in weather, the night sky, and seasons.	27, 51, 53, 58, 64–65, 75, 99, 107, 108–109, 110–111

(2.8) **Science concepts.** The student distinguishes between living organisms and nonliving objects.

The student is expected to:	Teacher Edition pages
(A) identify characteristics of living organisms; and	27, 30, 31, 34, 35, 51, 53, 69, 71, 72, 88, 89, 90, 107, 127, 132, 133, 137
(B) identify characteristics of nonliving objects.	30, 31, 35, 127, 132, 133

(2.9) **Science concepts.** The student knows that living organisms have basic needs.

The student is expected to:	Teacher Edition pages
(A) identify the external characteristics of different kinds of plants and animals that allow their needs to be met; and	27, 31, 53, 69, 79, 107
(B) compare and give examples of the ways living organisms depend on each other and on their environments.	27, 53, 56–57, 69, 72, 73, 75, 96–97

(2.10) **Science concepts.** The student knows that the natural world includes rocks, soil, water, and gases of the atmosphere.

The student is expected to:	Teacher Edition pages
(A) describe and illustrate the water cycle; and	75
(B) identify uses of natural resources.	27, 53, 59, 73, 74–75, 89, 96–97, 102, 110, 111, 117, 122

SOCIAL STUDIES

(2.2) **History.** The student understands the concepts of time and chronology.

The student is expected to:	Teacher Edition pages
(B) use vocabulary related to chronology, including past, present, and future;	38, 42, 70–71, 90–91, 92, 94, 102, 104, 122, 137, 139
(C) create and interpret timelines;	93

(2.4) **History.** The student understands how historical figures and ordinary people helped to shape our community, state, and nation.

The student is expected to:	Teacher Edition pages
(A) identify contributions of historical figures such as Henrietta King and Thurgood Marshall who have influenced the community, state, and nation;	82b, 115, 122b, 122, 128, 138
(C) explain how local people and events have influenced local community history.	90–91, 138–139

(2.5) **Geography.** The student uses simple geographic tools such as maps, globes, and photographs.

The student is expected to:	Teacher Edition pages
(A) use symbols, find locations, and determine directions on maps and globes; and	22, 42, 62, 82, 102, 122, 128, 129, 135, 139, R2, R3

(2.6) **Geography.** The student understands the locations and characteristics of places and regions.

The student is expected to:	Teacher Edition pages
(B) locate the community, Texas, the United States, and selected countries on maps and globes;	22, 42, 62, 82, 102, 119, 122, 135, 139

(2.8) **Geography.** The student understands how humans use and modify the physical environment.

The student is expected to:	**Teacher Edition pages**
(B) identify ways in which people have modified the physical environment such as building roads, clearing land for urban development, and mining coal;	71, 94–95, 96–97

(2.14) **Citizenship.** The student understands important customs, symbols, and celebrations that represent American beliefs and principles and contribute to our national identity.

The student is expected to:	**Teacher Edition pages**
(B) identify selected symbols such as state and national birds and flowers and patriotic symbols such as the U.S. and Texas flags and Uncle Sam; and	30, 66–67, 82b, 115, 122b, 128–129, 138
(C) explain how selected customs, symbols, and celebrations reflect an American love of individualism, inventiveness, and freedom.	128, 138

(2.15) **Culture.** The student understands the significance of works of art in the local community.

The student is expected to:	**Teacher Edition pages**
(A) identify selected stories, poems, statues, paintings, and other examples of the local cultural heritage;	22, 24, 28, 40, 46, 51, 58, 62, 66–67, 76–77, 82, 86, 90–91, 96–97, 100, 110, 117, 124, 128, 131, 134–135, 136–137, 138–139

(2.16) **Science, technology, and society.** The student understands how science and technology have affected life, past and present.

The student is expected to:	**Teacher Edition pages**
(A) describe how science and technology have changed communication, transportation, and recreation; and	56–57

(2.17) **Social studies skills.** The student applies critical-thinking skills to organize and use information acquired from a variety of sources including electronic technology.

The student is expected to:	**Teacher Edition pages**
(A) obtain information about a topic using a variety of oral sources such as conversations, interviews, and music;	37, 39, 40, 51, 60, 77, 80, 97, 100, 117, 131
(B) obtain information about a topic using a variety of visual sources such as pictures, graphics, television, maps, computer software, literature, reference sources, and artifacts;	22b, 22d, 22, 23, 30, 31, 36, 37, 42b, 42d, 42, 43, 50, 51, 56, 57, 59, 62b, 62d, 62, 63, 70, 71, 76, 77, 82b, 82d, 82, 83, 86, 90, 91, 92, 95, 96, 97, 102b, 102d, 102, 103, 110, 116, 117, 119, 122b, 122d, 123, 128–129, 135, 138, 139
(C) use various parts of a source, including the table of contents, glossary, and index, as well as keyword computer searches, to locate information;	xx–xxi, 22, 23, 42, 43, 62, 63, 82, 83, 102, 103, 122, 123, R3–R13

(2.18) **Social studies skills.** The student communicates in written, oral, and visual forms.

The student is expected to:	**Teacher Edition pages**
(A) express ideas orally based on knowledge and experiences;	24, 39, 44, 64, 84, 104, 124